Makers of Modern Theatre

Who were the giants of the twentieth-century stage, and exactly how did they influence modern theatre?

The key theatre-makers who shaped the drama of the last century are Konstantin Stanislavsky, Vsevolod Meyerhold, Bertolt Brecht and Antonin Artaud. Robert Leach's *Makers of Modern Theatre* is the first detailed introduction to the work of these practitioners. In it, Leach focuses on the major issues which relate to their dominance of theatre history:

- What was significant in their life and times?
- What is their main legacy?
- What were their dramatic philosophies and practices?
- How have their ideas been adapted since their deaths?
- What are the current critical perspectives on their work?

Never before has so much essential information on the making of twentieth-century theatre been compiled in one brilliantly concise, beautifully illustrated book. This is a genuinely insightful volume by one of the foremost theatre historians of our age.

Robert Leach is a theatre director and author, currently teaching drama at the University of Edinburgh. His earlier books include *Revolutionary Theatre* (1994) and *A History of Russian Theatre* (2000).

Makers of Modern Theatre
An introduction

Robert Leach

 Routledge
Taylor & Francis Group

LONDON AND NEW YORK

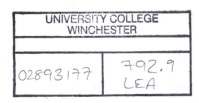
First published 2004
by Routledge
11 New Fetter Lane, London EC4P 4EE

Simultaneously published in the USA and Canada
by Routledge
29 West 35th Street, New York, NY 10001

Routledge is an imprint of the Taylor & Francis Group

© 2004 Robert Leach

Typeset in Goudy by BOOK NOW Ltd
Printed and bound in Great Britain by
TJ International, Padstow, Cornwall

British Library Cataloguing in Publication Data
A catalogue record for this book is available from the British Library

Library of Congress Cataloging in Publication Data
Leach, Robert, 1942–
    Makers of modern theatre/Robert Leach.
        p. cm.
Includes bibliographical references and index.
1. Theater–History–20th century. 2. Stanislavsky, Konstantin,
1863–1938–Criticism and interpretation. 3. Meyerhold, V. E.
(Vsevolod Emilevich), 1874–1940–Criticism and interpretation. 4.
Brecht, Bertolt, 1898–1956–Criticism and interpretation. 5. Artaud,
Antonin, 1896–1948–Criticism and interpretation. I. Title.
    PN2189.L37 2004
    792'.09'04–dc22   2003026488

ISBN 0-415-31240-X (hbk)
ISBN 0-415-31241-8 (pbk)

To Natasha, Nick, Becky and Dan

Contents

Illustrations

Boxes

1 Modern theatre ... Modernist theatre

The modern theatre is the theatre of today. 'Modernist' theatre refers to the theatre of the first fifty or so years of the last century, when Stanislavsky, Meyerhold, Brecht, and Artaud flourished. Their Modernism, however, infiltrates and influences all aspects of modern theatre. They bestride the gap between 'Modernism' and the modern. That is why they were, supremely, the 'makers of modern theatre'.

Modernism is usually – and correctly – associated with startling novelty, with art which deliberately shocks or which deliberately – even joyfully – breaks conventions. It is often designed to be partial, contentious, and challenging. Modernism created the 'avant-garde': those who not only introduced new subject matter to art, but did so by the use of new methods and new forms. They were the Symbolists, the Futurists, the Expressionists, the Surrealists, and all the other innovators and iconoclasts of that period. The richness and originality which they brought to art and culture were almost overwhelming, and it often seems that artists ever since have been working out the implications of their ideas. Certainly in theatre, the giants of the end of the twentieth century, practitioners like Augusto Boal or Peter Stein or Lev Dodin, constantly if implicitly refer in their work to that of their precursors, and often specifically to the four practitioners who form the subject of this book. We may argue, for example, that Feminist theatre capitalised deftly on certain implications of Brechtian theatre, or that contemporary 'physical theatre' owes its birth to the experiments of Meyerhold – or, perhaps, Artaud. And so on. Thus the four may be regarded not only as the makers of *Modernist* theatre, but as the makers of modern theatre as well.

Modernism was perhaps most forcibly characterised by its awareness that the old certainties of life and society, religion and culture, were fractured for ever by the ideas of Darwin, Marx, Freud, and others. Post-nineteenth-century life, at least in Europe and America, became hard to anchor for many whose primary experience was of incoherence and fragmentation.

The avant-garde artistic movements of the Modernists, therefore, were not only themselves fragments of the greater 'Modernist culture', they were also responses to the perceived fragmentation of experience. And the four practitioners whom we have identified as 'makers' of modern theatre all felt the force of this fragmentation, though all, of course, responded to it differently. We might suggest that Stanislavsky wanted to heal it, that Meyerhold wanted to make it cohere beyond the stage in the spectator (in Roland Barthes' sense, he wanted 'the death of the theatre artist'), that Brecht wanted to use it for political purposes, and that Artaud wanted it to cauterise. Insofar as this was the case, between them these attitudes encompass the range of Modernist theatre.

And after Modernism?

Probably the most noticeable developments in the second half of the twentieth century were less in the arts themselves than in 'post-modernist' critical theories of the arts, though surprisingly little of this was initially devoted to theatre. There were, of course, a few significant essays by Freud and Benjamin, Barthes and Derrida, which pointed to ways forward, but only towards the end of the century, with the work of critics like Keir Elam, with his semiotic approach, and Sue-Ellen Case, with her feminist orientation, did theatre become consistently the subject of theoretical scrutiny. The most notable theorist, probably, was Herbert Blau, who developed an interconnected web of critical ideas to produce a formidable, if pessimistic, critique of drama and theatre. Some of these works are set into a context of past critical debates and theories in Marvin Carlson's anthology, *Theories of the Theatre*.[1] In the following pages, I have tried to sketch in very lightly the possible relevance of contemporary theory to Stanislavsky, Meyerhold, Brecht, and Artaud in the sections devoted to 'twenty-first-century perspectives'. While making no pretence to comprehensiveness, these sections do attempt to suggest possible approaches, as well as referring briefly to some more recent work done, especially on Brecht and Artaud.

But, in the end, the significance of these four men is to be found in their theatre practice. The starting point is to be found in their understanding that the theatre is always symbolic. It assumes that everything that happens on stage *stands for* something else. This is true even of the most naturalistic piece. As Magritte asked of the pipe, so Stanislavsky asked of the stage prop: is it a real thing (itself) or is it an illusion? And because the theatre is three-dimensional and freestanding, because the greasepaint really smells and the boards really creak, the answer is not easy to formulate. For Meyerhold, the prop was of the theatre, metaphorical, but not illusionistic; for Brecht, it was perhaps a signifier; for Artaud, perhaps, a reality. And what of the actor himself? Is he a cipher? A character? A convention? A type? These four practitioners all recognised the centrality of the actor in the theatrical process. Each helped to open up acting and to liberate it from old traditions. Each saw the actor as a creative artist in his own right.

Telling, too, was the influence these four men had on the form which drama was to take and the content with which it would wrestle. In terms of content, between them, Stanislavsky, Meyerhold, Brecht, and Artaud cover the political and the non-political, the rational and the anti-rational, the public and the private. Their practice explores the place of the individual in society, and society's responsibility to the individual (as well as the individual's total rejection of society); it examines problems of narrative and plot, as well as of feeling and 'historical fact'. Brecht noted how 'we / Who wanted to prepare the ground for friendliness / Could not ourselves be friendly',[2] and at the same time Artaud was developing a 'Theatre of Cruelty'. But both saw in Bruegel's painting, *Dulle Griet*, theatre swarming through life.

In terms of their ways of working, Stanislavsky and Artaud worked 'from the inside' outwards, whereas Meyerhold and Brecht worked in the contrary direction. For Stanislavsky, the actor's felt emotion was to be shared with the silent spectator, while for Artaud the physical experience was to sear in equal measure the actor and the spectator. And where Meyerhold's theatricality shadowed reality, and validated poetic truths and the fragility of being, Brecht's theatricality argued about reality, made it accessible to reason and therefore changeable. Meyerhold and Artaud were concerned with theatre as primarily physical, but Stanislavsky and Brecht used a non-physical starting point, the feelings or thought itself, as their springboard. In consequence, the practice of these four men raised all the problems of naturalism and non-naturalism, montage and the through-line, which we are still struggling with today. They each ask, What is theatrical truth? (And we hear Stanislavsky's voice urging self-doubt, echoing down the years: 'I don't believe you!')

It is perhaps surprising that these four men knew each other as slightly as they did. Stanislavsky and Meyerhold, of course, were more than mere acquaintances: they worked together from time to time, and at telling moments in their careers. Their parallel development has been documented elsewhere,[3] but their collaborations occurred as each set out on his professional career, at the Moscow Art Theatre between 1898 and 1902, as well as in the summer of 1905, and at the very end of their lives, in 1938. Between these times, their relationship was stormy, or distant, or hostile, or intense. They followed each other's work with hawk-like eagerness, and commented on and discussed each other's tendencies and predilections. There was, however, a human warmth and undoubted regard between them personally at all times, whatever the nature of their professional rivalry.

However, the paths of each of the others in this group of 'makers of modern theatre' barely crossed. Meyerhold and Brecht both attended the performance of Mei Lan-fang in Moscow in 1935, but even though both wrote thoughtfully about the performance, it is not clear that they actually met. When Meyerhold's theatre toured Europe in 1930, Brecht attended performances, but again there is no record of them meeting. Indeed, it is clear that throughout the 1920s and beyond, Brecht followed as best he could the progress of the revolutionary Russian theatre of which Meyerhold was the leading practitioner. But contact was never established between them. On the other hand, there were plenty of contacts between their worlds, if not between the two of them as individuals: for example, Edmund Meisel wrote music for the film *Battleship Potemkin* made by Meyerhold's former student, Eisenstein, and, about the same time, wrote music for Brecht's *Man Is Man*. And Asja Lacis, Bernhard Reich, Walter Benjamin, Erwin Piscator, Viktor Shklovsky, and Sergei Tretyakov were only some of their mutual acquaintances.

Artaud, too, saw the Meyerhold Theatre in 1930, and he also worked with Georges Pitoeff, who had been an actor at Vera Komissarzhevskaya's theatre in Meyerhold's period as artistic director there. He also may have seen Stanislavsky and the Moscow Art Theatre in France in the early 1920s, and he acted in the French version of Pabst's film of Brecht's *The Threepenny Opera*. But beyond these few chance contacts, there seem to have been no encounters, or near encounters, between these four men, though in passing one might note other fleeting conjunctions and influences between them. The Dada movement, for instance, embraced Artaud in France and impinged on Brecht in Germany. More telling, perhaps, was the interest all four shared in eastern theatre, including Balinese, Chinese and Japanese theatres, especially Kabuki and Noh, as well as allied practices like yoga.

Peter Brook, in asking 'How Many Trees Make a Forest?' suggested that: 'For Artaud, theatre is fire; for Brecht, theatre is clear vision; for Stanislavsky, theatre is humanity'.[4] Others might suggest that for Stanislavsky theatre is psychology; for Meyerhold it is art; for Brecht it is political disputation; for Artaud it is apocalypse. There may not be much to be gained from such formulations. However, it is worth remembering that each of the four suffered grievously at the hands of society. Stanislavsky's factories and home were expropriated by the Bolsheviks; and when he became their favourite theatrical guru, they confined him to 'internal exile', cut him off from the world, and allowed him access only to Party-approved doctors. Meyerhold was imprisoned by the Whites in 1919 and sentenced to death; he was arrested by the Communists, grotesquely tortured, and finally sentenced by them and actually shot in 1940. Brecht was exiled from his native land for thirteen years when he was at the height of his powers; as a writer his books were burned, and he died young, at fifty-eight. Artaud was confined to mental asylums, almost starved, and only released after he had been subjected to fifty or sixty electro-convulsion therapy treatments; his death at the early age of fifty-one was, some have argued, the result of the treatment he received.

In the end, however, each stands for himself, each offers the potential for development and extension. When theatre has no more use for Stanislavsky or Meyerhold or Brecht or Artaud, it will surely be a poorer institution than it is.

2 Konstantin Stanislavsky

Life and work

Konstantin Sergeyevich Stanislavsky was born on 5 January 1863. His real surname was Alexeyev, and he belonged to an extremely wealthy merchant–manufacturing family; but his maternal grandmother was a successful French actress who had married a Russian.

Figure 2.1 Konstantin Sergeyevich Stanislavsky.

Konstantin Alexeyev's childhood was happy, privileged, and serene, and revolved almost exclusively round the family. He adored his mother and feared his father. He remembered family members swimming in the river, sometimes with his cousins, sometimes for prizes, and a brass band playing for them! And he remembered dressing up on St John's Night, and he and his brothers and sisters leaping out at passers-by. They went to balls when 'instead of tablecloths there were roses brought by express trains from Nice and Italy',[1] travelled, read widely, and performed charitable works. What he remembered best in his childhood, he later wrote, were the emotions which he lived through, especially when he was obstinate or indulging in a tantrum: 'not so much the facts that caused' them, but the emotions themselves. His truth, even as a young child, was the truth of the emotions. 'I remember all the spiritual stages of my childish fit as if the thing took place today, and when I remember them I experience again an anguished pain in my heart.'[2]

Despite the progressive capitalism of the family, the young Alexeyev's childhood was lived with one foot in 'old' Russia. The serfs had only received their legal emancipation in 1861. It was a society dominated by the gold onion domes and swinging censers of the Orthodox Church, and indeed there are parallels to be drawn between Stanislavsky's later acting system and the practices of the Orthodox mystics. He remembered holidays from school: 'In the morning one must go again to church, rising early; then there is a long period of standing, the tasty holy water, the winter sun warming us through the cupola and gilding the iconostasis, around us people in their holiday best, loud singing'.[3] When he approached the entrance examination for the local *gymnasium*, 'so that the Lord might make me wise enough to pass the impending purgatory, my nurse hung a little bag with mud from Mount Athos around my neck, and my mother and sisters decorated me with holy images'.[4] Unfortunately, during the examination, he fiddled so much with the little bag that all the 'holy mud' ran away!

For Konstantin Alexeyev art and religion were near neighbours. One side of life was occupied with business, trade, money-making; the other centred on religion, art, the preoccupations of the spirit. 'We decided that if we were to occupy ourselves with art, no thought of money must enter our minds.'[5] He loved especially all the arts which involved performing. But it was quite natural after a visit to the circus, and the forming of a determination to run a circus later in life, that he should find it necessary to 'make my decision binding with an oath', and that the oath should involve taking an icon down and swearing by it.[6] Art and religion were bound together, but it was the religion of old Russia. Going to the theatre proper was also somehow part of the same old Russian world, even if the play to be seen was modern:

the young Alexeyevs were washed, and dressed in Russian blouses made of silk, velvet trousers, and soft chamois leather boots, and they wore white gloves on their hands. It was almost as if they were going to church.

Stanislavsky's Moscow

Moscow was the city of merchants: solid, old-fashioned, and very Russian. Its churches, epitomised by Ivan the Terrible's St Basil's Cathedral, were topped with gaudy onion domes, and Red Square (literally, 'beautiful square') was dominated by its ancient Kremlin, or citadel. The rich Russian art collectors, Sergei Shchukin, Ivan Morosov, and Pavel Tretyakov, were all based in Moscow.

Artistically too Moscow was traditionalist. The Maly Theatre was renowned for the homely realism of Mikhail Shchepkin's acting and merchant families' domestic dramas created by Alexander Ostrovsky. Isaak Levitan, supreme painter of the Russian landscape, and Sergei Rakhmaninov, composer and devout Russian Orthodox believer, were both Muscovites, and even when a new group of artists did burst onto the Moscow scene, it was somehow fitting that they should be 'Primitivists' – Natalia Goncharova, Mikhail Larionov, Kasimir Malevich, and Georgy Yakulov.

Only the astonishing serial music of Alexander Scriabin and, later, the hullabaloo of Futurism's poets, Vladimir Mayakovsky, David Burlyuk, Alexander Kruchonykh, and Velimir Khlebnikov, seemed able to scratch the image of the canny, but still colourful and vital, city.

All the Alexeyev children adored the theatre and dreamed of creating their own productions, and in 1877 their father went so far to gratify them as to transform one room in their *dacha* at Lyubimovka into a theatre. They all loved acting there, and Konstantin became the director, perhaps because his love was the greatest, perhaps because he had the most talent. They created 'the Alexeyev Circle' and performed for the public. Konstantin's attempts to train his siblings included going out in the evenings pretending to be tramps among real people, and later playing the same game for whole days 'in the character' of their current role. 'Living the part' even in adolescence was a serious business. By his later teens the Alexeyev Circle was more or less defunct, and Konstantin had begun to act with amateur theatre companies, some a little *risqué*. For him, theatre was serious. Found in a somewhat insalubrious performance place, he changed his stage name to 'Stanislavsky' and went on working at his acting. He took singing lessons with the leading professional, Fyodor Komissarzhevsky, and performed in some of the productions at the Mamontov Private Opera.

Savva Mamontov and Abramtsevo

Savva Mamontov's estate of Abramtsevo, north-east of Moscow, was a colony for artists, which attracted not only painters, including the group known as 'the Wanderers', but also writers, architects, musicians, and more, who together built the famous Abramtsevo church in traditional style.

In the early 1880s, their Sunday evening play readings grew into full stagings of plays, in which Stanislavsky, whose cousin was Mamontov's wife, often participated. Mamontov used artists in the colony to create stage designs, and in 1883 his Private Opera became professional, its first presentation being Rimsky-Korsakov's *The Snow Maiden*, designed by Viktor Vasnetsov. This was probably Russia's first attempt to adopt Wagner's idea of the *integration* of all the arts – text, acting, and design – into the theatrical performance, and it was taken on by Stanislavsky to the Moscow Art Theatre.

Abramtsevo was Moscow-centred and developed the 'Russian' style in contradistinction to the cosmopolitanism which had dominated Russian culture for nearly two hundred years. It was thus a catalyst which helped to change the nature of art in Russia.

In 1887, he and Fyodor Komissarzhevsky, with Alexander Fedotov, a former actor with the Maly Theatre, who was trained in the ways of Shchepkin and Ostrovsky, established the Society of Art and Literature, largely with Stanislavsky's money. In 1889 he married one of the actresses in the company, Maria Petrovna Perevostchikova, known as Lilina. In 1893 his father died, and he took over as managing director of the business. But nothing could divert him from the theatre. Fedotov's professionalism was a revelation, his cavalier way with a playtext startling: he cut and changed it simply to suit the *theatrical* conception he had envisaged and was now striving to create. For ten years this formidable amateur group, which Stanislavsky ran by himself once Komissarzhevsky and Fedotov had fallen by the wayside, provided a significant training ground for him. Its standards were as high as any professional theatre, and Stanislavsky's fanaticism, together with his wealth, ensured that it flourished.

Naturalism

Naturalism in the theatre was above all a reaction against the conventions of melodrama, escapism, 'stock types', and the like. It aimed to create stage performances which gave the spectator the illusion that he was watching real life unfold before him. Acting, stage settings, dialogue, costume – everything was to be 'true to life'. This, it was felt, would enable the theatre to confront serious ideas and controversial contemporary opinions, such as Comte's determinism, Marx's political theories of class struggle, or Darwin's ideas of evolution.

Advocated powerfully by Émile Zola and August Strindberg, leading Naturalist playwrights included Henrik Ibsen (especially in his 'middle period'), August Strindberg, Anton Chekhov, Maxim Gorky, Gerhardt Hauptmann, and George Bernard Shaw. Among the theatre companies which strove to find convincing ways of presenting work by these authors were the Duke of Saxe-Meiningen's company, André Antoine's Théâtre Libre in Paris, Otto Brahm's Freie Buhne in Berlin, and J. T. Grein's Independent Theatre in London.

The Moscow Art Theatre followed these pioneering companies, but it was Stanislavsky whose system really revealed how to present naturalistic drama convincingly. Ironically, Stanislavsky himself always wished to escape what he regarded as the Naturalist straitjacket and avowed that his system was equally applicable to any sort of drama. It was, so long as the style of presentation was to be fundamentally illusionist.

This was the period when Naturalism was in the ascendant. In 1890, the company of the German Duke of Saxe-Meiningen appeared in Moscow. The company was renowned as the world's leading exponents of 'Naturalism', and Stanislavsky eagerly attended their performances, noticing how every character seemed to be alive, even the 'extras' in the crowd, and how groupings and movements acquired a kind of casual spontaneity. He was also struck with the way Ludwig Chronegk, their director, conducted rehearsals. He was strict to a fault, beginning the rehearsal precisely on time and drilling the actors unmercifully to achieve the effects he wanted. Chronegk's tyranny in rehearsal, added to Fedotov's way with the script, gave Stanislavsky's theatre work in the 1890s its special flavour, and enabled him to achieve results he had previously barely dared to hope for.

For instance, for his 1896 production of *Othello*, he drilled his probably inadequate amateur actors unmercifully, and presented the play in what was actually an inadequate translation, which, however, had the merit of allowing him to create, as it were, his own play. Modelling himself on a handsome Arab he happened to meet in Paris, flaying himself intellectually, and wearing himself out physically ('After a long rehearsal I was forced to lie down with a quickened heart, and I would choke as if I had asthma'), he presented an understated, doting, but ultimately insecure Othello, which professionals like Ernesto Rossi admired, students like Vsevolod Meyerhold rhapsodised over, and Nikolai Efros recorded was such as 'Moscow had never witnessed'.[7] Later that year, he presented *The Polish Jew*, again following Fedotov's style, in a manner more suited to his performance than to the author's conception, and even admitted himself in his self-denigrating style that he had acted 'not badly'. *Russki Listok* recorded that he 'conveyed the agonising delirium' of Matthias 'with exceptional "realism"',[8] while the German actor, Ludwig Barnay, told him he was 'first rate'.[9] Here was an amateur who was yet as brilliant a star as any professional on the Moscow professional stage. His next step was both logical and inevitable.

On 22 June 1897 he agreed to meet Vladimir Nemirovich-Danchenko for lunch at Moscow's Slavyansky Bazaar hotel, a sober hostelry frequented mostly by financiers, businessmen, and stock brokers. Stanislavsky at the time was thirty-five years old, very tall, graceful, alert, a heavy smoker, with grey hair but a black moustache. Nemirovich-Danchenko was five years his senior, shorter, stockier, also a heavy smoker, with a full beard. This first meeting between them lasted into the early hours of the following morning. They had taken a private room in the restaurant, and they talked eagerly, while first they ate lunch, and then drank coffee. They continued talking into the evening, and discovered they had better eat their evening meal here too. After that, and more coffee and cigarettes, late in the evening, they took the forty-minute train ride to the station nearest to Lyubimovka. From the station a *droshky* bore them on to the Alexeyev *dacha*, where over early breakfast, as dawn broke, they carried on talking, arguing, planning, discussing. 'It was something extraordinary', exclaimed Nemirovich-Danchenko.[10]

He had opened the conversation somewhat patronisingly by sounding out Stanislavsky, the 'gifted amateur', but he soon found someone he could relate to, and whose ideas chimed with his own to an extraordinary degree.

Vladimir Nemirovich-Danchenko

Born in 1858, Nemirovich-Danchenko began his long career in the arts as a writer. He also joined the Board of the Maly Theatre, and taught drama at the Moscow Philharmonia Music and Drama School, where his students included Meyerhold, Olga Knipper, and Ivan Moskvin.

In 1897 he met Stanislavsky at the Slavyansky Bazaar in Moscow, for the long discussion which led to the foundation of the Art Theatre, but after a few years the two began to find each other difficult to deal with. Nemirovich knew that Stanislavsky's genius was what made the Art Theatre into the foremost theatre in Russia, perhaps in the world, but he found his restless artistic questing infuriating. For his part, Stanislavsky found Nemirovich intolerant, inflexible, and rude. Matters came to a head when Nemirovich sacked Stanislavsky from the cast of *The Village of Stepanchikova*. The breach was irreparable, and though the two continued jointly to head the Art Theatre, they no longer spoke to each other.

In 1919 Nemirovich set up the Moscow Art Theatre Musical Studio, later the Nemirovich-Danchenko Musical Theatre, and he directed the controversial opera, *Lady Macbeth of Mtsensk* by Shostakovich, which triggered Stalin's persecution of the arts. Nevertheless, as a member of the Communist Party, Nemirovich himself escaped censure, and indeed in 1936 he was among the first to be awarded the honorific title 'People's Artist of the USSR'. He died in 1943.

Once they got to Lyubimovka, Stanislavsky began to write down what were effectively a series of revolutionary conclusions. They agreed that a new theatre should be established, where the art of the theatre should take precedence over the requirements of the box office: the administration should serve art, not the other way round. They agreed that every production should be a fresh creation; that the staging, the decor, the costumes – everything – should be created anew, even down to the programme the spectator would read. This meant a new emphasis on rehearsals, and dress rehearsals, which in turn implied an ensemble company, not one composed of stars and extras. Thus they would on the whole employ Stanislavsky's best amateur colleagues, and the best students from Nemirovich-Danchenko's classes at the Philharmonic, in preference to established professionals, who had the old bad habits of the theatre ingrained in their approach. The theatre would show a new respect for its audience, who would be admitted at 'popular' prices; but they would not be admitted at all if they were late, and the auditorium, and even the corridors, would have their lights dimmed at the start of the performance. Nemirovich would be responsible for the repertoire, while Stanislavsky would be responsible for the stage productions. The theatre would be financed by a company of share-holders. They gave themselves a year for the venture to get under way.

The Moscow Art Theatre assembled the following summer in a group of buildings a couple of miles from Lyubimovka, and began rehearsing the new season of plays. In October they opened with Alexey Tolstoy's historical drama, *Tsar Fyodor Ionnavich*. This was well, though not ecstatically received, and was followed by a judicious mixture of classical and modern plays, which failed to make the significant impact the company's finances required. In December they presented *The Seagull* by Anton Chekhov, which proved to be a triumph, and secured the future of the theatre. For the next few seasons, Chekhov's plays formed the centrepiece of an increasingly confident and successful venture which, by the time of his early death in the summer of 1904, was firmly established, with a reputation for modernity, honesty and quality second to none.

Anton Chekhov

Chekhov was born on 17 January 1860 in Taganrog, a busy port on the Azov Sea, near Rostov. One of six children, his parents were quarrelsome, and his father tyrannical and improvident. Chekhov himself, though, grew up lively and amusing, as well as observant and intelligent, with a strong sense of responsibility towards others, particularly his family. His parents moved to Moscow, but he stayed in Taganrog to complete his schooling, following them only in 1879 to train to be a doctor. Even as a student he supported his family, working long hours on medicine and spending much of the night writing little stories, squibs, joke satires, and even short stage farces, all of which he sold for whatever he could get.

By the middle 1880s, he was practising as a doctor, and writing stories notable for their compassion and clarity. He was regarded as perhaps second only to Tolstoy among living Russian writers. His first performed full-length play, *Ivanov*, was successfully premiered at the

Korsh Theatre, Moscow, in 1887, but his next, *The Seagull,* first performed at the Alexandrinsky Theatre in St Petersburg in 1896, was much less successful, and Chekhov swore to write no more plays.

But in 1898 Vladimir Nemirovich-Danchenko persuaded him to let the new Moscow Art Theatre attempt *The Seagull,* and the production was a triumph. He returned to writing plays, and Stanislavsky and the Art Theatre were responsible for the premieres of his later plays – *Uncle Vanya* (1899), *Three Sisters* (1901), and *The Cherry Orchard* (1904). These are works of great subtlety and resonance, and were all well received when first performed, even though Chekhov disliked what he regarded as Stanislavsky's lugubrious style: to him, these plays were ironic comedies.

From at least the early 1890s Chekhov suffered from tuberculosis. By 1904 he was dying. That summer he went to Badenweiler, by the Black Forest, with his wife, the Art Theatre actress Olga Knipper. On the night of 1–2 July, he awoke, shared a drink of champagne with her, and died.

Stanislavsky, as the chief stage director, remained true to his earlier methods, and was a dictatorial director whose justification was to be seen in his results. He was not cruel or unpleasant to his actors, but his approach was to prepare a 'production plan' or *mise-en-scène* before the company met, and then to use rehearsals to ensure that the actors conformed to this plan. The plan included everything from the characters' motivations, through the scenery, to the atmospheric sound effects; nothing was left to chance. But from the beginning there were mutterings of opposition to this method, and to the attribution of success to them. Meyerhold, for instance, who played Treplev in the original *Seagull,* thought that it was the actors' own sensitivity to Chekhov's rhythms, 'not the *mise-en-scènes,* nor the crickets, nor the sound of horses' hoofs on the bridge',[11] which captivated the spectators. But Meyerhold and a number of others were virtually expelled from the company in 1902, when it was reorganised into something approaching a co-operative, and in the meantime Stanislavsky's reputation was growing. His acting was outstanding. He presented especially memorable characters in Dr Stockman in Ibsen's *An Enemy of the People,* Astrov in *Uncle Vanya,* Satin in *The Lower Depths* by Maxim Gorky, and Vershinin in Chekhov's *The Three Sisters.* He was at the height of his powers.

Symbolism

Symbolism, perhaps the first self-consciously 'Modernist' movement in the arts, was founded by the French poet, Stéphane Mallarmé. It developed some of the theatrical ideas of Richard Wagner and Friedrich Nietzsche in deliberate opposition to the Naturalism of Zola. It championed in particular the drama of the Belgian, Maurice Maeterlinck, typified by plays such as *Interior*, *The Sightless*, and *The Death of Tintagiles*. Its most significant French practitioner was Aurélien Lugné-Poë, and later Symbolist playwrights included Hugo von Hofmannsthal, W. B. Yeats, and Paul Claudel. Perhaps more significantly, Ibsen in his last plays, and Chekhov, especially in *Three Sisters* and *The Cherry Orchard*, used symbolism in apparently more naturalistic dramas to add unexpected resonances and depth.

Yet, as always with Stanislavsky, he was dissatisfied. Something was missing. He felt an emptiness at the heart of his own best performances. At first he wondered whether this was the result of the kind of play he was specialising in: perhaps he, and the Art Theatre, should be directing their attention to the more modishly modern Symbolist drama of writers such as the Nobel prize-winner, Maurice Maeterlinck. But when he directed a triple bill of Maeterlinck's *The Sightless*, *Interior*, and *The Intruder* in October 1904, the result was hugely disappointing. The following spring he met the dismissed Meyerhold again. Meyerhold had had some success with Symbolist drama and was now full of enthusiasm for them. Stanislavsky suggested setting up a Theatre Studio attached to the Art Theatre, and letting Meyerhold lead a company there which would concentrate on this 'new' drama. At his own expense he hired Meyerhold, a company of actors, designers, and others, and found a theatre in Moscow for them to perform in. In the summer of 1905, under Stanislavsky's watchful eye, the Theatre Studio company prepared four productions. But when Stanislavsky saw them in the big Moscow Theatre he had hired, he found them unconvincing. At the same time, Moscow was in turmoil as the people revolted for better living conditions and democracy, and against the disasters of the war with Japan. The new productions were shelved and the Theatre Studio company was disbanded.

The first Russian revolution, 1905

In 1904 Japan attacked the far eastern Russian naval base at Port Arthur to devastating effect. All Russia was caught on the hop, and the tsar declared war on Japan.

But the Russian people, exploited and hungry, were not in favour, and opposition to the war was quickly and effectively organised. Demands for civil rights, for political freedoms and democracy, were made with increasing stridency, while the war with Japan went from bad to worse. On 22 January 1905 a peaceful demonstration of workers was shot at and dispersed by the tsar's troops, with many casualties, on what became known as 'Bloody Sunday'. Strikes were organised, terrorist atrocities perpetrated, and people's soviets (councils) were roughly elected by popular mandate, Lev Trotsky becoming president of the St Petersburg soviet.

In August 1905 the tsar concluded the Treaty of Portsmouth with Japan, but it was too late. The people were in furious revolt, and a general strike forced the tsar to concede a popularly elected Duma (parliament) for the government of the country.

The fact that he slid away from his commitments over the following years, so that effectively the 1905 revolution achieved nothing, was one major reason why twelve years later the people revolted again.

That winter the Art Theatre undertook its first foreign tour, to western Europe. It was an unexpected success, and in Germany the Kaiser himself attended performances and indicated his pleasure. But Stanislavsky was not particularly consoled. The following summer he went to Finland with a notebook and pencil, and tried to focus on how – or why – his dissatisfactions had arisen. The problem seemed to centre around the twin challenges of 'truth' (emotional truth, as Stanislavsky conceived it) and spontaneity. He needed to find a way to ensure these two were always present in his performances. This was the first inkling of the system he was to devise over the next six or eight years. On his return to Moscow he discussed his problems and his new understanding with his personal assistant, Leopold Sulerzhitsky, whose support and enthusiasm re-energised him. In September 1908 they directed Maeterlinck's children's fantasy drama, *The Blue Bird*, together, and in the production the following year of *A Month in the Country* by Ivan Turgenev, Stanislavsky began consciously to apply his new 'system'.

Contrary to Art Theatre habit and perhaps principal, *A Month in the Country* was rehearsed behind closed doors. Stanislavsky began with a series of sessions when all the actors sat round a table and he conducted detailed discussions of the play. First he addressed each character's 'through-line', how each changed and developed emotionally, how each scene related to the others. Then he split the text down into 'bits' and established both a mood for each bit, and a 'task' for each character within each bit. It was weary work. Only after two months was Stanislavsky satisfied, and the actors were allowed to stand up and begin to 'move' the work. Another two months went by, and at last the production was ready. It opened on 9 December 1909, and was an immediate success. The detail was clever and attractive, and the final performances assured and emotionally profound and gripping, none more so than Stanislavsky's own performance as Rakitin. Despite the sweat and tears (and there had been plenty of each along the way), and despite the many doubts, especially among the established players, who had felt no need to change their ways and were unable to understand Stanislavsky's apparently irrelevant theorising, the new 'system' was beginning to bear fruit.

Nevertheless, Nemirovich-Danchenko was thoroughly suspicious of Stanislavsky: 'I find that in the last few years our theatre has fallen short of its purpose', he wrote severely in 1909; and 'We must stop shilly-shallying in search of form.'[12] He was determined to get the Art Theatre back onto the track he (Nemirovich) desired. The bitterness between the two men grew. What Stanislavsky needed was space and time to experiment, but this was no longer available in the main Art Theatre where Nemirovich's malign influence inhibited him. Consequently, after he had assisted in bringing Gordon Craig's extraordinary *Hamlet* to completion, he decided to create his own laboratory, or Studio, wherein the 'system' could be developed, tested, and perfected. Therefore, on 1 September 1912, the First Studio of the Art Theatre was established, financed by Stanislavsky himself (later the Art Theatre took over the budget), with Sulerzhitsky in charge, and an enthusiastic group of young actors and students eager to begin work.

Leopold Antonovich Sulerzhitsky
Gorky nicknamed Sulerzhitsky 'Suler'. Born in 1872, he was a small man with bow legs, but strong, energetic, and good-looking. He trained to be a painter, but was expelled from art school for political activities. He became a merchant seaman, developed an interest in eastern philosophies, and adopted what would now be called 'Green'

politics, tinged with revolutionary tendencies. He was even confined to a lunatic asylum in 1896 for his views.

Through Tolstoy's daughter, a fellow student at art college, Sulerzhitsky met the great writer, and in 1899 he assisted him in the project to resettle in Canada the controversial peasant religious sect known as the Dukhobors. Tolstoy largely paid for them to emigrate in an epic journey, beset with hardship, sickness, storms at sea, cold, and hunger. Afterwards Tolstoy commented that Sulerzhitsky was 'the purest man I have ever known'.

Gorky introduced him to Stanislavsky after a performance of *An Enemy of the People*. They talked in Stanislavsky's dressing room, in the cab going home, and almost through the night, and a friendship developed in which Sulerzhitsky came to be more and more important to Stanislavsky. In 1908 Sulerzhitsky went to Paris with Vakhtangov to direct Maeterlinck's *The Blue Bird*, and later he assisted with the Art Theatre productions of *A Month in the Country* and *Hamlet*. When Stanislavsky established the First Studio in 1912, Sulerzhitsky was the obvious man to head the project. His influence was immense, many of his ideas became integral to Stanislavsky's system as it developed, and he was also behind the idealistic attempts to build a theatre colony in Evpatria in southern Russia. But on 17 December 1916, before any of his projects had reached fulfilment, he died of the chronic kidney disease which had plagued him for years.

For four years, until the death of Sulerzhitsky in December 1916, the First Studio was a unique creative centre where the ideas of Stanislavsky were worked through and developed, through classes, workshops, experimental sessions, discussions and arguments, and rehearsals. An open book in which members of the Studio were to contribute their ideas, disagreements, and suggestions was kept, and even today makes fascinating reading. And the achievements of the Studio were novel, unexpected, and brilliant. Sulerzhitsky was a superb leader, his warm personality and eager enthusiasm sparking a similar commitment from the others, and the dream of a self-sustaining theatre collective almost came to fruition when Stanislavsky purchased land at Evpatria by the Black Sea. Studio members went there each summer to learn through physical labour: they adapted the place as a theatre haven, with sleeping quarters, cultivated areas to grow their own food, and a theatre for visitors, who would spend days (and nights) here.

This dream was never quite realised. But when the First Studio presented an adaptation of Charles Dickens's *The Cricket on the Hearth* in Moscow in November 1914, Stanislavsky felt his search for a system had been finally justified. He wrote: 'In this production . . . there sounded for the first time those deep and heartfelt notes of superconscious feeling in the measure and the form in which I dreamed of them.'[13]

Two years later, Sulerzhitsky died, and Evgeny Vakhtangov took over as leader. Though a greater theatrical practitioner in every way, Vakhtangov was less in sympathy with Stanislavsky than Sulerzhitsky had been. The First Studio began drifting away from Stanislavsky. Or, to put it another way, Stanislavsky was growing beyond the First Studio. His ideas were changing, developing. He established a Second Moscow Art Theatre Studio, more like a traditional school, and taught master classes there. Then a Third Studio was created, and after the revolution a Fourth was also established.[14]

But while the studios were responding to Stanislavsky's extraordinary creative drive, and bringing the system to its highest and most successful levels of achievement, Stanislavsky himself was finding his acting increasingly problematic. His Salieri in Pushkin's *Mozart and Salieri* in 1915 was overburdened by his attempts to work out all the finer details of his theory on himself, and his next part, Rostanev in his own adaptation of Dostoevsky's *The Village of Stepanchikova*, was so painful that in the end Nemirovich-Danchenko removed him from the cast and gave the part to another actor.

Figure 2.2 The Cricket on the Hearth, First Studio of the Moscow Art Theatre, 1914.

Soon after this, Russia dissolved into revolution, Stanislavsky was dispossessed of his factories and his home – a new one was found for him only by the new commissar in charge of the theatres, Anatoly Lunacharsky, with the personal backing of Lenin himself – and the Art Theatre seemed on the point of splitting asunder. One group of most of the best actors, headed by Vasily Kachalov and Chekhov's widow, Olga Knipper, was caught by the Civil War on the 'wrong' side of the combat lines, and seemed lost, and in the spring of 1921 the Art Theatre's subsidy was withdrawn (though it was restored before the year was out). Meyerhold wrote an article which he entitled 'The Solitude of Stanislavsky', in which he depicted Stanislavsky as a prisoner in his own theatre, using his 'system' to defend himself against Nemirovich-Danchenko's misconceptions of literature. Even the Studios were collapsing, and its members abandoning Stanis-lavsky's ideas for Meyerhold's 'Modernism'. It was his lowest point.

But in the late spring of 1922 the so-called 'Kachalov Group' returned to Moscow, without too many defections to the west, and a foreign tour was hastily arranged for the reintegrated company. In September 1921 they left for Europe, and did not return to Russia until August 1924, having toured not only western Europe, but America twice. Artistically, their visits across the Atlantic had been profoundly successful and influential, and if not much profit had accrued, Stanislavsky had been inveigled into writing his first book: not quite the one he wanted to write, but his self-critical artistic autobiography, charting his path towards the 'system', *My Life in Art*.

When Stanislavsky returned home, he seemed to have new purpose. The artistically impressive performances in America and elsewhere were actually based on productions from the very earliest days of the Art Theatre – *Tsar Fyodor*, Chekhov's *Three Sisters*, and so on – and Stanislavsky seems to have wanted to create something fresh with his system. His chance came when Nemirovich-Danchenko himself went abroad with his Art Theatre Music Studio, leaving the main Art Theatre in Stanislavsky's hands. In one of his most productive periods, he now created a series of productions which were innovative and widely acclaimed, including a re-thought revival of *Uncle Vanya*, new productions of old plays, such as Ostrovsky's *A Burning Heart* and Beaumarchais' *The Marriage of Figaro*, operas like *The Tsar's Bride* and *La Bohème*, and, most interestingly, new Soviet plays, including Mikhail Bulgakov's *The Days of the Turbins* and Vsevolod Ivanov's *Armoured Train 14–69*.

He was also beginning to document his methods, dividing them into two parts, consisting, first, of the actor's work on himself, and, second, of his work on the role. These writings became in English *An Actor Prepares*, *Building a Character*, and *Creating a Role* – works which stimulate and infuriate in almost equal measure. They treat the problems of acting through the fictitious development of a student actor (modelled on the remembered ambitions and questions of the young Stanislavsky, of course), who attends the classes of a 'Master' (the mature Stanislavsky). Because he was writing them at a time when he was still working, still developing his ideas, they possess no finality, and consequently sometimes seem contradictory, sometimes almost impenetrable. They remained unfinished at Stanislavsky's death, but still they are the nearest we can get – and that is quite close if we read them creatively and with care[15] – to a genuine manual of Stanislavsky's practice.

This was a new Stanislavsky, with a new purpose, and working on new developments to his system. But in October 1928, at the thirtieth-anniversary celebrations for the Art Theatre itself, he suffered a massive heart attack which effectively ended his professional career. After rest and recuperation he took up his self-imposed tasks again, but not as a full-time working member of a company. Nevertheless, this semi-retirement enabled him to develop a new 'Method of Physical Actions' for actors, which effectively completely superseded the old 'system' worked out in the First Studio. Meanwhile, significant and threatening changes were occurring in the Soviet Union.

At the time of the revolution, and for a few years after it, every 'old' idea had been castigated, scoffed at, and discarded. In the theatre this included Stanislavsky's ideas: it was the time when the members of the various Studios were giving their loyalties to Meyerhold. But as society settled down to the new order, and especially after Lenin's death and Stalin's acquisition of power, experiment became less acceptable, and by the end of the 1920s a new kind of cultural (as well as political) conservatism was setting in. In the arts, innovation became gradually intolerable, and all who wanted to work in any artistic sphere had to join the monolithic union for workers in that sphere, and then had to create 'art' which was 'Socialist Realist' in accordance with the policy which the Communist Party laid down. Experimentation, unpredictability, and 'difficult' work were no longer to be countenanced. Stanislavsky's 'system', however, was pronounced not only acceptable, but actually the *only* acceptable method of work for actors.

Socialist Realism
Socialist Realism grew out of the same nineteenth-century Realism as Stanislavsky's acting system. It was marked by didacticism, social involvement, and a sort of naturalism in which the content was easily assimilable because of its surface likeness to 'reality'.

Socialist Realism, which was promulgated by Stalin's Culture Minister, Andrei Zhdanov, built on these characteristics, which was why it was so easy for the Communists to take ownership of the Stanislavsky system. But Zhdanov stressed also typicality, optimism, and 'revolutionary romanticism' as necessary to *Socialist* Realism. Hence the Charter of the Union of Soviet Writers, drawn up in 1934, insisted that the Soviet artist must give 'a true, historically concrete depiction of reality *in its Revolutionary development*' and emphasised that the 'truth and historical concreteness of the artistic depiction of reality must be combined with task of the ideological transformation and education of the workers in the spirit of Socialism'.

By thus simplifying the Realist artist's 'task', and by insisting that this was the *only* acceptable method for the Soviet artist to adopt, Zhdanov's policy inevitably led to a standardisation in the arts, even when it did help – or seemed to help – popular understanding. In the end, Socialist Realism came to be aligned with sentimentality and facile optimism, so that effectively it left little of value behind.

Meanwhile, Stalin decided to take the Art Theatre under his personal wing, and re-named it the 'Moscow Academic Art Theatre of the USSR', adding the name of Gorky, his favourite playwright, to this title after Gorky's death in 1936. In the time of the Great Terror, therefore,[16] the Art Theatre was held up as a model of Soviet Theatre, its productions were greeted with sycophantic awe, its subsidies were increased, and its leading players were expected (perhaps required) to sign letters of congratulation to Stalin each time more show trials and death sentences were announced.

To his credit, or perhaps because he was now virtually confined to his flat, if not his bed, Stanislavsky did not sign such weasel-worded missives. But he was virtually a prisoner in his own home, isolated, neutralised, and condemned to a kind of 'internal exile'. Nevertheless, even under these abnormal conditions, he was developing new ideas with a few trusted co-workers. No-one heard about his latest innovations, but they informed his last work, most notably the unfinished *Tartuffe*. They came to be codified as 'The Method of Physical Actions', and they form the main subject of Vasily Toporkov's *Stanislavsky in Rehearsal*,[17] as well as being often behind the thinking in *Creating a Role*, his third book in the English-language sequence. The method is new and daring and owes something to the work of his former employee, long-time ideological opponent, and newly befriended colleague, Vsevolod Meyerhold. *Creating a Role* puts new emphasis on Meyerhold's techniques of improvisation and scenic movement. But in the end, the Method of Physical Actions is Stanislavsky's own, and contains perhaps his most constructive ideas for actors.

In January 1938 Stanislavsky was seventy-five years old. The street where he lived was re-named Stanislavsky Street, and Stalin bestowed upon him the uniquely prestigious Order of Lenin. But he was still immersed in his work, and even appointed Meyerhold, whose own theatre had been liquidated, to a directing post in the Stanislavsky Opera Theatre. Meyerhold was, he told Yuri Bakhrushin, his 'sole heir'. Despite his isolation, his projects must have appeared to Stanislavsky to be going well in his last year. His works were being published, his ideas were flowing, but physically he could no longer bear up. In the summer he weakened, and on the afternoon of 7 August 1938, as his nurse came to take his temperature, he shivered, suffered one convulsion, and died.

The key questions

All his life Stanislavsky remembered that he was born in the year the great 'Realist' Russian actor, Mikhail Shchepkin, had died. Stanislavsky recalled Shchepkin's dictum: 'It is not important that you play well or ill; it is important that you play truthfully.'[18] The key question for him was how to play 'truthfully'.

His early career coincided with the rise of Naturalism. It was Emile Zola in 1881 who declared: 'The impulse of the century is toward naturalism.' It had apparently arrived in the novel, but, Zola continued,

> I am waiting for someone to put a man of flesh and bones on the stage, taken from reality, scientifically analysed, and described without one lie. I am waiting for someone to rid us of fictitious characters, of these symbols of virtue and vice which have no worth as human data. I am waiting for environment to determine the characters, and the characters to act according to the logic of facts combined with the logic of their own disposition . . . I am waiting for a dramatic work void of declamations, majestic speech, and noble sentiments, to have the unimpeachable morality of truth and to teach us the frightening lesson of sincere investigation.[19]

Though Zola was seeking a new dramaturgy, which was perhaps to be fulfilled by Ibsen and, later, Chekhov, his despairing hope could also be seen to be answered by the advent of Stanislavsky and the Moscow Art Theatre.

From his very early experiments on the stage, Stanislavsky kept notebooks in which he tried to analyse his acting. In an early note, he wrote, significantly: 'Herein lies the problem: to bring life itself on to the stage, but avoid routine (which kills this life), while transgressing none of the stage rules.'[20] Life in this sense, and truth, became almost synonymous for Stanislavsky. He recalled his early career in terms Zola would certainly recognise: 'The virtue of my work then lay in the fact that I tried to be sincere and sought truth, and banished lies, especially theatrical, crafted ones. I began to hate the theatre in theatre, and sought in it living, genuine life.'[21] 'Living, genuine life' for Stanislavsky incorporated Russian notions of the 'soul' as well as his often reiterated aim of 'embodying the life of the human spirit' in the character on stage. The truth Stanislavsky sought overlapped with this; it included, first, 'emotional' truth, but also other kinds of truth: 'spiritual' truth, 'intellectual' truth. These three together, he believed, amounted to 'inner' truth, to what was true to the imagination, to what was to be imagined.

Truth and life. Stanislavsky believed that inner truth became accessible on stage when the actor 'lived' the part. The idea of 'living' the part, or perhaps 'living through' the part, is an uneasy one. The very word which Stanislavsky used for this, *perezhivanie*, has caused much controversy: it is in fact quite likely that Stanislavsky was being deliberately vague, since what he is referring to is virtually impossible to pin down, though an actor who has experienced it knows exactly what he means. It is something to do with creating and experiencing simultaneously, and it also includes a fierce sensation of being 'in the present'. The audience feels it as the *immediate* communication of 'felt' experience.

Stanislavsky's question, therefore, was how to achieve this, how to 'live the part', and thereby replace theatrical falseness with 'inner' truth.

Stanislavsky's answers

'There is no actual method yet', Stanislavsky said in 1924; 'there are only a number of basic principles and exercises'.[22] This was after nearly twenty years of work on what here he calls his 'method'!

Stanislavsky knew precisely and always what the questions were he was trying to answer, but his solutions were always tentative, temporary, and developing. He never found a single answer which he could stick to. His career shows a restless striving, a discontent with whatever had been done, and a new searching for other, better ways forward. He took inspiration from many areas, and borrowed magpie-like from whatever he found useful, including modern psychology, theatre tradition, the practices of the Orthodox Church, the eurhythmics of Jaques-Dalcroze, ancient Hindu yoga techniques, contemporary Tolstoyan philosophy, and more. He took most, probably, from Leopold Sulerzhitsky, his assistant, though whether everything he got from Sulerzhitsky was ultimately helpful might be argued. Sulerzhitsky believed that art was to do with emotion and its purpose was to provide spiritual enlightenment, both familiar positions for Stanislavsky. But the question of the place, use, and function of emotion became one of the most vexed in all his work.

One feature of that work which did not change, however, was the relationship between truth and life. The actor's inner truth penetrated real life and thus led to the life of the theatre. But the ordinary actor – and Stanislavsky made a distinction between the geniuses of the stage, like Tomasso Salvini, and the run-of-the-mill actor, like (as he perversely saw it) himself – could never be sure at any given time *how* to penetrate that inner truth. That was what Stanislavsky's system addressed. The system was to provide the actor with the means and the technique to be able consistently to create life on stage. The actor must be alert and 'in the present' all through every performance. His 'system' was to be the unseen engine which allowed the vehicle (the actor in the play) to move smoothly. It was the grammar which made sense of otherwise arbitrary words and phrases. He wanted it to provide a route by which the actor would be able to experience, to *live through* the part.

The system (or the Method of Physical Actions, as it developed into) was rooted in the belief that the body and the mind are indissolubly one. What affects one affects the other. But because the path Stanislavsky saw went 'from the conscious to the unconscious', he began by asking the actor to work physically on himself. He sought a good level of physical alertness in the actor, for without it nothing else was likely to happen. Relaxation of the muscles became one of the Stanislavskian actors' prime requirements, and techniques of physical relaxation were regarded as highly important. The sheer good sense of this emphasis is clear to anyone who attends the theatre. It is easy to spot an actor whose body is tense, or physically 'bound', or whose voice slides into the wrong register, or who shouts too much, imagining that intensity is a substitute for what Mihkail Chekhov called 'ease'.

Only the relaxed actor, Stanislavsky maintained, could focus his attention properly, and attention was the next part of the actor's work on himself. An actor must focus absolutely, and not allow his attention to wander, most especially not to let it wander out into the auditorium. Attention is of course related to concentration, and the actor is equally required to concentrate unremittingly on the stage action and what his playing partner is doing, observing, listening, and responding truthfully.

In real life there are always plenty of objects that fix our attention, but conditions in the theatre are different, and interfere with an actor's living normally, so that *an effort* to fix attention becomes necessary. It becomes requisite to learn anew to look at things on the stage, *and to see them.*[23]

Finally, the actor must train his imagination. Stanislavsky puts considerable emphasis on this, for without being able to imagine the truth of a situation, how can an actor embody it? The basic technique he advocates involves what he calls 'the Magic If': *if* this canvas was a real castle wall, how would I act? Stanislavsky calls this *if* 'a kind of lever to lift us out of everyday life on to the plane of imagination'.[24] His explanation is unequivocal: 'In order to be emotionally involved in the imaginary world which the actor builds on the basis of a play, in order to be caught up in the action on the stage, he must believe in it.'[25] Thus, an actor needs not only to train himself to be physically alert and relaxed, not only to develop his ability to concentrate, he must also know how to use his imagination productively. These are the basic areas of the actor's work on himself.

The second part of the system was more controversial, and indeed here is where Stanislavsky worked hardest, and was least satisfied with himself. It concerned the actor's work on the role, and centred on the relationship between action and feeling, stage action and the actor's feeling. Essentially Stanislavsky believed that an action stems from a feeling – that one runs away, say, because one is feeling frightened. 'The right and logical process [is] the inner experience comes first and is then embodied in an external form', he said.[26] Only *genuine* feeling ('inner experience') could stimulate genuine action. This inevitably gives rise to the question: how does the actor genuinely feel the role? Of course the imagination plays a significant part in this process, and Stanislavsky suggested that if the actor broke down the emotion into *things to do*, small bits, then this was a possible route to truth. Thus, when discussing 'love', he insisted on discussing it in terms of the incidents which comprise it:

First, it was the meeting between 'her' and 'him'. Either immediately, or by degrees . . . the attention of either or both of the future lovers is heightened. They live on the memory of every moment of their meeting. They seek pretexts for another meeting. There is a second meeting. They have the desire to involve one another in a common interest, common action which will require more frequent meetings, and so on . . . The first quarrel, reproaches, doubts . . . The first kiss. Growing demands on each other. Jealousy. A break . . . They meet again. They forgive each other. So it goes on.

If you carry out in your imagination – with the right basis of detailed circumstances, proper thinking, sincerity of feeling – each step in this series of actions, you will find that first externally and then internally you will reach the condition of a person in love.[27]

However, the imagination employed thus is not the only way, nor indeed is it perhaps the best way, to arouse genuine emotion.

A more favoured technique, at least for a number of years, was what Stanislavsky called the 'emotion memory', which derived from the contemporary French psychologist Theodule Ribot, whose works he studied. Ribot described two men who had been stranded on a desert island; one remembered what he had done to try to escape; the other remembered how he had felt – 'delight, apprehension, fear, hope, doubt and finally panic'.[28] The latter's was an emotion memory, which is actually accessible to all of us. If you blush at the memory of some moment when you made a fool of yourself, or if your palms sweat at the memory of an incident when you were in great danger, you are experiencing something through your emotion memory. 'In time of actual danger a man may remain calm, yet faint away when he recalls the memory of it.'[29] Such experience can be harnessed by the actor.

Stanislavsky also pointed to the 'sensation memory' as a useful tool for the actor. This could be useful for the actor who has to sit down to what is in reality a meal made of painted papier mâché. He needs to convince the audience that it is delicious, mouth-watering food. To do this, he may need to bring to mind some memory of a particularly delectable meal he has enjoyed, thereby giving his expressions of delight a kind of reality through his 'sensation memory'. In justification for this approach, in *An Actor Prepares* Stanislavsky wrote: 'Always and for ever when you are on the stage, you must play yourself.'[30] Later he came to modify his view of the utility of the actor's memory as perhaps unreliable, perhaps likely to bring other unwanted connotations with it, and in any case perhaps too easily prone to betray the truth of the stage encounter the actor was attempting to create.

But however created, the actor's emotions were to spark his stage actions. Each bit of the actor's action on the stage was the result of a feeling, or rather was the result of a task which sprang from the feeling. If I love you, I want to smile at you, offer you a chair, make you a cup of coffee, sit beside you, hold your hand, and so on. Each is a piece of action which stems ultimately from my emotion of love for you. My love *justifies* a string of actions on my part. The emotion stimulates the motion. In other words, Stanislavsky noticed that there was a world of difference between lighting a fire, and lighting a fire to keep warm. The latter action has a justification, and is interesting. The former does not, and is not. Stanislavsky was quite adamant about this: 'All action in the theatre must have an inner justification', he said.[31] It was, he believed, at the heart of the fundamental theatrical negotiation between actor and spectator. So what one watches as a spectator in the theatre, the actor *doing something*, is inextricably linked to the emotion he feels, and thus to the 'inner truth' which is at the core of his art. Such was Stanislavsky's reasoning.

His system, therefore, comprises, first, the actor training himself to relax and concentrate, and then to set his imagination free by means of the Magic If. He is now in a *creative mood*. This enables him to access the truth of feeling in the role which alone can propel him into the truth of action. The truth of action thus embodies the inner truth which Stanislavsky believed was what the actor aims to communicate.

Theatre practice

Stanislavsky's professional theatre career, which began with the formation of the Moscow Art Theatre in 1898, may be divided into three phases. The early years at the Art Theatre, when he directed most of the productions, and acted in many of them too, was characterised by autocracy. He worked out a production plan, or *mise-en-scène*, before the cast assembled. When he met them, they sat round a table while he explained what he wanted from them. Then they got up and, under his guidance, did what he asked them to do. This was the approach employed, for instance, for the famous production of Chekhov's *The Seagull*, which purportedly 'saved' the Art Theatre from ruin, and it is well documented in *'The Seagull' Produced by Stanislavsky* which was published in the 1930s.[32]

After a very few years, however, Stanislavsky became dissatisfied with such dictatorial methods, and from about 1907 he modified his practice. The new phase reached its highest and most impressive point in the work he did with the First Studio of the Art Theatre in the years immediately after its foundation in 1912. It was here that what is usually known as Stanislavsky's 'system' was at its finest and its clearest, and it is towards this achievement that his autobiography, *My Life in Art*, leads. The practice of the 'system' from the period of the First Studio up to about 1930 is largely (but by no means exclusively) behind his two English-language books, *An Actor Prepares* and *Building a Character*.

Stanislavsky's last phase, when he developed the Method of Physical Actions, is what is documented mostly in the third English-language book, *Creating a Role*, which, however, was not published until nearly a quarter of a century after his death. It is easy to see, therefore, that any attempt to crystallise his practice is fraught with problems. It should also be noted that he always argued that his system was a tool, not an end product; a guide, not a gospel. To sum it up, therefore, to strike the right balances, to adopt the

correct tone, poses almost insuperable challenges in any attempt to
it. Nevertheless, and despite these difficulties, its centrality to the d⌐⌐⌐
ment of twentieth-century Western theatre makes the attempt to describe
it inescapable as well as worthwhile. And at least one may note that from
the outset, and consistently throughout his career, Stanislavsky's aims
remained the same. As Balukhaty put it in his Introduction to *'The Seagull'*
Produced by Stanislavsky, it was 'to convey by means of scenic devices the
truth of the emotional experiences of the characters in the play'.[33]

Very early Stanislavsky was aware that the actor needed a driving force,
or an enthusiasm, for his work, and he isolated three 'inner motive forces'
which the actor could use for this – the *feelings*, which were significant but
not easily controlled; the *mind*, which could guide and point the work; and
the *will*, the key motivating force. When these worked in harmony, they
provoked the 'creative mood' which the actor needed. When the feelings or
the mind (or both) awoke the will to action, the relationship between
the psychological and the physical became clear. These two features – the
psychological and the physical – of the human being were interdependent,
according to Stanislavsky, but it was the psychological which stirred
the physical to action: if the action were true, it in turn confirmed the
'inner truth'.

It was in his production of *A Month in the Country* in 1909, in which he
himself played Rakitin, that Stanislavsky first put his ideas into practice.
The process as he conceived it involved the actor working in rehearsals
with other actors, but also crucially at home alone. His idea of what the
actor should do as his 'homework' at this point consisted of six steps which
would take him to the first night. They were: first, the arousal of the actor's
'will', his enthusiasm for the play to be performed; second, his search for
useable psychological material to help him with his role; third, the
'invisible' creation of his character in his own imagination; fourth, his
physicalisation for himself of what he conceived to be the truth of the
character; fifth, the synthesising of these last two stages, that is, the melding
of the imaginative creation and the physicalisation; and sixth, the final
performance before the audience.

Meanwhile the process of company rehearsals proceeds in two stages. In
the first, the company sits round the table to discuss the play. In fact, during
A Month in the Country, they found it practically impossible to *discuss* the
play: almost always Stanislavsky himself did most of the talking, as the
play's superobjective and the characters' through-lines were decided, and
then the play was split, first into episodes, and then further into 'bits'. The
second stage of the process consists of more conventional rehearsing. In *A*
Month in the Country, Stanislavsky insisted in this phase that the actors
concentrate on playing the actions worked out round the table. This was

pursued strenuously, and in extraordinary detail, and in the end each line, even each phrase, was clearly 'justified'. And the result was a performance of which Stanislavsky was justly proud.

But the company of experienced actors was emotionally exhausted by this process, and by no means convinced that the same (or better) results could not have been achieved by more usual means. So Stanislavsky established the First Studio, where young actors, without the experience to make them question his ideas, could work on the system, and here, under the guidance of Leopold Sulerzhitsky, it was rapidly developed. As presented in *An Actor Prepares* and in such accounts as survive, it seems that the emphasis in the First Studio was on experimentation, self-discovery and improvisation, and the atmosphere was intense and focused.

The system first asks the actor to work 'on himself', and to begin in apparently the simplest way, by learning to relax the muscles. Muscular tension not only makes the actor look unnatural on the stage, it also distorts all his training and rehearsal work. In *An Actor Prepares*, Tortsov, the 'Master', asks one student to lift the piano and simultaneously perform a complicated mathematical exercise, or describe a row of buildings he knows, or sing a particular aria. The student is unable to. "'So you see," said Tortsov, "that in order to answer my questions you had to let down the weight, relax your muscles, and only then could you devote yourself to the operation of your five senses. Doesn't this prove that muscular tautness interferes with inner emotional experience?"'[34] His students are required to perform regular relaxation exercises, a simple one being to lie on the back on the floor, note any muscular tensions, and consciously relax them. From this, they should contract and then relax each muscle in their bodies in succession – not an easy task! Stanislavsky also points out that purposeful action can itself relax the muscles. A student is asked to reach up to pick an imaginary peach. If performed 'truthfully', that is, if the student 'believes in' the peach, superfluous tensions recede, and the muscles behave completely naturally. Relaxation is to an extent governed by correct breathing. Control of the breath leads to control of the energy flow, so that a relaxed body, breathing correctly, is poised, alert, but at ease. This observation derives from the principles of yoga, where breathing is related to balance and to an understanding of the centre of gravity. Consequently, members of the Studios were encouraged to practise yoga.

Yoga

Yoga means union, or one-ness. It is a Hindu concept which refers to the union of the spirit with the body, and the soul with the universe, their mutual identity, and is brought into being by means of contemplation and mental and bodily balance and tranquillity.

The practice of yoga stems from the teachings of Goraksha, who united in himself a Buddhist upbringing with his later conversion to Shaivist Hinduism, Shaivists being followers of Shiva. It consists of three parts: posture, developed from the yoga exercises known as yogasana; breathing; and meditation, developed through psychophysical exercises. All these were used creatively by Stanislavsky and Sulerzhitsky as they developed what came to be the Stanislavsky system.

Breathing led naturally to consideration of the problems of voice and speech. 'Speech is music', Stanislavsky said,[35] and he urged his students to 'feel' the language. He knew that 'words and the way they are spoken show up much more on the stage than in ordinary life'.[36] He made sure members of the Studio were aware of their personal problems in this area, and saw that they received individual attention from a specialist. He pointed to mechanical repetition of lines, for instance, as a problem for any actor, and he warned against lazy articulation, inadequate volume control, and more. Students worked on diction and articulation in extraordinary detail, as a glimpse of Tortsov at work in *Building a Character*, demonstrates:

> Do you realise that an inner feeling is released through the clear sound of the A? That sound is bound up with certain deep inner experiences which seek release and easily float out from the recesses of one's bosom. But there is another A sound. It is dull, muffled, does not float out easily but remains inside to rumble ominously as if in some cavern or vault. There is also the insidious A A A which whirls out to drill its way into the person who hears it. The joyous A sound rises from one like a rocket, in contrast to the ponderous A which, like an iron weight, sinks in to the bottom of one's wellsprings.[37]

After a while thus examining the letter A, the class passes on to the letter B, and Tortsov has much to say about this letter too, and its potential. At last he asks the students to put the two letters together. The class blurt out 'Ba-a-a' like a herd of sheep, but Tortsov makes them intone it in different ways to convey, first, a buoyant greeting, and thus feel:

> how way down inside me a booming B has come to life, how my lips can hardly stem the force of the sound, how the obstacle is broken through

and from my opened lips, as from outstretched arms or the doors of a hospitable home, there emerges to meet you, like a host greeting a dear guest, a broad, generous A, exuding welcoming spirit.[38]

He continues by showing how variations of intonation just with the letters *BA* can be achieved, and how each conveys a different meaning.

But this is by no means all he taught about voice and speech. For instance, he examines in detail the pause, having fun with the sentence supposedly written by the tsar in answer to a prisoner's plea for pardon: *Pardon impossible send to Siberia*. If a pause is placed after 'Pardon', the prisoner is saved. If a pause is placed after 'impossible', the prisoner is damned. He distinguished between the 'logical pause' and the 'psycho-logical pause', which might be anything but logical. And these again were to be distinguished from the *'luftpause'*, which is 'the briefest of rests, just sufficient for a quick intake of breath'.[39]

Stanislavsky pointed out how pause and intonation combined to create meaning, indeed that mere gibberish, if intoned correctly and given pauses, could easily provide meaning. He had his students speak particular sentences with different intonations to create different meanings. This work was related to the work on stress put into a line or a sentence. He advocated finding the 'key word' in a sentence, and stressing only that, which did not preclude vocal 'colouring' for other parts of the sentence. One way of stressing a word, he pointed out, was to change the tempo at the point of stress. He wanted his actors to be aware of the part played by rhythm in speech: lack of rhythmic awareness made a speech resemble the walk of a drunkard.

Stanislavsky also trained his actors to pay attention, to concentrate, to focus on the particular, and to avoid generalising, at all times. There were many exercises developed in the First Studio for this. For instance, at night in bed, go over in your mind everything that has happened during the day *in detail*. Feel the carpet on your bare feet as you got out of bed in the morning, taste again your breakfast coffee, remember the pattern on the cup, the colour of the carpet and where it was worn, and so on. This exercise also encourages 'public solitude', Stanislavsky's name for an actor's total absorption in what he is doing on stage, to the exclusion of all else. Public solitude requires absolute attention and concentration. He compared the kinds of concentration to the circles of light cast by different lamps. The table lamp casts only a small circle of light around itself, like the basic circle of concentration of the actor around himself. The standard lamp casts a greater circle, which takes in furniture and perhaps another person. The ceiling light covers the whole room, which the good actor can sometimes encompass, even though soon he is likely to withdraw to a smaller, more manageable circle of attention.

The ability to concentrate was necessary if two of Stanislavsky's key ideas were to function properly. They were the Magic If, and the Given Circumstances. The Magic If is that supposition which enables the actor to believe without taking a lie for the truth. In other words, it is a *supposition* upon which all his work is based. '*If* there were a madman outside the door, what would I do?' The 'Magic If' is a means of releasing the actor's imagination: 'What if . . .?' He can explore a fantasy without its being fake. But, importantly, the Magic If only operates successfully when used in conjunction with the 'Given Circumstances', that is, the context within which the action of the play proceeds.

The Given Circumstances provide the answers which set the parameters for the imaginative responses to the Magic If. They tell, for example, *where* the action takes place: what country it happens in, in rural or urban surroundings, indoors or out, in what room, or in a garden or wood or field or shrubbery. These considerations make increasingly nuanced differences. Australia is, for instance, very different from Poland, and people's behaviour is different. But the kitchen is very different from the bedroom, and people behave differently in each. The same is true of time. What century do the events take place in? What year? What is the season? Which day of the week is it? What time of day or night? Again, life in 1901 was very different from life in 2004. People are often different on Sunday compared to, say, Monday. In the morning they behave differently from the evening. And so on.

It is important to notice that the Given Circumstances also incorporate the *theatrical* context of the actor's work. So he needs to take into account, for instance, the design of the set, the nature of the props, and the cut of his costume, as well as the director's conceptions in terms of blocking, rhythm, his use of music, and so on. Indeed, sometimes Stanislavsky seems to stress this more than the fictional circumstances of the play itself. What is significant, however, is the interdependence of the two conceptions, as Tortsov says to his students: 'By using the word *if* I frankly recognized the fact that I was offering you only a supposition. All I wanted to accomplish was to make you say what you would have done *if* the supposition about the madman were a real fact, leaving you to feel what anybody in the given circumstances must feel.'[40]

The exercise involving the madman was also a way to stimulate the actors' emotions. Exploring emotion was obviously central to Stanislavsky, though he knew finding the right emotion was not easy. Imagine searching a house with many rooms, in each of which are many cupboards, in each of which are many boxes, and in one box is the bead you seek, the emotion you need. He used 'emotion memory' as a tool in this work and believed it could be trained. Thus Studio members were encouraged to mime a simple action, say, making a bed or frying an egg, so that this might conjure up an emotion experienced while performing the action for real. Perhaps you made love in such a bed, or quarrelled while making breakfast. 'Don't think about the feeling itself', he urged, 'but set your mind to work on what makes it grow, what the conditions were that brought about the experience'.[41] Other exercises brought the situation closer: actors were asked to sit beside a bed and imagine their father was in it and dying; or they had to say goodbye to a loved one. Finally, actors were encouraged to discover emotional resources in 'life around you, real and imaginary, from reminiscences, books, art, science, knowledge of all kinds, from journeys, museums and above all from communication with other human beings.'[42]

The emotions thus conjured into being had also, of course, to be communicated, but often they had to be communicated by means other than simply words. When Masha discusses Gogol in front of Tuzenbach and Chebutykin, how does she communicate her despairing love to Vershinin in *Three Sisters*? For this, an approach to what became known as the 'subtext', Stanislavsky went back to yoga, perhaps under the influence of Sulerzhitsky, and explored the idea of prana rays. These, he believed, were initially energy flows between people, which could actually carry messages in some subtle way. They were rays which could be emitted and received as they streamed from person to person, or actor to actor, and from stage to auditorium. They were related to the prana, or life energy, because they were controlled by, or through, the breathing. The idea may sound far fetched, but the fact has been demonstrated many times that two people can communicate without looking at each other or making any sound. Stanislavsky sought to exercise this faculty and thereby make it more accessible. This was the kind of work explored quite open-endedly in the First Studio.

Putting on a play was a different exercise since it had a clear end in view. It began with the 'table' work first used in *A Month in the Country*. The Studio, however, aimed to make this phase of rehearsing more democratic, so that the whole group might share insights, interpretations, and ideas, thus making them feel that the play and the production belonged to them all, and creating a constructive ensemble out of a cast.

First, the company was to decide the play's 'superobjective', that is, what the playwright had been trying to say. In *Three Sisters*, for example, Chekhov might have been commenting on the way the minutiae of living destroy wider potentials. From this is derived each character's 'fundamental objective' – what each wants as a guiding principle. This was to be expressed actively: 'I want . . .'. Stanislavsky describes how the original rehearsals for *Three Sisters* ground to a halt as the play's superobjective weighed them down. It was only when the actors realised that their characters' fundamental objectives involved *wanting happiness*, even though the play's superobjective emphasised their *un*happiness, that their work began to cohere. Thus, the play's superobjective was not the same as the characters' fundamental objectives. Stanislavsky also noted that the character's fundamental objective was not always quite what it seemed. Thus, Argan's objective in Molière's *Le Malade imaginaire* was not, as it first seemed, 'I want to be ill'; rather, it was 'I want people to think I am ill'. In Goldoni's *La Locandiera*, Ripafratta's fundamental objective was not 'I want to hate women', it was 'I want to woo them secretly'.[43] One might note, too, that there seems to be some confusion in Stanislavsky's terminology here, though this may be the responsibility of the translator: often the character's 'fundamental objective' is translated in *An Actor Prepares* as his 'super-objective', the same word used to describe the aim of the play itself.

The more detailed text analysis and research focused first on the Given Circumstances of the play – when it happened, where, and how, as well as discussion of settings, costumes, music and so on. The text itself was broken down, first into 'episodes' – large pieces of text which sometimes coincided with a whole scene – but then into smaller units, or 'bits'. Each bit – or 'bead' on the string – contained a single action. It was given a caption which indicated this, but which also pointed to the particular task the characters were to address specifically and at that moment. Thus, though in the episode one character may want to seduce the other, this must be divided into bits, each bit comprising, as it were, a step in the seduction. She takes his coat, offers him a cup of coffee, engages in conversation, closes the curtains, and so on. Each 'bit' includes a specific 'task' (to help him relax, to put him at his ease, to make him feel important, to cut out the outside world, and so on), and also the action which is taken to fulfil the task. Every action must be in response to a task. This is the iron rule of Stanislavsky's system. No action may be performed without a clear justification. One must not simply shut the door, one must shut it to keep out the draught, or to prevent the people in the next room from hearing what is to be discussed. One might perhaps think in terms of tactics and strategy. The strategy is to seduce the man; the tactics are to make him coffee, shut the curtains, and so on. In *A Month in the Country*, Stanislavsky noted that Natalia Petrovna uses 'in turn mockery, irony, an open and frank tone, the tone of a great and upright gentlewoman, with folded arms',[44] and more, in order to get her way. These are the tactics she uses to accomplish her strategy.

Action and activity

Action is the heart of Stanislavsky's system. An actor/character performs an action in order to fulfil a task: an action is performed *for a purpose*. It is expressed by an active verb. A complete performance can be seen to consist of a chain of actions, a through-line of actions, which can be considered the actor's *score* (as a musician in an orchestra plays a score).

An activity in Stanislavsky's terms is, as it were, what the actor/character 'does with his hands'. It is not part of his score in the sense that it does not matter in terms of the development of the play whether he performs these things or not. He lays the table, reads the newspaper, peels an orange. Masha takes snuff in *The Seagull*, Gayev pretends to play billiards in *The Cherry Orchard*. These are inconsequential activities which may be personally revealing, but have no purpose beyond themselves.

Stanislavsky also insisted that, as with the fundamental objective, each task be expressed with an active verb ('I want . . .') and laid down a number of conditions which each should fulfil: they should be 'on our side of the footlights', 'personal' to the actor, yet 'analogous' to the character, 'truthful', 'clear cut', and so on.[45] And once the task had provided the actor with the necessary action, the idea of a self-contained 'bit' was erased, so that the play would actually run smoothly from one action to the next through a whole episode. Moreover, it was in the process of fulfilling the tasks that the 'character' appeared. Stanislavsky stressed that for the actor to think in terms of building a character who was angry, or long-winded, or introverted, or whatever, was to approach the problem from the wrong end. If he fulfilled the tasks properly, taking into account the Given Circumstances, and also the homework he was to have done on the character's biography and so on (described below), the character (or 'image') would appear. He was quite categorical about this:

> One should not act an image . . . Carry out all your planned actions correctly, penetrate into and sense all the thoughts contained in your role while you are on the stage, analyse your attitude . . . and as a result of all that you will achieve an image. Don't force yourself into any schematic form on the stage.[46]

At the same time as the actor was analysing the play round the table in rehearsals, he was also expected to be working at home. Indeed, sometimes it seemed to Stanislavsky that rehearsals existed mainly to point out what the actor needed to work on at home. The homework involved extensive use of the imagination, trying to imagine the character's home life, his family, his hobbies, preferences, likes and dislikes. He was also to imagine the character walking in the streets, visiting a restaurant, calling on other characters in the play, and so on. All this was carried on alone, using the 'inner eye': a kind of filmstrip which the actor would not only watch, but would also activate in his brain. Such visualisation also, of course, helped the actor later when he had to describe on stage something that had happened, perhaps in the playwright's imagination, such as Clarence's dream in *Richard III* – he could, and should, visualise it to make it vivid and 'present'. What was created in the exercises of the imagination away from the rehearsal room was what the actor had then to 'embody' on the stage, when finally the moment came to get up from the table.

In the embodiment there were three factors to be aware of. The first was the 'through-line of action', the series of actions which comprised the performance. The through-line of action had to be logical, coherent, and consistent, so that it would clarify the whole conception of the part, and reveal the character's fundamental objective, the 'inner truth' of the part. The second factor was the 'inner truth' to be found in the subtext, which had its own 'through-line'. It

> flows uninterruptedly beneath the words of the text, giving them life and a basis for existing. The subtext is a web of innumerable, varied inner patterns inside a play and a part, woven from 'magic ifs', given circumstances, all sorts of figments of the imagination, inner movements, objects of attention, smaller and greater truths and a belief in them, adaptations, adjustments and other similar elements. It is the subtext that makes us say the words we do in a play.[47]

The third factor was the tempo-rhythm of the performance. By 'tempo' Stanislavsky meant the outward speed, referring it to the development of the through-line of action. By 'rhythm' he meant the development of the 'inner' action, that is, the emotions. Many examples of how these differ might be adduced: imagine waiting at the train station to welcome home your lover, a soldier, who has been away fighting a war for six months. The train is late, the tempo is therefore slow. But your heart is racing; the rhythm is therefore fast. The tempo-rhythm referred to both the inner and the outer progression of the part.

Probably this description oversimplifies Stanislavsky's system, and also makes it appear neater and more coherent than ever it was in practice through the 1910s and 1920s. As has been made clear, it was a constantly evolving, constantly changing approach, which by the early 1930s Stanislavsky himself had effectively outgrown. Now he was moving to a fundamentally different method, as different from the so-called 'system' of the previous years as that system was from the autocratic approach of the 1890s and 1900s. This was what was to become known as 'The Method of Physical Actions'.

On one level, this name is misleading, for the process is open, fluid, and anything but methodical. But if it is seen as a method of rehearsing (as opposed to training actors), the term is more accurate. Indeed, this may suggest (correctly) how it complements rather than supersedes, Stanislavsky's earlier system. Sharon Carnicke points out that Stanislavsky himself suggests that it involves 'taking action', rather than 'acting',[48] and Bella Merlin explains that this makes it *immediate*: 'The actor didn't ask, "What would I do *if* I were in this situation?" but simply said, "Here I *am* in the concrete reality of this stage environment, so what do I do *now?*"'[49] This indicates vividly how, in this way of working, acting and experiencing virtually merge.

The process is actually comparatively simple. The actors read the play, or the scene, together. They discuss it, in order to agree on what happens. They may also discuss fundamental objectives for their characters, though these may be modified as the rehearsals proceed, and the Given Circumstances, the immediate 'facts', which will affect what they do. Then they get up and try to recreate the scene through improvisation. The process is known as 'Active Analysis': they analyse the scene, not 'passively', round the table, but actively in improvisation.

The first improvisations are usually short and perhaps rather strange; the actors may break down, they may omit more than they include. But after the first attempt to create the scene, they return to the script, re-read it, compare what they did with this original, and then try again. Soon the actors find, for instance, where the role overlaps with their own experience. They begin to find the rhythm, structure, conflicts, and action and counteraction of the portion of the play being addressed. They may need different props, or to spend a little time discussing the author's language or rhythm. And they improvise again.

The work may be interspersed with freer improvisations and études which in Stanislavsky's late years often pre-empted the imaginary explorations and meetings of the old system's actor's homework. More 'facts' are gradually unearthed, and more research is pursued into areas which seem to be relevant. But basically this work, which may continue for days, even weeks, is posited on the idea that the event being dramatised is in essence a series of physical actions. The improvisation enables the actor to discover *in himself* the justification for the action, and the tasks which motivate it, so that the emotion and the action acquire an organic unity in the actor's body. Stanislavsky encouraged his actors to write down the 'score' of the actions, and then to test them in a 'silent étude': they were asked to perform the actions without the benefit of words to examine its coherence, logical progression, and ability to communicate.

In the Method of Physical Actions, the actor quickly penetrates to the heart of his creative problem. He listens to and reacts with his partner, honestly and truthfully, and if this varies from what happens in the script then together they examine why and how. There is a truth in this work, if it is done properly, an immediacy and a specificity, which actors constantly seek. Moreover, the knotty relationship between psychology and physicality, mind and body, disappears and the two complement one another from the start. Gradually, if the improvisations have continued long enough, and if the playwright is good enough, the two will merge into one imperceptibly. That at any rate is the aim. The actors' improvisation will inevitably come to need the playwright's words. It rarely happens, of course. But the fact that such a notion can be entertained shows how the new method works.

Sadly, Stanislavsky did not live long enough to see his final production of Molière's *Tartuffe* reach the stage, and demonstrate – or destroy – the credibility of his final method. In fact it may be questioned whether he really wanted it to come to performance, since by now he was entirely caught up by the *process* of rehearsing (something which had always fascinated him). But his work was carefully and interestingly documented in Vasily Toporkov's *Stanislavsky in Rehearsal*, and the production was presented to the public over a year after Stanislavsky's death, having been completed, with little further experimentation, by his assistant Mikhail Kedrov. The acclaim which greeted it was probably genuine, though in the climate then prevailing in the Soviet Union one can never be sure. And perhaps the uncertainty suits Stanislavsky's cast of mind best.

When the final productions which Stanislavsky did present are considered, however, his achievement was impressive, and for different reasons. People remembered *The Seagull*, for instance, because of the 'atmospherics' it created. This was thanks to Simov's designs as well as to Stanislavsky's direction, and to the sound effects and lighting as well as the acting. Everything was detailed and specific to the point of laboriousness, because Stanislavsky at that time believed that outer verisimilitude, human interactions in real places, and their rhythm in real time, was the path which led to inner truth. Never before had the Russian stage been so bathed in an 'atmosphere', with its revealing and dynamic pauses, but also its contrasting stage movement. Stanislavsky

> seemed to be anxious that there should be a great deal of movement during the performance, uninterrupted movement, in the course of which the significance of the inter-linking of word and gesture, not to be broken for a single moment, should be clearly brought out. In a Stanislavsky production the characters always speak while doing something, i.e. either moving about, or gesticulating, or miming. And if there is an interruption in the dialogue during a pause, it mostly happens with the aim of eliciting the greatest possible significance from the gesture which at that time forms the pivot of the action on stage.[50]

Balukhaty adds to the above: 'With Stanislavsky, movement is to the highest degree exact and naturalistic.'[51]

What did *The Seagull* look like to those first Art Theatre audiences of 1898? According to Nemirovich-Danchenko, Nina's strange, possibly absurd monologue, in Act 1, provoked

> not the shadow of a smile, not the least hint of anything untoward. Then ensued the bitter outburst between mother and son; then, as scene followed scene, the more intimate these people became to the spectator, the more perturbing became their fits of anger, half-phrases, silences, the more powerful there rose from the depth of the spectator's soul the perceptions of his own unhappiness and anguish. And when at the end of the act Masha, restraining her tears, said to Dorn: 'Please help me, or I'll commit some stupidity, I'll laugh at my own life,' and then flung herself on the ground near the bench, weeping, a repressed, tremulous wave swept through the audience.[52]

Stanislavsky's own description evokes the elusive subtlety of Chekhov, and his attempt to realise this:

> To the accompaniment of tasteless conversation and jokes, the domestic spectators take their places on the long bench and the tree stumps, their backs to the public, very much like sparrows on a telegraph line. The moon rises, the sheet falls, one sees the lake, its surface broken with the silver gleams of the moon. On a high eminence that resembles the base of a monument, sits a grief-stricken female figure wrapped in manifold white, but with eyes that are young and shining and cannot be grief-stricken.[53]

Figure 2.3 The Seagull, Moscow Art Theatre, 1898.

Stanislavsky believed his system reached its finest expression in the First Studio's production of *The Cricket on the Hearth*, presented in 1914. This production had the advantage of a small, intimate theatre, but its warmth and sincerity gave it, Stanislavsky said, 'those deep and heartfelt notes of superconscious feeling in the measure and the form in which I dreamed of them'.[54] In the cheerful glow of the Peerybingle parlour or Caleb Plummer's toyshop, lighting, set, props, and costume combined to spellbinding effect. Mikhail Chekhov, who played Caleb, made all the toys in his shop himself, even the scenery was created by the actors, and the whole was imbued with the Tolstoyan generosity of spirit which Sulerzhitsky brought to the First Studio. Stanislavsky too worked on bringing out the play's superobjective, and on the actors' sincerity, with exercises as well as encouragement. In performance, Vakhtangov's Tackleton, a 'suffering and condemned man, crippled by a capitalistic city',[55] was all angularity and staccato rhythms, contrasting with Chekhov's Caleb, who presented a flowing, curvilinear toymaker. According to the critic Nikolai Efros, *The Cricket on the Hearth* was the best production he saw in 1914.

Equally impressive, perhaps, though for slightly different reasons, was Stanislavsky's 1927 production of *Armoured Train 14-69* by Vsevolod Ivanov. Once again using his old designer Viktor Simov to create a romanticised, almost stylised, set, Stanislavsky only conducted a few rehearsals, yet stamped his ideas on the final production indelibly. Using improvisation much as in the final Method of Physical Actions, he created an opening scene in a flower shop in which something of the old 'atmospherics' was discernable. The rather stereotypical characters became genuinely interesting, especially the Bolshevik Peklevanov, his peasant protégé, the apolitical Vershinin who becomes a Bolshevik hero, and their antagonist Nezelasov. Vershinin was played by the veteran Art Theatre star Vasily Kachalov, who managed to attain a

> charismatic dignity which made entirely credible the character's influence on the peasants of Eastern Siberia (where the play was set). This feature of Kachalov's playing was best seen in the 'Belltower' scene in which Vershinin sets up his headquarters on the low, sloping roof of a village church which has been left in ruins by the Japanese. From this vantage point he surveys and addresses the swelling ranks of his peasant army. The episode presented an opportunity for the Art Theatre to return to one of its great traditions, namely the massive crowd scenes that had featured in many productions.[56]

Melodramatic mass action, descended ultimately from the nineteenth-century work of the Duke of Saxe-Meiningen and melded to psychological acuity, made the production not only typical of Stanislavsky, but also important for the Soviets. Allied to suitably heroic pseudo-propaganda, and with a kind of popular vernacular humour, this production became a prototype for the coming Socialist Realism. Did Stanislavsky see the full implications of what he was creating? Probably not. He was trying to achieve an inner truth which would transcend any theatrical falseness.

Figure 2.4 Armoured Train 14-69, Moscow Art Theatre, 1927.

Stanislavsky after Stanislavsky

Stanislavsky's legacy was complicated partly because of his own inconsist-
encies and enthusiasms, but partly also because of the vagaries of world
history. This is easily seen in the case of his books. First to be published was
My Life in Art, which appeared in America in 1924, and attempted to
describe how he had come to develop his system. It was aimed at the
American audience which was simultaneously being swept off its feet by
productions which had not employed that system. In 1936 the English-
language *An Actor Prepares* appeared two years before the Russian original,
An Actor's Work on Himself, Part 1, was published. And the original turned
out to be almost twice as long as the 'translation'. Moreover, by this time
Stanislavsky had left behind the system which it described, and was working
feverishly on his Method of Physical Actions. To complicate matters
further, *'The Seagull' Produced by Stanislavsky*, describing his earliest
Chekhov work and including the production plan which he had imposed on
his actors in 1898, was published in Russia in 1938, forty years later, and
taken by many as reflective of his new work.

The rest of his writings appeared after his death, and caused inevitable
reinterpretations. *An Actor's Work on Himself, Part 2*, was published in
Russia in 1948, ten years after the appearance of Part 1, and this was made
into the (again much shorter) *Building a Character*, published in America in

1949. His descriptions of the Method of Physical Actions, as well as various other writings, were brought together to make *Creating a Role*, which was not published until 1961. Books about Stanislavsky's working methods by some of his collaborators also appeared sporadically, but because most of them did not attempt to place what they described in the complicated story of Stanislavsky's development, they too, in a sense, added to the confusion.

For many the true legacy was handed on through continuing practice, though here again history played its slightly cynical part. While America responded to Stanislavsky's interest in psychology, the apparently Marxist Soviet Union preferred the materialism of concrete physical actions. Meanwhile, some of his productions froze in the repertoire of the Art Theatre like the permafrost of Kolyma. In 1987 I saw Stanislavsky's production of *The Blue Bird* by Maurice Maeterlinck at the huge Soviet-built new Art Theatre building in Moscow, a full *eighty years* after its premiere! Has the system actually done 'as much harm as good', as Peter Brook has argued?[57] The final account, perhaps, has still to be rendered.

Perhaps more influential than Stanislavsky's books in the spread of the system was the word of mouth of some of the First Studio's brightest lights, though inevitably each of them had their own angle on Stanislavsky's work, and each developed it in his own way. Richard Boleslavsky emigrated soon after the revolution, and took his version of the system to America, where he was joined in teaching it by Maria Ouspenskaya. Mikhail Chekhov stayed in Russia until 1928, where he taught his own system, outlined in his books.[58] The third star of the First Studio, Evgeny Vakhtangov, died in Russia in 1922, having founded the Art Theatre's Third Studio in order to pursue his attempt to inject some of Meyerhold's ideas into the Stanislavsky system. His influence both in Russia and beyond remained long after his demise and clearly informed the Sovietised 'Stanislavsky'.

It was this Stanislavsky who was increasingly revered and invoked as the inspiration for the Soviet theatre, especially in the training of actors. But what the Soviet authorities meant by this was a sort of filleted Stanislavsky – the materialistic elements of his system, notably the emphasis on 'physical action' implied by his last works, accentuated to the exclusion of its more spiritual parts and the emphases on the non-material aspects of acting.

For decades after his death, Russian and Soviet theatre was dominated by those who had trained in the Soviet version of his system, especially at the Art Theatre's own school. Notable names from the 1940s included Nikolai Khmelev, Mikhail Kedrov, and Maria Knebel, all of whom worked with Stanislavsky. Khmelev promoted Andrei Lobanov, who became known for his illusionist style derived from his use of the material elements of the techniques of Active Analysis. Lobanov became artistic director of the Ermolova Theatre, before being sacked and driven to his death by the

Soviet authorities in 1954. More acceptable to them was Alexei Popov, who had been a member of the First Studio, and was artistic director of the Central Theatre of the Red Army from 1936 to 1958. The Russian 'stars' of the period, such as Alla Tarasova and Angelina Stepanova, were also products of the Stanislavsky school.

In the 1950s, Maria Knebel, who by the way had worked extensively with Mikhail Chekhov as well as Stanislavsky, and continued to use his ideas throughout her career, introduced to the Central Children's Theatre, which she ran, two men who were destined to become significant forces in Soviet theatre in the post-Stalin Communist period, Anatoly Efros and Oleg Efremov, from the Moscow Art Theatre School. In 1957 Efremov founded the Sovremennik ('Contemporary') Theatre, and went on to become artistic director of the Art Theatre itself; while Efros directed the Lenin Komsomol Theatre, though he was dismissed from this position in 1967, and went on to the Malaya Bronnaya Theatre. Efros's work was notable for its psychological strength and use of Freudian or at least sexual motivations. A third force in Soviet theatre at this period was Georgy Tovstonogov, a former student of Alexei Popov, who was appointed to the Leningrad Bolshoi Drama Theatre in 1965, and employed the Soviet version of the Method of Physical Actions relentlessly. He asserted:

> Not long before his death, Stanislavsky developed the basis of theatre art. He determined the essence of his teaching as 'The Method of Physical Actions.' This method is now the only one, and there is nothing to equal it in the field of an actor's art that existed or exists in the world Theatre.[59]

The influence of these three directors was immense and long-lasting. Even after the collapse of Communism, their work and methods, which derived from the Sovietised Stanislavsky, were pervasive throughout Russia and eastern Europe, as the case of Albert Filozov demonstrates. Bella Merlin describes how she met and was taught by this leading actor in the 1990s. His techniques, she reports, derived from his personal fusion of what he had learned from Mikhail Kedrov, Evgenia Maryes, and Maria Knebel, all of whom were personally trained by Stanislavsky, and all of whom had slightly different approaches to his ideas.[60] The point is that it was Stanislavsky's ideas that were behind *all* of this.

In the rest of Europe Stanislavsky's influence was never as pervasive. This was partly for political reasons, but it was also partly because Europe had its own theatrical masters – Copeau, Dullin, Jouvet, St Denis, Mnouchkine in France; Piscator, Brecht, and Stein in Germany; Strehler and Fo in Italy. Later, especially with the publication of his books, his influence was detectable, but never so all-encompassing as in Russia or America. But it is significant that even such an avant-garde practitioner as the Polish Jerzy Grotowski acknowledged that he had been 'possessed' by Stanislavsky when he was a student, and throughout his life he acknowledged Stanislavsky as the primary influence on his work. This was, of course, in eastern Europe, where the Soviet empire dominated all aspects of cultural and artistic life. But even before the Second World War the Stanislavsky influence was noticeable. In Czechoslovakia, for instance, Maria Germanova's Prague Group of the Moscow Art Theatre, which was descended from the Kachalov Group who had been cut off from Moscow at the time of the Russian Civil War, flourished for many years. When the company visited Britain in 1928 and 1931, it received some notably good reviews: 'The characters live when they are on stage and go on living after they have left it . . . These Russian actors have wandered far from Moscow, but they still go round Stanislavsky.'[61] In fact, Germanova herself, trained and favoured by Nemirovich-Danchenko, was never a favourite of Stanislavsky, but his influence still ran deep through the troupe.

However, Britain on the whole remained singularly uninterested in Stanislavsky, or at least in the real Stanislavsky. This was partly because of the influence of Fyodor Komissarzhevsky, who, having left Russia after the Bolshevik revolution, reincarnated himself as Theodore Komisarjevsky, and introduced Chekhov to Britain in a series of revelatory productions in a small former cinema in Barnes, north London, in the mid-1920s. His productions tended to be slow, even tragic, with a sad and wistful mood which was, at least on the surface, rather reminiscent of Stanislavsky's productions (and which were consequently far from Chekhov's ideas of brisk-paced, ironic comedy). This tone and tempo seemed to suit the post-war British intelligentsia's nostalgia, and created the style for British Chekhov which lasted for decades. Komisarjevsky was taken as knowing about Stanislavsky, though he had never worked with him, and indeed he had had the impudence to publish a small book on the system in Russia in 1917, which had so infuriated Stanislavsky that he had considered suing him over it. Britain, however, knew nothing of this.

The British theatre has always resisted systems, and even technique, preferring to believe in the myth of the untutored genius. Nevertheless, a few practitioners acknowledged Stanislavsky's mastery. The first to do so in England were the pioneering founders of Theatre Workshop, Joan Littlewood and Ewan MacColl. Littlewood always insisted that her actors define their objectives in Stanislavskian terms to give their work real urgency, and she also employed improvisational études to deepen and strengthen the actors' understanding of situation and character. Michael Redgrave also adopted at least some of Stanislavsky's ideas, which he advocated in his 1955 book, *The Actor's Ways and Means*. And Peter Brook, who has recorded his surprise that Stanislavsky was 'virtually unknown' in Britain when he began his career in the 1940s,[62] used Stanislavsky's system frequently and successfully. His formulation – 'in everyday life "if" is an evasion, in the theatre "if" is the truth'[63] – brilliantly restates one of the system's central concepts. Sadly, Brook had to move to Paris to pursue his unconventional career.

Meanwhile in America Stanislavsky's ideas had been developed differently. Richard Boleslavsky had left the Bolshevik Republic in 1920, but when the Art Theatre arrived in New York in October 1922 he rejoined them while they were in America. He acted on the tour, assisted with directing work, but most importantly, with the backing of Stanislavsky, he began to explain the principles of the system. Americans devoured it greedily. In 1923, Boleslavsky secured backing for a Laboratory Theatre where he and Maria Ouspenskaya began to teach what they understood to be the system, till the venture died in 1930. Boleslavsky subsequently published *Acting: the First Six Lessons*[64] which employs Stanislavsky's fictional method with student and teacher asking and answering questions to outline his syllabus.

Boleslavsky and Ouspenskaya inspired a group of Americans, including Harold Clurman, Lee Strasberg, Stella Adler, and Francis Fergusson, to set up their own 'Group Theatre' in 1931, modelled on their idea of the Moscow Art Theatre. Here they consciously attempted to apply what they had learned of the Stanislavsky system first from seeing the Art Theatre eight years earlier, and then from sitting at the feet of Boleslavsky and Ouspenskaya. They based their work in improvisation and 'emotion memory', and noted immediately how they were able to achieve something beyond any other contemporary American theatre:

> The effect on the actors was that of a miracle. The system . . . repre-
> sented for most of them the open-sesame of the actor's art. Here at last
> was a key to that elusive ingredient of the stage, true emotion. And
> Strasberg was a fanatic on the subject of true emotion. Everything was
> secondary to it. He sought it with the patience of an inquisitor, he was
> outraged by trick substitutes, and when he had succeeded in
> stimulating it, he husbanded it, fed it, and protected it. Here was
> something new to most of the actors, something basic, something
> almost holy. It was revelation in the theatre.[65]

The Group created some of America's finest drama in the period of the Depression, and over the decade of its existence their company helped to shape the careers of such significant artists as Clifford Odets, Morris

Carnovsky, Mordecai Gorelik, John Howard Lawson, Elia Kazan, Franchot Tone, and others.

Meanwhile, America's knowledge of Stanislavsky was widening with the arrival of other former Art Theatre members – most notably Michael Chekhov, whose Moscow Art Players also brought Andrius Jilinsky and Vera Soloviova. All three set up as teachers, Chekhov initially in England, but he returned to the United States at the outbreak of the Second World War. Others to work as acting teachers in America included Maria Germanova, and, more successfully, Tamara Daykarkhanova. Though Jilinsky and Chekhov made some impact, it was Boleslavsky's protégés, through the Group Theatre, who carried the greatest influence, even though they were riven with personal as well as ideological quarrels. The most notable of these came when Stella Adler brought back from France news – and some experience of – Stanislavsky's new techniques, which were to coalesce into the Method of Physical Actions, which clashed with Strasberg's emotion-based approach.

A few years after the Group Theatre's demise in 1941, some of the same group, notably Harold Clurman, Cheryl Crawford, who had administered the Group Theatre, and Robert Lewis, set up the Actors' Studio in New York to continue the work on Stanislavsky's system in an American context, with its concomitants, as the American saw it, of socially aware drama and the values of the ensemble as opposed to the star system. The Actors' Studio soon became the base for Lee Strasberg, whose 'fanaticism' had by no means dwindled. It was largely here that what came to be known as the 'American Method', based essentially on emotion memory and a Freudian approach to psychology, was evolved. It was bigger than one man's vision, however, and somewhat different directions, still recognisably forms of 'the Method', were taught by other former members of the Group Theatre, including Robert Lewis, Sanford Meisner at the Neighborhood Playhouse, New York, and Stella Adler at the Conservatory named after her. Mention should also be made of Uta Hagen, who largely rejected 'emotion memory', at the HB Studio, and Sonia Moore, who began her career at the Third Studio of the Moscow Art Theatre under Vakhtangov, at her American Center for Stanislavski's Art. However, it was from the Actors' Studio that almost all of America's greatest actors of the second half of the twentieth century – Marlon Brando, Dustin Hoffman, Robert de Niro, and many more – came.

But by the 1960s socio-political developments, as well as new artistic urges, began to undermine the primacy of the Method in America, notably through the work of Julian Beck and Judith Malina at the Living Theatre, and Joseph Chaikin at the Open Theatre, so that by the end of the century, though it was certainly true that Stanislavsky's flame still burned brightly, for example, in the work of directors like Ned Mandarino, it – and its offspring, the Method – were no longer dominant.

But more and more, and throughout the world, in film and television as well as on the live stage, the attempt to create the illusion of reality predominated, and wherever it did so, there Stanislavsky's ideas about acting remained inescapable and fundamental.

Twenty-first-century perspectives

What place should Stanislavsky have in the theatre of the twenty-first century? In some ways he seems to be old-fashioned, and in others out of touch. For example, his thinking is rooted in the Enlightenment of the eighteenth century. He sees the world as whole, objective, and real, and the human personality as, potentially at least, integrated. Truth is in the world, and can be apprehended as such. Consequently, he sees that a role has a through-line which is logical and coherent, and that the actor's job is to find it.

But this basic attitude is refined by his Romanticism. His belief, for instance, in the need to identify bits to make the episode, and episodes to make the through-line, which conversely can only find its logic and its coherence through the discovery of its episodes and bits, echoes uncannily Schleiermacher's view of the whole and the parts. Friedrich Schleiermacher was the leading German Romantic critic, who pointed to the 'hermeneutic circle', that in order to understand a work of art one must see it whole; but in order to do so, one must see each part of which it is constituted; but each part can only be understood in the light of the whole; and so ad infinitum. The notion is related to Romanticism's other idea, to which Stanislavsky also subscribes, that one must travel through the particular to reach the universal.

Hence Stanislavsky's focus is on the individual. For him, the individual's experience is vital, and art is a process of self-discovery. He asserts forcefully and continually that the actor is an artist, and as such must be 'sincere'. This is a problem for the actor, who is also an individual human being, but it lies behind, for instance, Stanislavsky's demand for 'truth': 'I don't believe you', he frequently complained to his student actors. We may trace the demand for sincerity through Tolstoy to the Romantic poets, such as Wordsworth, whose 'emotion recollected in tranquillity' also resonates with the idea of 'emotion memory'. Stanislavsky's ideas that art is a special privileged form of human activity, and that the spectator as well as the actor must 'identify' with the role, are also fundamentally Romantic.

When it comes to more detailed work, Stanislavsky's ideas may seem more up to date, more in touch with the work of some of the twentieth century's most typical thinkers. For instance, his understanding of the human psyche has much in common with Freud's ideas, rather than those of later, perhaps more subtle, psychologists. Today, Freud is seen increasingly as misogynistic and class-biased. His work seems to reinforce certain kinds of apparently undesirable stereotypes, and to offer little help in prising open unexpected or liberating perspectives. Similarly, Stanislavsky's phenomenology has much in common with Heidegger's, with its interest in individual consciousness and how lived experience interacts with the 'real' world.

Stanislavsky's work also implicitly investigates the problematic relationship between theatre and life. The title of his autobiography implies the ambiguity inherent in much of his work: *My Life in Art*. The possessive pronoun, 'My', focuses inevitably on the value of individual experience, but there is also an implication that my 'life' only has meaning 'in art', that 'art' has perhaps produced 'my life'. Stanislavsky's conception of the actor 'living the part' also suggests that life is produced in the practice of the art of acting. This of course privileges art in a thoroughly Romantic manner. Theatre is transitory, and each moment on stage is to be 'lived', not merely to be recreated from yesterday, or from rehearsals. But life, too, is transitory, and must be lived every day.

Finally, notice might be taken of two other strands of Stanislavsky's work which suggest possibly fruitful connections with more modern ideas. First, his abiding belief that a play is structured by its actions, which is the core of the Method of Physical Actions, might lead him towards a Structuralist position, which itself would open up new perspectives on his practice. And, second, his attitude to the unconscious and to the individual seems to take him some way towards the Lacanian modification of Freudianism. Lacan's paradox is that the unconscious is the kernel of the self, but that since it is linguistic in its essence, and language exists as an entity entirely without it, there is no separate self. Traditional notions of character are then no longer valid. Stanislavsky's idea that character exists *in action* may not undermine Lacan's thought, but it does introduce a new dynamic into the conundrum.

All this suggests that Stanislavsky's work, though in some respects seemingly old-fashioned, might reward re-examination. In particular, his ideas point again to the crucial dilemma most convincingly expressed by Diderot:

> If the actor were full, really full, of feeling, how could he play the same part twice running with the same spirit and success? Full of fire at the first performance, he would be worn out and cold as marble at the third. But take it that he is an attentive mimic and thoughtful disciple of nature, then the first time that he comes on the stage as Augustus, Cinna, Orosmanes, Agamemnon or Mahomet, faithful copying of

himself and the effects he has arrived at, and constantly observing human nature, will so prevail that his acting, far from losing in force, will gather strength with the new observations he will make from time to time. He will increase or moderate his effects, and you will be more and more pleased with him. If he is himself while he is playing, how is he to stop being himself? If he wants to stop being himself, how is he to catch just the point where he is to stay his hand?[66]

When is an actor not an actor?

Stanislavsky's published work raises other questions connected with their form. Are they to be read merely as fiction? If not, who are Tortsov and Kostya? Are they to be seen as Socratic dialogue, opening up dusty corners and challenging complacency? They often seem to explore new, different ways of piercing, unveiling and shadowing the vexed relationship between the stage and the world. What is needed now, perhaps, is an extended and detailed examination of some of Stanislavsky's texts. Interestingly, a start has been made by Bella Merlin in her analyses of *'The Seagull' Produced by Stanislavsky* and *An Actor Prepares*.[67] This is certainly one way forward for those who still value Stanislavsky in his role as a maker of modern theatre.

Further reading

Stanislavsky's complete works were published in Russia in eight volumes between 1951 and 1964 as *Sobranie Sochinenii* (*Collected Works*). A new and fuller edition is being published in Moscow at the present time, under the same title, and has so far reached eight volumes.

In English, his major works are all published by Methuen and have been reprinted many times in the last two decades. They are:

My Life in Art
An Actor Prepares
Building a Character
Creating a Role

Selections from Stanislavsky's works have also been published as *An Actor's Handbook* and *Stanislavski's Legacy*. (It is worth noting that Stanislavsky's name on these works (and others) is usually spelled with an -*i* ending, though this is not in accordance with current transliteration practice.)

Between 1918 and 1922 Stanislavsky gave a series of more or less informal talks to members of the Bolshoi Opera Studio. These were taken down almost verbatim, and form the basis of:

Stanislavsky, Konstantin, *Stanislavsky on the Art of the Stage*, London: Faber & Faber, 1950.

Other books written by his colleagues bearing directly on his work, some more reliable than others (Gorchakov's account, for instance, has been heavily criticised for inaccuracies) include:

Balukhaty, S. D., *'The Seagull' Produced by Stanislavsky*, London: Dennis Dobson, 1952.
Gorchakov, Nikolai M., *Stanislavsky Directs*, New York: Funk & Wagnalls, 1954.
Stanislavski, Constantin, and Rumyantsev, Pavel, *Stanislavski on Opera*, London: Routledge, 1998.
Toporkov, Vasily, *Stanislavski in Rehearsal*, London: Routledge, 1998.

Biographies of Stanislavsky include:

Benedetti, Jean, *Stanislavski, a Biography*, London: Methuen, 1988.
Magarshack, David, *Stanislavsky: A Life*, London: Faber & Faber, 1986.

Other works, practical or theoretical, in English, which are worth consulting, include:

Benedetti, Jean, *The Moscow Art Theatre Letters*, London: Methuen, 1991.
Benedetti, Jean, *Stanislavski: An Introduction*, London: Methuen, 1982.
Benedetti, Jean, *Stanislavski and the Actor*, London: Methuen, 1998.
Carnicke, Sharon M., *Stanislavsky in Focus*, Amsterdam: Harwood, 1998.
Cole, Toby, *Acting: A Handbook of the Stanislavski Method*, New York: Crown, 1974.
Counsell, Colin, *Signs of Performance*, London: Routledge, 1996.
Edwards, Christine, *The Stanislavsky Heritage*, London: Peter Owen, 1966.
Gauss, Rebecca, *Lear's Daughters: The Studios of the Moscow Art Theatre, 1905–1927*, New York: Peter Lang, 1999.
Leach, Robert, *Stanislavsky and Meyerhold*, Bern: Peter Lang, 2003.
Levin, Irina and Igor, *Working on the Play and the Role: The Stanislavsky Method for Analysing the Characters in a Drama*, Chicago, Ill.: Ivan R. Dee, 1992.
Merlin, Bella, *Beyond Stanislavsky*, London: Nick Hern Books, 2001.
Merlin, Bella, *Konstantin Stanislavsky*, London: Routledge, 2003.
Sayler, Oliver M., *Inside the Moscow Art Theater*, New York: Brentano's, 1925.
Worrall, Nick, *The Moscow Art Theatre*, London: Routledge, 1996.

3   Vsevolod Emilievich Meyerhold

Life and work

Meyerhold was born on 28 January 1874 in the city of Penza, approximately 550 kilometres south-east of Moscow. Part German Jew and part Russian, Karl Fyodor Kasimir, as he was named, was the youngest of the eight children of Emile Fyodorovich Meyergold, a prosperous German vodka distiller, and Alvina Davidovna, née Hess, his wife. She especially loved the theatre: her youngest son, too, enjoyed street entertainers, and the travelling fairground shows he saw. He was, however, a studious boy, reading much, including Dostoevsky, being fluent in German as well as Russian, and playing the violin and the piano with almost equal facility. Still, he wanted to be an actor, and 'already at the age of seven, grown-ups would find me before the mirror trying to transform my childish little face. Later, there were other powerful attractions: to music (the violin), literature, politics, but the attraction to the theatre proved to be the most powerful of all.'[1] And while still in his teens, the young Karl Meyergold was acting on Penza's amateur stage.

In 1892, his father died. Circumstances straitened. Perhaps to avoid conscription into the Prussian army, Meyerhold took Russian citizenship, and changed his name to Vsevolod Emilievich. Three years later, he entered Moscow University to study law, and in April 1896 he married his Penza sweetheart, Olga Munt. But he was already dissatisfied with the idea of a career as a lawyer, and elected to follow his sister-in-law, Ekaterina Munt, into the Philharmonia School, to study acting under Vladimir Nemirovich-Danchenko. As a drama student he worked hard, even fanatically, acted and directed with an astonishing maturity, and graduated with the highest grades in 1898. That was the year Nemirovich-Danchenko and Stanislavsky established their new Moscow Art Theatre, and Meyerhold was invited to become a member. He accepted without hesitation, despite other more lucrative offers from other more established managements. Idealism, experimentation, even risk were what he sought, then and

Figure 3.1 Vsevolod Emilievich Meyerhold.

throughout his career. 'We are striving to create the first rational, moral and public-accessible theatre and we dedicate our lives to this high goal', he informed his wife after the company began to rehearse.[2]

This was at Pushkino, a country estate next to the Alexeyev (Stanislavsky) estate. Years later, Meyerhold remembered the 'dusty summer day' when 'it all began'.[3] He drove in a cab to Moscow's Yaroslavl Station with Ivan Moskvin, also a graduate of the Philharmonia School. They caught the train together, and reached Pushkino where for the whole summer the company rehearsed the new theatre's new repertoire. They lived a communal life, sharing domestic tasks, discussing, arguing, planning and dreaming, and rehearsing daily from the imaginative production plans Stanislavsky drew up. 'We lived', Stanislavsky recalled, 'a friendly and a joyful life'.[4]

In the first years of the Art Theatre's existence, Meyerhold played a number of leading roles, including Treplev in *The Seagull* (his favourite part, he always maintained), Tiresias in *Antigone* by Sophocles, Malvolio in *Twelfth Night* and Tuzenbach in *Three Sisters*. He discovered that his ideas chimed with those of Anton Chekhov, with whom he developed a warm friendship. Decades after Chekhov's death, he asserted: 'Chekhov loved me. That is the pride of my life, one of my most precious memories.'[5] At that time, he was, he noted, 'rushing towards a vital life, towards thrilling, healthy labour. One wants to seethe, to boil, in order to create; not only to destroy, but to create in destroying.'[6] He was too much of a handful for the Art Theatre, and when the company was reorganised, despite Chekhov's protests, Meyerhold was not invited to become a share-holder. A meeting was held which, Olga Knipper wrote to her husband, Anton Chekhov,

> was not pleasant. Sanin and Meyerhold informed the management, officially, of their departure from the theatre. We all decided to ask them to stay as we need them in our work. Roksanova, Munt, Abessalomov and . . . Sudbinin were voted out. The whole proceeding was revolting. I am tired and my head is splitting.[7]

Meyerhold left the Art Theatre in the spring of 1902. In May he went to Italy where he read, enjoyed the street life, and came into contact with expatriate revolutionary politics. He returned to begin rehearsing with a new company he was forming with Alexander Kosheverov. They opened in Kherson, in September 1902, with a production of Chekhov's *Three Sisters*. The company, proudly calling themselves 'Comrades of the New Drama' played two seasons (1902–3 and 1903–4) in Kherson and one (1904–5) in Tblisi, Georgia, as well as touring various other provincial Russian cities. Meyerhold, who had been an assistant director at the Art Theatre, now began directing in his own right. By his own admission his first efforts slavishly copied Stanislavsky, but gradually he found his own way, and with it his own confidence. Since he was mounting two, three, or even sometimes four new productions a week, his progress was inevitably haphazard, but it was real enough, and the company retained his idealism both in its repertoire and in its developing style: Meyerhold experimented with Symbolist drama, mounting plays by Maurice Maeterlinck and Stanislaw Przybyszewski, before almost anyone else in Russia had approached this work.

Consequently, when in early 1905 Stanislavsky was considering establishing a 'Theatre Studio' to explore stage Symbolism, he invited Meyerhold to take charge. Meyerhold boldly proclaimed his aim: 'The Theatre-Studio should strive for the renovation of dramatic art by means of new forms and new methods of scenic presentation.'[8] The 'new forms' were evident in the repertoire, which was to include Maeterlinck's *The Death of Tintagiles*, Hauptmann's *Schluck und Jau*, and other ultra-modern works. The 'new methods of presentation' involved a new approach to both stage design and acting. In terms of stage design, Meyerhold abolished the meticulous maquettes of the Art Theatre, and substituted something much more impressionistic, with the artists merely submitting paintings which *suggested* forms and colours. As for the acting, this was to be based on improvisation, and Meyerhold coined a new term for his approach – the 'Theatre of the Straight Line'. This involved the director assimilating the work of the playwright – not just the play to be presented, but, if possible, his whole *oeuvre* – which he (the director) then presented to the actors. The actors, their enthusiasm fired by this, used the director's thoughts, ideas, and interpretations to make their performances, which were then presented to the audience. The 'straight line' went from playwright, through director, to actor, and then on to the spectator. It was a bold and original conception, one which formed the basis of Meyerhold's approach for the rest of his life. The crucial element in creating the performance was the relationship between the director and the actor: the director created the parameters within which the actor was to find his performance *through improvising*.

Stanislavsky hired a large Moscow theatre on Povarskaya Street for the young company, but when they rehearsed there, their delicate effects were lost in the vast auditorium. Then, on 14 October, armed revolt broke out in the city. The theatres closed, and Stanislavsky decided to use this as a reason for bringing the Theatre Studio experiment to an end. Meyerhold, whose mother had also recently died, was in 'emotional turmoil'; for him it was 'a personal tragedy'. But in a few months, he was able to see that the decision was correct. What was needed before such an original venture was attempted was a new kind of actor.

Meyerhold returned to the Art Theatre, but began to spend time in St Petersburg, with the artistic avant-garde. He also read Georg Fuchs's Wagner-inspired *The Theatre of the Future* which advocated a 'spiritual union' between actor and spectator. But his financial situation dictated that he return to the Comrades of the New Drama. By chance the company was booked to perform in a huge theatre in Poltava. Meyerhold built a forestage over the orchestra pit, dispensed with the front curtain and thus created a new kind of Fuchs-inspired configuration, dominated by a forestage upon which the dramatic action could take place.

Meyerhold's St Petersburg

St Petersburg was created by Tsar Peter the Great in 1703 as Russia's window on the west, and it always retained an air of Europeanism. In Russia's 'Silver Age' between two revolutions, it was decadent and cosmopolitan, fascinating and brittle.

At the Maryinsky Theatre, lit by electric lights years before Moscow's theatres were plugged in, Vaslav Nijinsky, Anna Pavlova, Tamara Karsavina, and Mikhail Fokin danced; while in her own dramatic theatre in Offitserskaya Street, the fantastic, fragile figure of Vera Komissarzhevskaya, idealistic, suffering, and incredibly beautiful, acted, winning and breaking the hearts of men and women alike.

Every Wednesday evening, Vyacheslav Ivanov held *soirées* in his 'Tower' apartment, when artists, intellectuals, poets, and writers met, to argue, plan, and amuse one another. Among them was the enigmatic but brilliant Mikhail Kuzmin, poet, musician, playwright, translator, whose openly homoerotic verse scandalised and titillated in almost equal measure. Meanwhile, the elegant Nikolai Evreinov, director of the satirical 'little theatre', the Distorting Mirror, propounded his theories of monodrama and the theatricalisation of life.

St Petersburg's name was changed to the more Russian-sounding Petrograd in 1914, and the city was never quite the same again.

This was to be pursued in the St Petersburg theatre of Vera Komissarzhevskaya, who appointed him to her company as actor and director. But Meyerhold had his own agenda and, as she noted, treated her theatre as his experimental laboratory. His most significant production, Blok's *The Fairground Booth*, did not even feature Komissarzhevskaya in the cast. This play is a wistful, ironic debunking of Symbolism's tendency towards mysticism by use of figures from the then highly fashionable *commedia dell'arte*. Even if it was the *commedia* of Callot's fantastical drawings rather than of the sweat of the real-life popular stage, it opened up to Meyerhold the traditional trestle stage, thrust out into a popular audience without wings or scenery, *commedia*'s characteristic reliance on the actors' improvisation *within a predetermined scenario*, and stock characters, Harlequin, Pierrot, and Columbine. Furthermore, the play's self-referential theatricality – the author interrupting the actors, a clown who bled cranberry juice, an ending in which all the scenery flew up into the flies – revealed possibilities which had hardly been dreamed of within the portals of the Moscow Art Theatre.

But Komissarzhevskaya had had enough, and on 9 November 1907 Meyerhold was given notice. Five months later, to the surprise of all, he was appointed to the heavily subsidised imperial theatres of St Petersburg, as actor and staff director. His work here over the next ten years gave Meyerhold unparalleled experience of directing excellent actors, with generous budgets and on big stages. Most significant, perhaps, were his productions of Wagner's *Tristan and Isolde* (1909), for which he had constructed a 'relief stage' in front of the main stage, together with *Don Juan* by Molière (1910) and *Masquerade* by Lermontov (1917), both of which used *commedia* motifs to unexpected advantage.

The Russian imperial theatres

Russian theatre in the tsarist period was dominated by the imperial theatres, which were directly subsidised and administered as if they were part of the imperial court. The Bolshoi ('big') theatre which staged mostly opera and ballet, and the Maly ('small') theatre, which staged straight drama, were in Moscow, while in St Petersburg there were three imperial theatres: the Maryinsky, for opera and ballet, the Alexandrinsky for drama, and the Mikhailovsky, which presented French and foreign drama. These theatres retained a monopoly until 1882, and even after that date they still dominated.

The question implicit in the existence of imperial theatres was whether they were toys of the court, or an aspirant 'national theatre'. They often seemed unenterprising and played to largely privileged and wealthy patrons. But they were also responsible for the primacy of Russian ballet, for the career of the extraordinary singer, Fyodor Chaliapin, and for the Maly Theatre, long known as 'Moscow's second university'. Their director from 1901 to 1917, Vladimir Telyakovsky, recruited the best talent available and tried to raise standards, while obviously forbidding anything politically suspicious or radical. In his time the imperial theatres' impressive international repertoire certainly played a significant part in the flowering of Russian culture in the 'Silver Age'.

Meanwhile, Meyerhold had the time and security to develop his experimental work outside the imperial theatres. In 1908, for instance, he directed popular and folk dramas in a 'little theatre', the Cove, as well as teaching acting at St Petersburg's Music and Drama School. In the autumn of that year, he tried to set up his own school with the musician Mikhail Gnesin and the dancer Valentin Presnyakov, and when that failed, in the autumn of 1909, he returned to teaching acting, this time at the Pollak

School of Music, Drama and Opera. In April 1910 he directed an intimate production of Calderon's *The Adoration of the Cross* at Vyacheslav Ivanov's Tower; in October he directed *Columbine's Scarf*, adapted from Schnitzler's *The Veil of Pierette*, at the House of Interludes; and in November 1911 he presented his most extreme *commedia* show, *Harlequin the Marriage Broker*, with Vladimir Soloviev at the Assembly House of the Nobility. Here, with a conventional *commedia* stage setting, plenty of improvisation, a traditional story, and a series of *lazzi* (set stage jokes), he created perhaps his most thoroughly 'grotesque' production. The following summer, with a group of friends, he took the Casino Theatre in Terioki, just over the border in Finland (later incorporated into Russia and re-named Zelenogorsk), and staged an experimental season including work by Wilde, Strindberg, and Shaw, as well as *Harlequin the Marriage Broker* again and his own pseudo-*commedia* scenario, *The Lovers*. In 1913 he published his book, *On Theatre*.

To save the imperial theatres embarrassment as he continued this work, Meyerhold had taken the stage name, Dr Dapertutto for his unofficial work, and in the autumn of 1913 he opened Dr Dapertutto's Studio. Charging its members a small fee, the Studio provided classes in the areas of practical theatre which Meyerhold deemed consequential: theatre history, with the emphasis on popular theatres through the ages; practical music and speech, taught by Mikhail Gnesin; *commedia dell'arte*, taught by Soloviev and Konstantin Miklashevsky; and Scenic Movement, taught by Meyerhold himself, though he was involved in all the other classes too. To these were added, as the Studio continued, classes in dance, in circus skills, and in stage management. Students demonstrated their skills in public in two exhibition performances, the first of which took place on 7 April 1914, when *The Fairground Booth* in a new staging, and *The Unknown Woman*, also by Blok, were presented, and the second a year later, consisting of a programme (which varied from night to night) of scenes, sketches, and études from the Studio's current work. Meyerhold also published a magazine, *The Love of Three Oranges*, in which he discussed his ideas, and the Studio was visited by prominent poets, artists, and musicians.

Russia in revolution, 1917

In November 1916, in view of the devastating losses in the war against Germany, but against his autocratic inclinations, Tsar Nikolai II summoned the Russian Duma (parliament). At its meeting, the Cadet Party's Milyukov vehemently attacked the government for incompetence and corruption. Faced with a crisis of confidence, the tsar resorted to repression, having workers' leaders arrested in Petrograd (St Petersburg) and elections in Moscow annulled.

But in February 1917 the Duma reconvened and Milyukov resumed his attack. Street demonstrations followed, and by 10 March people were electing their own soviets. Nikolai tried to dissolve the Duma, but it refused to be dissolved. Huge swathes of the army were deserting him for the forces of democracy. On 14 March, the Duma and the soviets collaborated in the formation of a new Provisional Government, and the tsar abdicated.

The new government was led by Prince Lvov, with Milyukov prominent in it. But the rising star was Alexander Kerensky, leader of the Social Revolutionary Party, a largely peasant-based quasi-revolutionary grouping. A general amnesty was proclaimed, freedom of speech and democratic rights were promised, and preparations were begun for the election of a genuinely representative Constituent Assembly.

In April, Lenin returned from exile, and began agitating and organising. And soon the Provisional Government began to fall apart. Milyukov resigned, Kerensky grabbed more power and instigated a new offensive against Germany. But this failed, and the troops were beaten back. Meanwhile peasants seized land, many factories were on strike, and the workers themselves took control of others. Soviets were organised, Trotsky returning as president of the Petrograd soviet. Lenin's Bolsheviks rose up, but they failed to gain power. Trotsky was arrested and Lenin escaped to Finland. In the aftermath, Kerensky became Prime Minister, even though he had no solution to the state's chaotic finances, nor to the problems of food distribution.

In September, General Kornilov tried to seize power. The people wanted – and the Bolsheviks promised – bread and peace. In October, they rose again and this time they succeeded. The Second Congress of the Soviets approved their actions on 7 November 1917, and though many Mensheviks and Social Revolutionaries withdrew in protest, and there was a brief but fierce battle for Moscow, by 15 November the new Bolshevik government under Lenin was effectively in control of Russia.

There followed a bloody Civil War, as the various defeated factions ('Whites') took up arms against the 'Reds', and the Germans, Czechs, British, Americans, and Japanese all tried to intervene. But in a series of campaigns the foreign interventionists and their Russian allies were defeated, and by October 1922 even Vladivostok was in the hands of the Bolsheviks.

Two days after Meyerhold's opulent production of *Masquerade* opened at the Alexandrinsky Theatre in St Petersburg (Petrograd) in February 1917, the monarchy fell. The revolution had begun which in November was to sweep the Bolsheviks into power. Meyerhold responded to the political whirlwind with energy and enthusiasm. His future step-daughter, Tatyana Esenina, remarked that 'he experienced a kind of rebirth'.[9] Immediately he declared for the new regime, and in August 1918 he became a member of the Party. He was appointed to the new Theatre Department of the Ministry of Culture and Education as a deputy to Olga Kameneva, wife of the new Moscow Party chief and Trotsky's sister, and determined to mount 'the first Soviet play', Mayakovsky's *Mystery Bouffe*, at one of the imperial theatres. The actors refused to co-operate, however, so Meyerhold resigned from his position and mounted it instead at the theatre of the Music and Drama Conservatoire on the first anniversary of the Bolshevik revolution. It was a noisy, blasphemous, rip-roaring hurrah of a play, a genuine slap in the face of conventional taste, in which Meyerhold put his *Commedia dell'arte* techniques to new, dynamic, up-to-the-minute use, and – implicitly – announced a new theatrical regime in Russia.

The Bolsheviks

In 1898 a group of nine Russian Marxist revolutionaries met in Minsk, Belorussia, and agreed to found the Russian Social Democratic Labour Party (RSDLP). Though virtually outlawed in Russia, it quickly attracted a number of members and held its first Congress in Brussels and London in the summer of 1903. At this Congress, two factions emerged. One, the bigger ('*bolshe*'), led by Vladimir Ilich Lenin, urged that the party should be small and tightly organised. Members should be militant, active, and disciplined. The other, smaller ('*menshe*') faction, led by Martov, preferred something much looser, more like a western social democratic party with a mass membership. This group's most prominent member was Lev Trotsky, who became president of the St Petersburg soviet in 1905.

Despite further differences in policy, the party remained nominally united in the Dumas elected after the abortive 'first revolution', but in 1912 the Bolsheviks expelled the Mensheviks, and became the RSDLP(B), while the Mensheviks were the RSDLP(M). It was the Bolsheviks who led the October revolution in 1917, by which time many Mensheviks (including Trotsky) had come over to them, and in March 1918 they became the Communist Party of Russia in their own one-party state.

The following year he hatched a plan with Kameneva to nationalise all the theatres in the country and thereby, of course, obtain control of them himself. The boldness of the plan was staggering, and was perhaps only foiled when he fell ill in May 1919 and had to leave Petrograd to recuperate in the south. As soon as he was gone, the senior members of the theatrical establishment – the esteemed actors and directors from the Maly, the Alexandrinsky, and even the Moscow Art Theatre – met with Lunacharsky, the playwright-Communist who was Lenin's Minister of Culture and Education and, in return for their agreement to put the theatre back on a 'normal' footing, the nationalisation plan was shelved.

Meanwhile, Meyerhold and his family were staying in Novorossiisk, north of Sochi on the Black Sea. In September, Meyerhold was arrested there by the White Army, imprisoned, and even threatened with death. He was held for four months, but escaped and went into hiding. In March, Novorossiisk was retaken by the Reds and Meyerhold emerged. He set to work immediately, mounting a production of *A Doll's House* and fighting against the Whites. In May, Lunacharsky asked him back to Moscow, and appointed him head of the Theatre Department. Noting the spreading 'theatre epidemic' – the unexpected rush in these revolutionary years by unskilled citizens to join amateur theatre troupes, actor training programmes, play-writing courses and the like – Meyerhold announced an 'October in the Theatre', like the 'October in the Countryside' campaign to win the peasants to the revolution. Meyerhold's campaign most visibly consisted of establishing a numbered series of Theatres of the RSFSR (Russian Socialist Federation of Soviet Republics), that with which he was professionally associated being Number 1. The implication was that these theatres would be favoured under the new regime, and a number of companies fell into line to become RSFSR Theatre Number 2, RSFSR

Theatre Number 3, and so on. On the third anniversary of the revolution, he presented an exemplary version of Emile Verhaeren's *The Dawns* as the inaugural production of RSFSR Theatre Number 1. Despite its popularity with many ordinary theatregoers, the production was not liked by the Party's elite, notably Lenin's wife, who loudly criticised it; and from that moment, Meyerhold's revolutionary star began a slow descent. By early 1921 it was obvious 'October in the Theatre' had failed. With the announcement of Lenin's New Economic Policy, which cut theatre subsidies to the bone, his position became untenable and he resigned. Though he mounted a revised version of Mayakovsky's *Mystery Bouffe* in May, by the end of the summer, RSFSR Theatre Number 1 had closed. [10]

Within a few weeks, however, a State Higher Directing Workshop (GVYRM) was set up with Meyerhold at its head. Reaffirming his dedication in the new Russia to the 'grotesque', Meyerhold sought 'pioneers' to find 'new paths' and a 'new theatre'. [11] The four ingredients in this new theatre would be theatricality, improvisation, 'physical culture', and 'tendentiousness'. [12] As with so many Soviet institutions in the early years of the new regime, GVYRM was re-named and reincarnated several times, but by the middle 1920s it had stabilised as GEKTEMAS ('State Experimental Theatre Workshop in the name of Meyerhold'), and it was here that Meyerhold's famous 'Biomechanics' was developed. In a sense, Biomechanics was a Sovietisation of Meyerhold's (or Dr Dapertutto's) Scenic Movement. It involved a new, Sovietised language, including algebraic formulations ($N = A_1 + A_2$), as well as including new elements deriving from 'Taylorisation' and Pavlov's experiments, and was first demonstrated in public in the summer of 1922.

Meanwhile, a 'free' workshop for his advanced students opened in December 1921, and this group became both an acting company proper and a more fluid laboratory, known as the 'Methodological Club Laboratory', committed to community participation and spreading the Meyerhold 'system'. This group provided most of the cast for the extraordinary productions of *The Magnanimous Cuckold*, perhaps Meyerhold's most astonishing work, staged in April 1922; *The Death of Tarelkin*, presented in November that year, for which Sergei Eisenstein was assistant director; and *The World Turned Upside Down* ('*Zemlya Dybom*') by Sergei Tretyakov, premiered in March 1923. These productions cemented the fusion of Meyerhold's experimental and public work, which had been separated before the revolution. They were startling, ironic, youthfully energetic, and life-affirming, like the hopes for the revolution itself. Something of their style can still be glimpsed in Russian silent films of the 1920s, especially Eisenstein's *The Strike* and Kuleshov's *The Extraordinary Adventures of Mr West in the Land of the Bolsheviks*.

Despite the failure of his 'October in the Theatre' campaign, Meyerhold was at this time enormously influential and charismatic. He attended all the premieres in Moscow, sitting in the front row of the stalls and clapping with his hands above his head if he approved of what he saw, walking out – even walking out early – if he did not approve. Gladkov recalled the *frisson* which ran through him – and the whole audience – when Meyerhold appeared in his own theatre:

> That evening I saw Meyerhold for the first time. He came out during the last act from a small door on the left, and standing on the little stairs, attentively watched the stage.
>
> I was sitting on the left side of the orchestra, and in the semi-darkness of the theatre I had a good look at the shock of gray hair, the huge nose, the firmly molded lips, the curve of the shoulders and the head proudly thrown back. I was not the only one who recognized him. A whisper of recognition ran through the audience.[13]

Figure 3.2 Cartoon of Meyerhold from the 1920s.

Meyerhold loved flowers and animals and was passionate about fine art, music, and literature, especially Pushkin who more and more came to influence him. He had a gift for friendship, but also a gift for quarrels. 'I love passionate situations',[14] he remarked. He fell headlong in love with one of his new students, Sergei Esenin's former wife, Zinaida Raikh. In a whirlwind, he divorced Olga Munt and married Zinaida, who was to remain the great love of his life. When her star appeared dim beside that of his greatest actress, Maria Babanova, in 1927, Meyerhold coldly dismissed the latter. Babanova never forgot the insult, and never quite recovered the youthful *élan* which had so distinguished her performances from her debut in *The Magnanimous Cuckold*. But maybe Meyerhold was not so much blinded by love as determined to move forward himself. Certainly some of Raikh's performances in the 1930s were unforgettable to those who saw them. In 1928 he staged the Russian classic, Griboyedov's *Woe to Wit* (as he retitled *Woe from Wit*), and some suggested that in the restless, satirical hero there lay a directorial self-portrait, especially as Erast Garin, who played Chatsky, made himself up to look like Meyerhold. He was a man 'constantly lacerated by dissatisfaction with himself',[15] as Meyerhold asserted the 'true artist' always was.

By the summer of 1928 Meyerhold's position was slipping. He and Raikh went to France, and from there he began to bargain for an increased subsidy for his work. Many thought he would follow Mikhail Chekhov and others into exile, but the government parleyed, and despite falling attendances at the Meyerhold State Theatre they agreed to write off most of its large debts. Consequently, when he returned to a hero's welcome in Moscow, he turned with fresh energy to a 'new' repertoire – plays by Mayakovsky, Tretyakov's *I Want a Baby*, Erdman's *The Suicide*, and more. But his hopes were soon squashed. The Tretyakov and Erdman plays were banned, and Mayakovsky's *The Bedbug* and the more brilliant *Bathhouse*, which received one of Meyerhold's most thrilling productions in 1930, were received sneeringly, even damningly, by critics who were beginning to flex their Stalinist muscles against the so-called 'avant-garde'. Later that year, the Meyerhold Theatre toured Germany and France, but the authorities recalled them before they could embark on the proposed American leg of the tour.

Vladimir Vladimirovich Mayakovsky
Mayakovsky was born in Georgia in 1893, and by the age of twelve (in 1905) was taking part in political demonstrations. He studied art and wrote poetry, and in 1912, with David Burlyuk, Velimir Khlebnikov,

and Alexei Kruchonykh, he published a 'Futurist' manifesto, *A Slap in the Face of Public Taste*.

By now his poems were appearing in print, and his first play, a tragedy, was performed in a double bill with Kruchonykh's *Victory Over the Sun* at Kommissarzhevskaya's former theatre in St Petersburg. Led by Mayakovsky, the Futurists became notorious for scandalous public readings and dramatic appearances. In 1915 he met Osip and Lily Brik: the former became his close friend, the latter his greatest love.

Mayakovsky embraced the revolution, and became its bard in poems, slogans and painted posters. His play *Mystery Bouffe* celebrated it, and almost all his work in the next few years argued for it.

By the end of the 1920s, however, his love life appeared to be collapsing, and his faith in Communism was dying too. Two more plays, *The Bedbug* and *The Bathhouse*, were mounted by Meyerhold, the second in a particularly vital production, but they contained bitter satire which the Stalinist *apparatchiks* were not able to tolerate. The critical reception was vicious. On 14 April 1930 Mayakovsky shot himself.

Back in Moscow, the Zon building which housed the Meyerhold Theatre was closed for refurbishment, and the Meyerhold State Theatre toured or performed temporarily in the uncongenial Passage Theatre. Meyerhold's plans for the Zon envisaged a truly modern theatre, where his work could be fittingly placed. His Biomechanics was being refined further, Zinaida Raikh was growing in stature as an actress, and his current repertoire, including *A List of Assets*, *Prelude*, and *The Lady of the Camellias*, was distinct and attractive. But there were unexpected tragic undertones in this clutch of plays, and besides, they, along with Tretyakov's *I Want a Baby* and others Meyerhold addressed, questioned the position of women in the new Soviet society at a time when Stalin asserted that the 'woman question' had been solved. Something was out of joint. In terms of theatre, Stalin sought portrayals of women in situations of domestic bliss. Meyerhold's response? 'I don't like sentimental art . . . Tears dampen the gunpowder.'[16]

In fact, he was desperately seeking new plays which would satisfy the authorities and yet be worth his attention. He knew he was in the firing line: 'I'm sure that if tomorrow I announced that the Volga flows into the Caspian Sea, then the day after tomorrow they'd start demanding an admission from me of the errors contained in this statement.'[17] In January 1936, *Pravda*, the Communist Party newspaper, attacked the opera *Lady Macbeth of Mtsensk*, by Meyerhold's close friend Dmitri Shostakovich. The following month the Second Studio of the Moscow Art Theatre was closed. The net was closing. Meyerhold felt constrained in March to deliver a speech, 'Meyerhold Against Meyerholditis'. Gladkov paints an unforgettable picture of him one evening that month, playing official host to André Malraux, the visiting French writer. He was a charming, serious, and interested host, but after Malraux left, he, Zinaida Raikh, and Boris Pasternak, his other guest, urgently and anxiously discussed his difficulties: whether he should approach Stalin, what he could say, and so on; but whenever he fetched more coffee 'he acted out for us waiters of different nationalities, going out and coming back each time as a new "character", pouring out liqueurs and cognac, doing tricks with a napkin and so forth'.[18]

Later that year he and Zinaida Raikh went to Paris again. He met Picasso and they discussed the possibility of the latter designing *Hamlet* for him. He was also making a new, creative relationship with Stanislavsky, and collecting together his articles for a new book on theatre. But the attacks on him as a 'Formalist' were all the time gathering pace, and the State Publishing House refused to publish his book despite its earlier promise. Finally, on 17 December, the attack came: *Pravda* accused his theatre of being 'alien' to the Soviet people. For three days his company held criticism and self-criticism sessions, but it was pointless. On 7 January 1938, the Committee for Artistic Affairs of the Peoples' Commissars of the USSR decreed the liquidation of the Meyerhold State Theatre. The performance of *The Lady of the Camellias* that evening was like a wake. At the end of the performance the audience crowded onto the stage. Zinaida Raikh fainted. The atmosphere 'resembled the mood in a family where someone everyone loved has just died: people were standing around in groups, smoking, saying nothing, thinking about things.'[19]

Stanislavsky offered Meyerhold a lifeline: a post in his Opera Theatre, and these two started to work together again. Stanislavsky even declared that Meyerhold was his heir, 'not just in this theatre, but in theatre as a whole'.[20] However, in August, Stanislavsky died, and though Meyerhold took over as chief director of the Stanislavsky Opera Theatre, and went with them on tour in southern Russia, he was effectively isolated. He wrote to his wife:

Me without you is like a blind man without his guide dog . . . I reached Gorenki on the 13th, saw the silver birches and gasped – surely these leaves are made of gold! . . . When I saw on the 13th in a fairy tale world the golden autumn, its miracle in all this, I whispered to myself: Zina,

Zinochka, look, look at these miracles and ... and don't leave me, *I love you*, you – my wife, sister, mother, friend, darling. *You are golden like this nature which creates miracles.* Zina, don't leave me![21]

In June 1939, he attended the All-Union Conference of Theatre Directors. Here, whenever he was noticed, his peers loudly applauded him, but on 15 June he made a sad speech, blaming himself for all sorts of mistakes. It was his last public appearance, and utterly out of character.

The Great Terror
In 1934 the Leningrad Communist Party boss, S. M. Kirov was murdered. Though there are good grounds for thinking Stalin himself was behind the murder, he used it as the excuse to 'purge' first the Party, and then society as a whole, of 'alien elements'. In 1936, the first 'show' trials began: in August, Zinoviev and Kamenev, two of Lenin's leading Bolshevik comrades, were arraigned for spying and 'Trotskyism', and executed, and in January 1937 Pyatakov, Serebryakov, Radek, and others followed them. In June 1937 the purges began to strike at the armed forces when seven leading generals were tried and condemned, and in March 1938, Bukharin, Yagoda, and Rykov were similarly despatched.

By now the purges had become the Great Terror. Quotas were set by Stalin: his regional governors had to execute so many per month, and arrest so many more. Literally millions lost their lives, and many millions more were sent to gulags or concentration camps. But the worst purges were of people nearest to Stalin. It is estimated that through 1938 90 per cent of the army's generals, 80 per cent of colonels, and 30,000 other officers in the Russian army lost their lives. Of the 138 members of the Communist Party's Central Committee in February 1937, ninety-eight were executed by firing squad.

Meyerhold was one among millions who were judicially murdered, Unlike many of Stalin's victims, at least his work and memory can be recalled and re-valued.

He travelled to Leningrad, where he was arrested and brought back to Moscow. On 14 July, Zinaida Raikh was brutally murdered, and the Meyerhold–Raikh flat appropriated and handed over to Lavrenty Beria, the Chief of Police. Meanwhile, on 23 and 27 June, Meyerhold was roughly interrogated, and a 'confession' obtained from him. But obviously the authorities wanted more. On 8 July he was tortured:

> They laid me face down on the floor and beat the soles of my feet and my back with a rubber truncheon. When I was seated on a chair they used the same truncheon to beat my legs from above with great force, from my knees to the upper parts of my legs. And in the days that followed, when my legs were bleeding from internal haemorrhaging, they used the rubber truncheon to beat me on the red, blue and yellow bruises. The pain was so great that it was like boiling water being poured on the tenderest parts of my legs (I screamed and wept with pain). They beat me on the back with the truncheon; they beat me about the face with blows from above.[22]

The process was repeated on 14 July, and more bogus 'confessions' were obtained. And so on.

By 20 August they had what they wanted. Meyerhold was prostrate in the prison hospital. In October he was formally indicted as a spy and supporter of Trotskyism. Further interrogations followed, at which he broke down humiliatingly, but also tried to retract his 'confessions'. To no avail. On 2 January 1939, and again on 13 January, he wrote to Vyacheslav Molotov, Stalin's Prime Minister, but on 1 February he was brought to 'trial', a ten-minute proceeding in the confines of the prison, and sentenced to death. He was shot the next day. His body was burned, and the ashes tipped into 'Common Grave Number One' in the Don Monastery cemetery.

The key questions

Within two or three years of his debut as an actor at the Moscow Art Theatre Meyerhold had begun to doubt the kind of theatre that was being created there.

The problem was to do with the nature of theatre itself. The Art Theatre raised the quality of the stage illusion to new heights. Their productions seemed as close to life as it was possible to be, both in terms of acting and of stage scenery, costumes, and so on. The audience peered through an imaginary fourth wall at actors 'living' their parts. Meyerhold himself could perform in this style brilliantly. His Treplev in Chekhov's *The Seagull*, for example, was 'weak and touching, a decadent *par excellence*'.[23] But to 'live' the part seemed to him to diminish the art and the theatricality of theatre.

Chekhov himself objected to these productions as much too one-sided. He saw his plays as comedies, and viewed the characters less as pathetic than ridiculous. The Art Theatre ignored the fact that he deliberately used traditional theatricalities: illicit lovers stumbled upon by a jealous rival; old men made fools of in pursuit of young women; two servants vying for one serving-maid's favours. Where in the Art Theatre's productions was the theatricality of such traditional moments, which Chekhov loved? Where, indeed, was Chekhov's irony, his humour, his symbolism, his ambivalence? Surely theatre which was true *to itself* would be able to spring these contradictions and provocations like a jack-in-a-box?

Meyerhold wrote to the author shortly before his death in 1904:

> Your play is abstract, like a Tchaikovsky symphony. Above all else, the director must get the *sound* of it. In Act Three, against the background of the mindless stamping of feet – it is this 'stamping' that must be heard – enters Horror, completely unnoticed by the guests: 'The cherry orchard is sold'. They dance on. 'Sold' – still they dance. And so on, to the end. When one reads the play, the effect of the third act is the same as the ringing in the ears of the sick man in your story *Typhus*. A sort of itching. Jollity with overtones of death. In this act there is something . . . terrifying.[24]

The terror, and the truth, Meyerhold argued, were obtained by Chekhov by purely *theatrical* means. And for Meyerhold such theatrical 'truth' might be found in the street puppet shows he had enjoyed as a boy, in the circuses and stage buffooneries of the popular fairgrounds, or in the golden ages of conventional theatre. But it was not found in a theatre which pretended it was real life.

In the late nineteenth and early twentieth centuries, questions were beginning to be asked in all the arts about the nature and supremacy of 'realism'. In Russia, the painter Vasily Kandinsky led the way: what was 'painterly' in painting? he asked. The young Formalist critics then followed with: what was 'literary' in literature?

Meyerhold asked: what is theatrical about theatre? How can theatre be true *to itself*?

Meyerhold's answers

> On a rainy autumn day a funeral procession crawls through the streets; the gait of the pallbearers conveys profound grief. Then the wind snatches a hat from the head of one of the mourners; he bends down to pick it up, but the wind begins to chase it from puddle to puddle. Each jump of the staid gentleman chasing his hat lends his face such comic grimaces that the gloomy funeral procession is suddenly transformed by some devilish hand into a bustling holiday crowd. If one could only achieve an effect like that on the stage![25]

Meyerhold wanted something more dynamic, more surprising, less safe than what the Art Theatre offered. For inspiration he looked at the medieval cathedral, with its lofty spires pointing to heaven and its snarling gargoyles, reminding us of hell. He recalled the baroque, which 'longs to enter into the multiplicity of phenomena, into the flux of things in their perpetual becoming'.[26] And he referred to the German cabaret of Ernst von Wolzogen, whose '*Uberbrettl* sought to invigorate modern art by refining the vitality of the popular variety stage, whose attraction lay in its vigour, geniality and adversarial stance'. Wolzogen presented 'recitations of poetry as well as erotic songs, literary parody, pantomime, one act plays and [the] rousing round dance, "The Merry Husband"'.[27]

All these were examples of the grotesque. According to Meyerhold, 'the grotesque mixes opposites, consciously creating harsh incongruity and *relying solely on its own originality* . . . It forces the spectator to adopt an ambivalent attitude towards the stage action [and] preserves this ambivalent attitude in the spectator by switching the course of the action with strokes of contrast.'[28] He therefore sought productions that would break up the flow of the drama unexpectedly. He learned to break up the plays he directed into quite short, self-contained episodes: in *The Forest*, for example, he divided the text into thirty-three film-like episodes, each of which was preceded by a title projected onto a screen in the blackout. One critic noted: 'Meyerhold cuts and edits his scenes like film; as in film he works through gesture; as in film he uses close-ups and long-shots; as in film he changes the location for each scene.'[29] Meyerhold noted that 'in genuine art the high and the low, the bitter and the funny, the light and the dark always stand side by side' and suggested that the grotesque was 'a theatrical style that plays with sharp contradictions and produces a constant shift in the planes of perception'.[30] 'No sooner has the pale, lanky Pierrot crept across the stage, no sooner has the spectator sensed in his movements the eternal tragedy of mutely suffering mankind, than the apparition is succeeded by the merry Harlequinade. The tragic gives way to the comic, harsh satire replaces the sentimental ballad.'[31]

This is the essence of theatrical grotesque, and it resides characteristically, if not exclusively, in the *commedia dell'arte*. Meyerhold therefore utilised elements of this form, starting with the forestage. Even in his production of Molière's *Don Juan* at the Alexandrinsky Imperial Theatre in 1910 he divided the stage into

the proscenium, constructed according to architectural principles, intended exclusively for 'reliefs' and the figures of the actors (who perform only on this area). The proscenium to have a forestage projecting deep into the auditorium. No footlights. No prompt box . . . [and] . . . the upstage area, intended exclusively for painted backdrops . . . not used by the actors at all, except in the finale (downfall and immolation of Juan), and even then they will appear only on the dividing line between the two areas.[32]

In later productions, such as *The Magnanimous Cuckold* or *The Forest*, the stage was used with much greater sophistication, but it was based on the same principles.

Commedia dell'arte and the theatres of the fairgrounds

Theatres of various sorts and sizes have operated in fairgrounds across Europe (and beyond) from very early times. In Russia, *skomorokhi*, travelling entertainers, were famous for music-making and ballad singing, clowning, tumbling, showing puppets, and dancing. The best-known European popular entertainment of this sort was probably provided by the *commedia dell'arte*, a form of theatre presented by itinerant Italian troupes in fairgrounds, market-places, tavern yards and village greens, from about 1550 onwards. *Commedia dell'arte* actors played stock characters (Harlequin, Pantalone, Pierrot, etc.) in masks and recognisable costumes, and improvised their performances from pre-conceived scenarios often based on popular tales. Performances usually included plenty of songs, spectacular tumbling, rope-walking, juggling, etc., and were filled with stage tricks (known as *lazzi*).

Later, *commedia dell'arte* was accepted in higher social circles across Europe, including Russia. By the middle of the eighteenth century *commedia* dramas began to be scripted, notably in the work of Carlo Goldoni (1707–98), though a movement to restore improvisation to *commedia*, led by Carlo Gozzi (1720–1806), met with some success. But *commedia*'s day was really over, and by 1800 it was virtually dead.

Also from the *commedia dell'arte* Meyerhold drew his ideas of character-isation. Instead of an individual psychology, he looked for the character's function in the drama. For instance, Astrov and Vanya in *Uncle Vanya* are lovers, who could be seen as variations on the *commedia* lovers, Harlequin and Pierrot, with Elena, the object of their passions, as Columbine. Characters exist in plays for a purpose. They function as heroes or spoilsports, confidantes or matchmakers, and this functional base should be drawn out and utilised. The same was true of situations. The jealous quarrel, mistaken identities, the cunning trick, all provide stock theatrical situations. There is no need to seek a spurious 'originality' in the presentation of the story: rather, the audience should be allowed to recognise for themselves the familiar theatricality in a new guise, and – perhaps unconsciously – compare, say, *The Magnanimous Cuckold*'s Bruno with Othello or Leontes or the absurd Master Ford in *The Merry Wives of Windsor*. These resonances, rather than a study of Bruno's sick mind, were what Meyerhold believed made for *theatrical* truth.

The *commedia dell'arte* technique of improvising was also useful. The *commedia* actors worked, not from a script whose lines they learned, but from a more or less detailed scenario, which gave clear outlines of the story but included virtually no dialogue. This enabled the actors to make up their dialogue, and to some extent their movements, as the drama proceeded. For a novice this was very difficult, but for a practised professional it provided the best kind of freedom, enabling the individual actor to create within clear, objective parameters, and setting store by his originality within the given situation and the given character. The *improvisator* needed both a sure knowledge of theatre history and a firm grounding in technique. The history led him to understand how stock situations could be developed and how he could use what Meyerhold called 'antics appropriate to the theatre'. Technique enabled him to perform these antics. Thus history taught him when to strut the stage, or to put a custard pie in his partner's face; technique allowed him to achieve the maximum effect with such an antic. The exercises in Meyerhold's Biomechanics were devised to give the actor the tools he needed for this kind of improvisational work. As Igor Ilinsky, one of the most talented Meyerhold-trained actors, noted:

> We were not to transfer these [Biomechanical] 'devices' to the stage, although in the beginning we sometimes demonstrated them in performances. These exercises were to train us and give us a state for a specific movement onstage. The exercises, partly gymnastic, partly plastic movement, partly acrobatics, were to teach acting students how to calculate their movements; to develop a keen eye, coordinate movements in reference to their partners, and in general give them flexibility so that in future performances the actor could move more freely and expressively in the scenic space. Similarly a person who has studied and knows many dance steps can more easily improvise and dance to music, endlessly varying these steps, than a person who cannot dance at all.[33]

Biomechanics, with its Soviet-seeming orientation, helped to bring Meyerhold's somewhat self-indulgent approach into the present. It was 'tendentious', and brought an unexpected sharpness to the metaphorical and playful elements of a theatrical style that played with contradictions and shifted the audience's perspective in unexpected ways. By so doing, it reasserted the audience's vital function. The audience was the fourth and final point in 'the Theatre of the Straight Line', which began with the playwright and went through the director to the actors, who 'reveal their souls' to the spectators. The *theatrical* theatre was inconceivable without spectators, crammed round the market-place trestle or relaxing in the pub, booing, hissing, or clapping energetically. Meyerhold liked best an audience which was not only vociferous, but which was divided in its reaction to the play, such as that at the end of *Don Juan*, which Yuri Yurev, who played Juan, recalled:

> When in the noisy applause at the end of the first performance, Varlamov and I went before the audience, a piercing whistle from the upper circle was suddenly heard: this served as a signal for other 'pro-testers'. One of them (as we then recognized, it was Prince Argutinsky), whistled especially hotly right in our faces, quite unembarrassed to give himself up to such behaviour.[34]

Meyerhold asserted: 'If everyone praises your production, almost certainly it is rubbish. If everyone abuses it, then perhaps there is something in it. But if some praise and others abuse, if you can split the audience in half, then for sure it is a good production.'[35] This is a reaction most likely to be provoked by a *theatrical* performance: one like *Don Juan* played out on the forestage, where actor and spectator can confront one another or conspire together unhampered by the proscenium arch.

What makes the theatre theatrical?

Meyerhold's answer was to combine in unexpected ways grotesque contradictions, a broken rhythm, the forestage, stock characters in stock situations, improvising actors, and a noisy, engaged audience.

And all were to be orchestrated by a theatrical Master.

Theatre practice

Perhaps Meyerhold's first moment of practical enlightenment came when he was working at the Moscow Theatre Studio on Maeterlinck's *The Death of Tintagiles*. He described it half humorously himself:

> In *The Death of Tintagiles* there are acts lasting ten to twelve minutes that take place in a medieval castle. But in order to change the scenery for the castle, it would be necessary to make the intermissions twice as

long as the acts, and this is absurd. Willy-nilly, we had to invent a 'stylised castle'.[36]

'Stylisation' was applied not just to the scenery, however: it was a key to Meyerhold's whole understanding of theatre. It was, for instance, central to the acting process as he began now to conceive it, and when the acting in *The Death of Tintagiles* failed to match his demands, he began to seek a new kind of actor. He soon realised that *technique* was the corner-stone for any development in acting. 'The duty of the comedian and the mime [in which categories Meyerhold included the actor] is to transport the spectator to a world of make-believe, entertaining him on the way there with the brilliance of his technical skill . . . the improvisations of the *commedia dell'arte* had a firm basis of faultless technique',[37] he wrote in 1912. And over twenty years later he remarked: 'An actor must study as a violinist does. You can't make yourself into an actor in three or four years.'[38]

His pre-revolutionary work on the technique of the actor was distilled in his Scenic Movement classes at Dr Dapertutto's Studio. Scenic Movement for Meyerhold was originally composed of three elements: improvisation, the mask, and rhythm. Practically, these three, treated together, focus on the actor's movement. Improvisation involves the actor *doing* something. If he wears a mask, this prevents him from relying on facial expression and forces him to use his whole body. Rhythm is what controls *how* he does it spatially as well as temporally.

But these basic properties need further refinement. Meyerhold soon discovered that movement requires stillness to be meaningful, and the pause came to carry deep significance in his system. The pause contains dynamic energy; it is the moment of refocusing, the 'still' picture in the moving pattern. 'Even in the pauses you have to know how to maintain the tempo of the dialogue', he said.[39] Also called by Meyerhold the 'raccoursi' and the 'silhouette', the moment of stillness was not only a sharp point in the forward rhythmic movement of the scene, it held *in itself* a key to meaning. For a brief slice of time the actor halts and we, the audience, note the gesture, the bodily posture, the stage grouping, before us; for an instant we receive an overall picture, which is yet charged with the dynamic of the scene, and our understanding is illuminated.

Meyerhold also taught the Retard and the Reject. The Reject referred to the actor's slight move away from the line of intended action before the move in the true direction. Thus the actor leans back before jumping forward, he leans left in order to point to the right, he draws his chin back before thrusting his face forward to stare at a disaster. The principle is that of the bent bow: it is impossible to fire an arrow without drawing back the bowstring.

The Reject was complemented by the Retard, a slowing down in the action. Meyerhold sometimes employed it to contrast with a previous or upcoming moment of excitement, energy, or simply speed. The sequence at the end of *Sister Beatrice* involved a typical Retard: the nuns wrap Beatrice in a linen shroud, carry her towards the Virgin, and kiss her hands, feet, and forehead. And these slowed-down actions, so clear and refined, provoked not only a strong emotional response in the audience, but also in the actors. Vera Komissarzhevskaya, who played Beatrice, was seen to be 'inwardly trembling with "creative tremor"'.[40]

Moments of stillness, Rejects and Retards all required the actor to master balance. Meyerhold's students walked tightropes, balanced billiard cues on their foreheads (and noses and knees and shoulders and other parts), and learned to stand on their heads and walk on their hands. They balanced a pitcher of water on their heads as they walked, and learned that asymmetrical stances – one arm out, the other close to the body, say, or one leg lifted up and bent, the other straight and carrying the weight – were to be preferred to simple soldierly symmetry. They discovered hand gestures, facial expressions, and even what to do with their eyes: 'I can always distinguish a genuine actor from a poor one by his eyes', Meyerhold said:

> The good actor knows the value of his gaze. With only a shift of his pupils from the line of the horizon to the right or the left, up or down, he will give the necessary accent to his acting, which will be understood by the audience. The eyes of poor actors and dabblers are always fidgety, darting here and there to the sides.[41]

Not only did they do basic gymnastics and acrobatics, the members of the Studio also played sports, boxed, threw the discus, and fenced.

Such work was clearly of use when Scenic Movement addressed the exploration of the potential of stage space in relation to a partner or partners. Meyerhold learned from the Italian Guglielmo Ebreo, who demanded that his actors were able to adapt themselves to the playing area. Thus an actor does not move naturally in a circular playing space in the same patterns as he does in a square one; he moves differently near the front of the stage from when he is at the back, and he is different again when alone compared to when he is in a crowd. Meyerhold also developed other partner exercises, such as the Slap in the Face, the Challenge, when one character hurls down a glove for the other to pick up, and the Flower Offer, when one character offers his beloved a flower.

Meyerhold's actors were not only aware of each other, they were also extremely self-aware. Training with stage props – letters, goblets, flowers, and so on – the actor learned that the prop is an extension of the hand, and must be as expressive. The hand, of course, is an extension of the arm, which is itself an extension of the whole body. The notion that every movement, however small, reverberates through the whole body, is a *sine qua non* of the Meyerhold system; and note how this work brings the student back to the question of balance. The same may be said of work with costumes. The trainee actor practised with a cloak, or with a hat, learning how these can be used to conceal or reveal, and to create patterns or character.

> The costume is also a part of the body. Look at the mountain dweller. It would seem that the *burka* must conceal his body, but usually it's sewn in such a way that when worn by a real Caucasian, it's all alive, all pulsating, and through the *burka* you can see the rhythmic waves of the body.[42]

Furniture, too, provided lessons: how to leap onto the back of a chair, or what variations might be contrived around a revolving door – always a favourite with Meyerhold, and used to wonderful effect in productions such as *The Unknown Woman* and *The Magnanimous Cuckold*.

To be aware of oneself as a physical entity in space and time was the aim of Meyerhold's training work. Much of it was done to music, partly to ensure that the actor did not become too absorbed in his inner self, but more importantly to develop rhythmic sensitivity. The actors worked to music played aloud, or to a drummed-out rhythm, or they hummed to themselves, in order to discover how to organise time creatively. Many of Meyerhold's productions, especially after his hugely impressive *Tristan and Isolde* of 1910, were arranged according to musical principles, and he wanted his actors to know 'how to act "with the music" and not "to the music"'. 'There is a colossal and not yet completely understood difference', he added.[43] The actor's self-awareness was also seen in Meyerhold's development of the oriental conception of 'self-admiration', which comes from the Chinese *yuan*, the ability to watch one's own performance while performing. It implies an objective gaze, but also a sense of complicity with the audience. As Brecht noted after watching Mei Lan-fang perform:

> The Chinese artist never acts as if there were a fourth wall besides the three surrounding him. He expresses his awareness of being watched . . . [He] observes himself. Thus, if he is representing a cloud, perhaps, showing its unexpected appearance, its soft and strong growth, its rapid yet gradual transformation, he will occasionally look at the audience as if to say: isn't it just like that? At the same time he also observes his own arms and legs, adducing them, testing them and perhaps finally

approving them. An obvious glance at the floor, so as to judge the space available to him for his act, does not strike him as liable to break the illusion.[44]

Meyerhold also called this 'mirrorising', and trained his actors to develop it. It was a trait the *commedia dell'arte* actor possessed. Meyerhold's view of *commedia* was certainly romantic. As Frost and Yarrow point out, it was

> conditioned by his acquaintance with a number of later European sources: the drawings of Callot, with their grotesque and malicious, sexual and scatological figures; the *fiabe* of Carlo Gozzi, with their deliberate room for the actors' improvisations, their poetic, magical delicacy . . . and finally the works of the Romantic E. T. A. Hoffmann, with their masked and transformed mysticism, their fascination with reality and its double.[45]

Jacques Callot
Callot was born in Nancy, in French Lorraine, in 1592 or 1593. As a young man he went to Italy, where he made etchings of the street life and festivals which fascinated him. He created surprising, often contorted, but expressive figures in wide piazzas, frequently from a moralistic or satirical viewpoint. His work shows him to have been one of the finest etchers in the history of art. In 1622 he returned to his native Nancy, where he continued etching, though now his work often took a darker, more savage tone. This was almost certainly a response to the brutalities of the Thirty Years War, which was raging in Lorraine at that time. Callot died in 1635.

Yet these forebears gave Meyerholdian theatre some of its characteristic brilliance: Callot's drawings, for instance, provided exercises, and not just in balance, for his students. The beginnings of a system in which the physical leads to the psychological may be discerned in Harlequin's flourish to denote his outgoing nature, or Pierrot's stance as the quintessence of introspection. In the pre-revolutionary period, Meyerhold used such traditions to assist in the creation of movement-based theatre. Beyond this, however, his actors learned traditional *lazzi*, antics appropriate to the theatre, which they could then use in performance: the Living Skeleton, the toys who come to life, the Chase, in which pursuer and pursued 'remain at a constant distance of about a foot from each other and run on the spot,

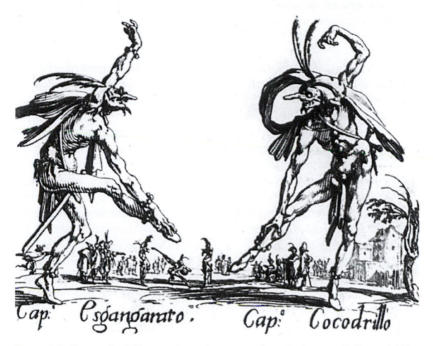

Figure 3.3 Commedia dell'arte-style performers: etching by Jacques Callot, c.1610.

concentrating more on making the spectators admire the rattling of their tambourines and their dazzling smiles than sustaining the psychology of the play'.[46] In 1908 Meyerhold learned from the Italian actor, Giovanni Grasso, what became one of his favourite exercises, the Leap on the Chest: one actor runs at another, and leaps on his chest, grabbing him round the neck while his partner clutches him round the knees. Another favourite from this period was Shooting the Bow, which developed into a complete étude, the Hunt, which included the prey's Dance of Death, and a triumphant Parade of Hunters. Such études led naturally on to the creation of whole pantomimes, perhaps from Gozzi's or other scenarios – simple stories rapidly transformed into *commedia dell'arte*-style performances, like *The Love of Three Oranges*, developed from Gozzi, which Meyerhold filled out and gave to Prokofiev as the basis for his opera. He was training twentieth-century 'cabotins':

> The cabotin is a strolling player; the cabotin is a kinsman to the mime, the histrion and the juggler; the cabotin can work miracles with his technical mastery; the cabotin keeps alive the tradition of the true art of acting . . . If there is no cabotin, there is no theatre either; and,

contrariwise, as soon as the theatre rejects the basic rules of theatricality it straightway imagines that it can dispense with the cabotin.[47]

Characterisation in *commedia dell'arte*, as already suggested, did not depend on psychology. Just the opposite: the *commedia* characters were recognised by their masks and costumes, and were deliberately presented as *types*. 'Typage' in this theatre depended on the character's function in the plot, his 'emploi'. Thus characters included the miser, the long-winded lawyer, the witty or cheeky maidservant, the braggart, and the gossip. Each of these is a character function. Individuality may be obtained by a secondary 'foible', such as particular movements or stances, like those of Harlequin and Pierrot already mentioned, or the drunk, characterised, according to Meyerhold, by the fact that 'all their segments of acting are unfinished as it were. You begin a movement and suddenly break it off. Or in the movement more energy is expended than necessary. Therein lies their comic essence.'[48] Gayev's foible in *The Cherry Orchard* is pretending to pot billiard balls, Sorin in *The Seagull* has a speech tic, constantly repeating 'And all that sort of thing'. Other foibles might be located in a costume – Meyerhold discusses how a tail coat affects an actor: 'In a tail coat one must keep to half movements. Elbows have to be held closer to the body. Gestural thrusts must be short, movements light'[49] – or in the hands, as with Stanislavsky's characterisation of Dr Stockman in *An Enemy of the People*: 'He decided to pick everything up with two fingers only. He practiced at home – his friends thought he had gone mad – and only when he could perform this action automatically, with dexterity, did he appear at rehearsals . . . The physical characterisation impressed everybody who saw it.'[50]

Speech was rarely seen by Meyerhold as a vehicle for emotion. Rather, he thought of speech musically, and considered that its primary function was to contribute to the temporal rhythm of the action. Thus actors in Dr Dapertutto's Studio in St Petersburg learned 'musicality', and the voice and speech work was incorporated into a course called 'The Musical Interpretation of Drama', taught by the composer Mikhail Gnesin. Gnesin included in his classes simple and complex forms of choral speech and plenty of singing, and indeed he analysed speech as song, so that actors often sang longer speeches for an exercise. Meyerhold was always adamant, however, that emotional colouring must be omitted from the voice. As early as 1906, Vera Komissarzhevskaya as the Virgin Mary in Maeterlinck's *Sister Beatrice*, spoke with a depersonalised sound, like the 'pure sound of an unknown musical instrument'.[51] Thirty years later, in a rehearsal for Dumas' *The Lady of the Camellias*, his approach still sought musical, not emotional, qualities. 'There's one drawback in what you're doing', he told Lev Snezhnitsky: 'The way you say your lines, all of them sound the same, they all sound equally important . . . Instead, we should hear a difference between the main word or phrase and its embellishments.'[52]

Meyerhold embraced the revolution of 1917 with ardour, and it not only gave a far sharper focus to his work, it also gave it a new social dimension. The need for precision led him to examine the minutiae of the acting process as he expounded it, and to come up with what he came to call 'Biomechanics'. Biomechanics codified this practice as it refined it. Meyerhold's actor, in a state of 'reflex excitability', received a stimulus to which he reacted with a three-part response. First he determined what to do, the 'intention'; second, he did it, the 'realisation'; and third, he came to rest, the 'reaction'. According to Igor Ilinsky, Meyerhold's leading actor in the Soviet period, Biomechanics assumed that 'Acting consists of coordinating the manifestations of [the actor's] excitability'. He continued: 'An actor representing fear must not experience fear first and then run, but must first run (reflex) and then take fright from that action. Translated into today's theatrical language this means: "One must not experience fear but express it onstage by a physical action".'[53] The acting cycle was only possible when, inventing a quasi-algebraic formulation, the actor (N) was able to understand what he had to do (A_1) and had the physical capacity to do it (A_2). Meyerhold thus created the equation:

$$N = A_1 + A_2$$

Meyerhold's explanation referred back to the work of Constant-Benoit Coquelin, who wrote:

> The arts differ according to the nature of their medium; well, the actor's medium is – himself. His own face, his body, his life is the material of his art; the thing he works and moulds to draw out from it his creation. From this it follows the existence of the comedian must be dual. One part of him is the performer, the instrumentalist; another, the instrument to be played on.[54]

Ilinsky illustrates the implications of this in a discussion of the end of *Othello*.

> Othello strangles Desdemona; the skilled actor must convey the utmost of his part, at the same time being in possession of himself so that he does not really strangle his partner. Here lies the difficulty. Biomechanics shows the actor how to control his acting, how to coordinate his acting with his partner and with the audience, how

to understand the expressive function of the sets, movements, perspective, etc.[55]

As this implies, Biomechanics was above all practical. It was designed for only one reason – to help the actor. Consequently, it was never a fixed set of principles or exercises or approaches, a fact which has often misled commentators. Meyerhold noted in the 1930s that he had found about 'twelve or thirteen' basic rules, but, he continued, he was likely to reduce this, perhaps to eight. Actually, 'the basic law of Biomechanics is very simple: the whole body takes part in each of our movements. The rest is elaboration, exercises, études'.[56]

The exercises and études taught three attributes which Meyerhold especially valued: balance; rhythmic awareness; and responsiveness, to one's partner(s), to the audience, and to external stimuli. The first two of these were addressed initially in the basic movement work – running, jumping, spinning, gradually more advanced gymnastics, all performed to music. Biomechanics also employed stick work, with many variations of tossing and catching the stick, as well as balancing it. The set exercises (which, by the way, were often first taught in Scenic Movement classes in St Petersburg before the revolution) are what Biomechanics is probably best known for, such as the preparatory exercise, the Dactyl. Ilinsky suggests the range of these:

> In a particular manner [the actor] grabs the body of his partner, who is lying on the floor, throws it over his shoulder and carries it off. He lets the body fall to the floor. He throws an imaginary disc and draws an imaginary bow. He slaps his partner (in a certain manner) and gets slapped. He jumps on his partner's chest and gets jumped on in return. He jumps on his partner's shoulders, and his partner runs around with him, etc. There were simpler exercises: take the partner's hand and pull him to the side, push the partner away, grab him by the throat, etc.[57]

Biomechanics: the Dactyl

The Dactyl is the most basic set exercise in Biomechanics, and is usually used as a preparatory exercise; or else as a conclusion, to something more complicated.

Stand firm but relaxed, feet about 30 centimetres apart, arms loose at the sides, head up, facing front. There are no pauses in the exercise; the whole movement flows through the moments isolated here. The tempo of the exercise may vary, but initially at least it is quite slow and relaxed, at least until the first clap, when it might speed up and be performed with a degree of taut intensity.

1 Both arms swing in a wide arc from beside the body backwards, knees bend, torso leans forward, head forward.
2 Both arms remain straight as they swing forward and up high; the knees straighten as the hands reach up, but the feet remain flat on the ground.
3 The arms are brought straight down in front of the chest with bent elbows, the torso inclines forward, the head begins to bend forward.
4 As the hands reach a point about level with, or an inch or two above, the groin, they clap energetically.
5 Immediately after the clap, the body partially straightens again, the elbows bend up, the hands are drawn up towards the chest, the head lifts.
6 Immediately the body bends again, the head lowers, the elbows straighten and the hands drop, clapping energetically again at about the level of the groin. (The effect of 4 and 6 is of two quick, strong claps closely following one another.)
7 Relax back to the starting stance.

Each set exercise was taught initially strictly according to its form and tempo, but once the actor had mastered this, he could vary it to suit his own rhythms or mood, and even add or subtract extra movements, so long as the main lines of the exercise were preserved. Any of these exercises might then be developed into a self-contained étude, a theatrical miniature, melo-dramatic or comic, as the Hunt developed from Shooting from the Bow. This provided a dynamic theatricality as well as emotional colouring to what might otherwise appear to be an arid exercise. Jonathan Pitches, who trained in Biomechanics, has recorded how he learned its value while working on a production of Gogol's *The Government Inspector*:

At the beginning of the process there was no conceivable link between the workshops and the rehearsals on Gogol's text – the work on the étude merely acting as a diversion from the real matter in hand. It was my belief that as the pressure built on the schedule we would be forced pragmatically to lose the 'luxury' of the biomechanical training in order to devote all our time to the blocking of the text. But this scenario did not play itself out. As the language of the étude began to establish itself the biomechanics became progressively invaluable. The rewards of the training in terms of concentration, ensemble discipline, rhythmic understanding and gestural expressivity were too great to be lost. We had no choice but to continue with the two hour workshop right up to the week of performance, a total of four months.[58]

Meyerhold's attitude to characterisation shifted over his career. His earliest concern was with the mask itself, and the *emploi*, the character's function in the action. After the revolution, the character's function began to assume a new *social* dimension, and to Biomechanics, it was suggested, 'sociomechanics' might now be added. Thus a new series of types, such as the capitalist in the top hat, the worker in the cloth cap, the revolutionary cadre with his red scarf, now clichés, but then startlingly satirical and original, was evolved, not just by Meyerhold, but more or less simultaneously by several revolutionary theatres. Consequently, in the period of the early 1920s, the *emploi* was related less to the play's action than to the world beyond the theatre. At the same time Meyerhold's individual characters became less simplistic: in *The Government Inspector* in 1926, for instance, Erast Garin as Khlestakov appeared at one moment as a dandy, at another as a lover, at a third as a glutton, and at a fourth as a trickster.

This process, more sophisticated both theatrically and psychologically, led on, perhaps inevitably, to the last addition to the Meyerhold system, noticeable certainly from 1930: the increasingly subtle use of psychology to reinforce the Meyerholdian physicalisation of character. Effectively, while retaining the idea of the set role, Meyerhold added a new concern for the physical circumstances of the action, and he encouraged actors now to think about the character's biography, his life before the action of the play, in order to give the details of the action a level of psychological truth. In other words, he insisted now that the sly and witty maidservant must be seen in a specific place – say, a hot kitchen. And the actor must know, say, that she has migrated from a rural village where her father was a peasant labourer. This might mean that her set role will have to be adjusted, say, to that of the traditional cook, sweaty and raucous; or perhaps to that of the peasant girl, durable and sensible. It also suggests that she will want to keep cool. She might take off her cardigan, imitating her mistress; or she might blow up her face as ploughmen (peasants) do at work. The set role gives the overall sense of the part, but the details are more likely to be governed by an individual psychology.

Meyerhold's practice was inevitably affected by the company he worked with. With his own actors he was a wizard; but it is worth noticing that he worked well with other actors too. And almost all actors loved working with him. 'Each rehearsal was a major holiday for all of us', Boris Zakhava said.[59] They loved him partly because he worked so hard himself, and was so obviously deeply engaged imaginatively in the production. It was also partly that he genuinely valued each actor's creativity, and expected each to be prepared to experiment and improvise. He himself was intensely creative in rehearsals. He arrived without detailed preconceived ideas, with no notes, but with his enormous theatrical intelligence and imagination. During rehearsals he encouraged, cajoled, demonstrated. Gladkov remembered 'many rehearsals when he never sat down at all. Such was the nature of his temperament. He encouraged the actors with his unchanging, characteristic, sharp and abrupt "Good!" or he ran up onto the stage and demonstrated, demonstrated, demonstrated.'[60] Mikhail Sadovsky described how he

> jumped from his seat, took off his jacket, and rushed to the stage. He made a few comments, then ran back into the auditorium just as quickly, bent over someone there, and whispered something in his ear. A moment later he was at the opposite end of the auditorium and only his sharp voice was heard calling: 'All right! Bravo! Terrific!'[61]

Meyerhold's rehearsal practice came of age at the 1905 Theatre Studio. Here, and always in the future, he saturated himself in the author's work and other material before the first rehearsal. The aim was to winkle out, and ascertain, the production's 'key idea', to which everything else was subordinate. Thus, in *Magnanimous Cuckold*, the key idea was the destructiveness of bourgeois property relations; in *The Government Inspector* the rottenness of imperial tsarist grandeur. The actors themselves were to saturate themselves in the material which yielded the key idea too: in *The Death of Tintagiles*, for instance, each read passages of Maeterlinck aloud to the others (some even read in French, apparently), and discussion ensued concerning Maeterlinck's world, his ideas, what was typical of him, or useful or right for the production, and so on. All this took place before the text was read. Meyerhold had little patience with reading and discussion round the table. Usually he was too impatient, and wanted to be up and rehearsing, though sometimes, as when he directed Mayakovsky's plays, he did allow a more prolonged period of discussion, partly because he found Mayakovsky's ability to illuminate his own texts helpful. Some discussions were always necessary, for Meyerhold wanted to extract through discussion the form and structure of the play, and then he was able to divide it into segments, or episodes. Beyond that, it was subdivided into 'motifs', each a manageable bite to begin rehearsing.

Next the actors improvised the scenes experimentally, trying to find the structure, the tone, and the other significant features isolated in discussion. They also improvised 'parallel scenes', to investigate relationships, use of the voice, and so on. And the improvisations were discussed and tried again. This process, which obviously pre-dates Stanislavsky's 'Method of Physical Actions', was bounded less by the script than by limits carefully prescribed by the director. As in *commedia dell'arte*, where the actor was constrained by the pre-existing scenario, and worked from a storehouse of already existing *lazzi* and other antics appropriate to the theatre, so Meyerhold's actors created within the spirit of the director's understanding, and using the techniques developed and honed in the Meyerhold Workshop. Meyerhold thus encouraged creative actors, was always delighted by the unexpected in rehearsals and was very quick to recognise what would aid the production. He never came to rehearsals with a prepared plan. Few of his preserved rehearsal scripts have many notes written on them, and he stated baldly: 'It's very bad when a director works with the blinders of a preliminary plan on his eyes and doesn't know how to use what the course of a rehearsal sometimes brings about by chance.'[62] But, it must be added, he never came to a rehearsal without having thought deeply in advance about the scene he was going to work on.

It seems that the general shape of the scene was in the director's mind before the rehearsal, and it was within this that the actor was expected to improvise. He was thus both restricted and free. Meyerhold said: 'Self-restriction and improvisation – these are the two main working requirements for the actor on the stage. The more complex their combination, the higher the actor's art.' And: 'By self-restriction within the given temporal and spatial composition, or within the ensemble of partners, the actor makes a sacrifice to the whole of the production. The director makes a similar sacrifice in allowing improvisation. But these sacrifices are fruitful if they are mutual.'[63] The collaboration between actor and director was in practice often less equal than is implied here, usually because Meyerhold's fantastic imagination and huge experience put his imagination far ahead of the actor's, especially as he was usually more deeply saturated in the material than the actor. Transcripts of his rehearsals frequently show his imagination engaging with a problem or possibility, then accelerating, freewheeling already well beyond anything the actor has conceived. The actor was also constrained because, between these freewheeling moments, Meyerhold placed 'breaks' in the scene which often encapsulated a key idea in a picture or silhouette. Between these breaks the actor was encouraged to invent, but it was the breaks which actually gave the scene shape and resonance. Often using paintings as models, Meyerhold composed each with painstaking care to be visually striking, and to create particular scenic effects.

When rehearsing, Meyerhold did not begin at the first scene and continue through the play chronologically. He rehearsed whichever scene he felt the actors were ready for. Often he spent inordinate amounts of time on apparently trivial moments, and equally often he staged the 'big' scenes extremely quickly and notably brilliantly. He was concerned to establish the play's meaning through an ever-changing pattern of pictures and movement, and noted: 'The essence of human relationships is determined by gestures, poses, glances and silences. Words cannot say everything.'[64] Once each scene had found an adequate shape, experimenting tended to be reduced, and Meyerhold began a series of runs-through. Most important here was to find the rhythm and the tempo, which was often quite jagged and uncomfortable: 'The swifter the text, the more distinct the breaks must be: the transitions from one segment to another, from one rhythm to another. Otherwise the motivation is lost, the living breath of meaning vanishes.'[65] But Meyerhold was also keen to leave the actors room for improvising, even in performance: 'The good actor is distinguished from the bad by the fact that on Thursday he doesn't play the same way he did on Tuesday. An actor's joy isn't in repeating what was successful, but in variations and improvisations within the limits of the composition as a whole.'[66] Sadovsky recalled him saying in the mid-1930s: 'The actor must not rivet his role tightly, like a bridge builder with his metal construction. He must leave some slots open for improvising.'[67] This is the same voice as that which introduced the Theatre of the Straight Line three decades earlier: 'The task of the director . . . is to direct the actor rather than control him.'[68] Few actors would have been surprised by Gladkov's diary note for 18 December 1936: 'Yesterday there was a remarkable rehearsal of the Boris and Shuisky scene [in *Boris Godunov*]. Already staged. Bogolyubov and Zaichikov rehearsed with great finesse. V. E. demonstrated magnificently. Inimitable hours. There was excitement, almost to the point of tears.'[69] Mikhail Sadovsky recorded another rehearsal, this time for *The Lady of the Camellias*: 'There was a torrent of fun on stage – singing, dancing, pounding music, and Meyerhold, high above it all, like a maestro, conducting a symphony in a creative ecstasy.'[70]

If the actor was the key component in Meyerhold's theatre, however, it is clear from this description that it was still the director who was the driver. Indeed, from the 1920s, he called himself 'the author of the production'. And those productions were, as surviving accounts from spectators testify, often extraordinary.

For example, his third production for the Theatre of Vera Komissarzhevskaya in St Petersburg was Alexander Blok's *The Fairground Booth*, which had its premiere on New Year's Eve, 1906. This was perhaps the first time that Meyerhold was able fully to realise the theatrical grotesque on stage. The play uses a group of mystics, a flustered author, Harlequin, Columbine, and Pierrot, and maskers at a medieval ball to raise problems of purity and lust, dreams and unconventional behaviour, banality, self-pity and the impossibility of true love, or indeed of true artistic originality. It is pervaded equally by self-disgust and amusement, but what is astonishing about it is that the terms it uses are throughout wholly theatrical.

Alexander Blok

Born in 1880 into an intellectual family (his grandfather was rector of St Petersburg University), Alexander Blok was perhaps Russia's greatest poet of the early twentieth century. His parents divorced when he was nine years old, and in 1903 he married Lyubov Mendeleyeva, daughter of the famous chemist, Dmitri Mendeleyev. She became his muse, incarnating for him divine wisdom and earthly beauty, but the marriage probably remained unconsummated, and Blok was known to frequent prostitutes. His poetry often shows his unhappy strivings with divine as well as carnal love. He and Lyubov formed a desperate triangle with Blok's friend, the poet Andrei Bely, reflected in the Harlequin–Columbine–Pierrot triangle in *The Fairground Booth*.

Blok's relationship with Meyerhold was also vexed and erratic, partly because his actress wife worked with him and adored him, while he fell in love with another of Meyerhold's actresses, Natasha Volokhova. Meyerhold himself said that 'in criticising me, Blok was fighting certain traits in himself. We had a great deal in common.'

Blok accepted the Bolshevik revolution, and wrote his greatest work, *The Twelve*, about it, but the severe deprivations of this time brought on the illness from which he died in 1921.

Meyerhold himself played Pierrot, and directed the play to emphasise the grotesque. Thus Mikhail Kuzmin's sweet, languorous music unexpectedly gave way at moments to harsh or dissonant chords. At the beginning, the mystics were seen almost in silhouette, facing the audience, waiting. When they bowed their heads, or moved otherwise, it became gradually apparent that their evening suits were actually cardboard cut-outs, painted and fixed, behind which the actors sat. When Pierrot awoke, Meyerhold made a strange, strangely beautiful, strangely fearful movement with his long white sleeve, which somehow conveyed to the audience the character's hope, but also the hopelessness of a *clown's* hope. Crude danger and delicate longing co-existed. The romantic ballroom scene contained nightmarish undertones, the beautiful Columbine appeared as Death, the fairground farce illuminated the nature of pure love. The teasing was incarnated in overt theatricality. The clown bled cranberry juice. Harlequin jumped through the window, which turned out to be paper. And at the end, after the scenery was suddenly whisked to the flies, Pierrot softly played his reed pipe and asked the spectators: 'Are you laughing at all this?'

Nevertheless, *The Fairground Booth*, for all that Blok described Meyerhold's production as 'perfect', represented a fairly crude beginning to his experiments with theatricality and the grotesque. Especially after the revolution, his work became bolder, and on occasions more extreme, especially when it was intended as experimental. His method was described in Sergei Eisenstein's article, 'The Montage of Attractions', which perhaps articulates the process more precisely than anything Meyerhold himself ever wrote. Making a clear distinction between 'narrative, figurative theatre', which he categorised as 'static' and 'domestic' (naturalistic), on the one hand, and 'the theatre of attractions, dynamic and eccentric' (Meyerholdian), on the other, Eisenstein suggested that this second mode of theatre depended, first, on the 'attraction'. An 'attraction' was 'any aggressive moment of theatre', anything which 'subjects the audience to ... specific emotional shocks'. These, Eisenstein explained, could be the unexpected colour of a costume, a roll on the drums, a clown's pratfall: in other words, an antic appropriate to the theatre. The production was then built as a montage of such attractions, or antics, and it was in the construction of the montage – its rhythm – that Meyerhold challenged, provoked, and teased out responses from his audience.[71]

In no production was this clearer than in *The Magnanimous Cuckold*, staged by Meyerhold in 1922. This play, set in a windmill, recounts the doings of Bruno, an unnaturally jealous husband, who cannot believe that any man could not fall for his beautiful wife. With burgeoning cruelty, his jealousy reduces and humiliates her until she decamps with the cowherd on condition that he will allow her to be faithful to him. Out of this earthy, comical fable, so like a *commedia dell'arte* scenario, Meyerhold fashioned one of his most brilliantly theatrical productions, in which one attraction followed another with almost bewildering speed and in riotous variety. There was an exhilarating chase sequence involving perhaps thirty actors doing leaps, somersaults, leapfrogs, and more, all over the stage; a comic, mechanical dance, the 'Chechotka', of the queuing husbands; acrobatic

Figure 3.4 The Magnanimous Cuckold (second version), Meyerhold State Theatre, 1928. Igor Ilinsky as Bruno, Zinaida Raikh as Stella.

leaps, as when the cooper suddenly leaped onto Bruno's chest, and, even more spectacular, the leap by Stella, the wife, onto the cowherd's shoulders before they ran away together; and outright clowning, as when the women beat up Bruno with loaves, or the mayor bowed goodbye, his backside hitting the revolving door, which flew round and hit Peter's backside, knocking him forward into Estrugo, who fell flat on the floor.

It was the way these disparate attractions were put together, however – the montage effect – which challenged audiences to think. Did bourgeois morality really rely on property relations? Was violence inherent in having possessions? Yet, because of the energy and high spirits of the dynamic performers, these serious questions did not lie heavily with the audience, but rather co-existed with the 'sheer joy of movement and rhythm'.[72] In fact, the theatricality 'furnished clear and convincing proof that the actor himself contained the magic power of transforming the wasteland of the stage . . . into something living'.[73]

Virtually Meyerhold's last, and some argued his greatest, production was Dumas *fils' The Lady of the Camellias*, with Zinaida Raikh as Marguerite, which opened on 19 March 1934. Here it seemed all the strands of his complex theatricality reached their apogee. He subtly evoked theatrical tradition, for instance in his borrowings from Eleonora Duse's famous performance of Marguerite, and set these side by side with new ideas, devised through improvisation and chance happenings in rehearsals. The frantic action of *The Magnanimous Cuckold* was juxtaposed to the elusive teasing of *The Fairground Booth*. The whole was structured through an extremely sophisticated musical score,[74] which existed in dialectical relationship to the fragmented montage of attractions which made up the action. Furthermore, the production was created when Meyerhold's theatre company was homeless and peripatetic, lacking any proper rehearsal space. Yet the detail was meticulous, from Prudence's long exit, taking a couple of cigarettes as she went, in Act 2, to the asymmetrical stances achieved by the actor, Lev Snezhnitsky, as Armand. And the large-scale effects were unforgettable. Marguerite's first entrance, bursting in on a slow, reflective conversation, driving two of her admirers as horses with a whip, shrieking with laughter, while beside her ran her friend with a scarf ready to wrap round her should her illness reassert itself, was one. Her death, surrounded by well-wishers, was another. Marguerite was turned half away from the audience, who only saw her wrist fall from the arm of her chair when she died. The well-wishers backed half a step (the Reject), before coming to her aid. The effect sounds cheap, but to those who witnessed it, it was devastating.

The audience at *The Fairground Booth* had hollered for Meyerhold and fought battles in the aisles. The Soviet Minister of Culture had decried *The*

Figure 3.5 The Lady of the Camellias, Meyerhold State Theatre, 1934. Zinaida Raikh as Marguerite.

Magnanimous Cuckold, which had provoked argument and fury as well as astonishment and delight. After *The Lady of the Camellias*, the Communist playwright Alexander Afinogenev jealously protested:

> [It] is the subtle poison of decay. This is how the old world lured people, with sparkle, velvet, silk, and shiny things . . . And the audience clap with delight and shout bravo . . . That's just the way that after the fall of the Paris Commune the bully-boys and their wives and prostitutes lived it up . . . And now this is being presented as a pearl of something. You are expected to take it as your standard and learn from it.[75]

He might have paused to wonder why the Soviet audience, with Stalin at the height of his powers, 'clapped with delight and shouted bravo'. Maybe at that dark time Meyerhold's playfulness, his joy, seemed to assert the value of living, not simplistically, but through images and the embodiment of the metaphor.

Meyerhold after Meyerhold

After Meyerhold's death, his work almost wholly vanished. Those few productions of his which still ran, such as *Masquerade* in Leningrad, had been directed by no-one if the programme was to be believed. Most of his papers had been gathered up and hidden by Sergei Eisenstein in the false roof of his out-of-town *dacha*. Plenty of his followers, former actors and colleagues, were still active in the Russian theatre: Petrov, Radlov, Vivien and many others in Leningrad, Gripich, Okhlopkov, Garin, Pluchek, and more in Moscow. But of their relationship with Meyerhold they said nothing. When Radlov mounted *Hamlet* at the Lensoviet Theatre in 1942, it was an almost wholly conventional production, with Dmitri Dudnikov a keen if gloomy prince. All traces of 'Meyerholditis', of which he had been accused in the 1930s, were wiped out.

In 1953, immediately after Stalin's death, the Theatre of Satire presented *The Bathhouse* by Vladimir Mayakovsky. Nothing so strange about this, perhaps: Mayakovsky was officially esteemed in Communist circles. But the production was by the Meyerhold-trained directors Sergei Yutkevich and Valentin Pluchek, the latter of whom had played Momentalnikov in Meyerhold's 1930 version. Two years later, the same pair mounted *The Bedbug*, and two years after that, on the fortieth anniversary of the revolution, they presented *Mystery Bouffe*. It was an overt attempt to resurrect Meyerhold in the theatre.

It coincided with other efforts to rehabilitate him. On 10 January 1955, Meyerhold's step-daughter, Tatyana Sergeyevna Esenina, wrote a letter to the Chairman of the Council of Ministers, Nikolai Bulganin, requesting consideration of the question of the rehabilitation of Meyerhold. In July she was told the matter was being reconsidered, and that references from those who had known or worked with Meyerhold would be helpful. With initial assistance from Alexander Fevralsky, the Meyerhold Theatre's archivist, and Mayakovsky's sister Ludmilla, they began to collect support. From Leningrad, Nikolai Cherkassov, Eisenstein's Ivan the Terrible, Leonid Vivien, and Andrei Golubev, *The Fairground Booth*'s original Harlequin, who had married Ekaterina Munt, sister to Meyerhold's first wife, immediately came forward. They were followed by Pavel Markov at the Moscow Art Theatre, Shostakovich, Mikhail Gnesin, Boris Pasternak, Ilya Erenburg, and many of Meyerhold's actors, including Maria Babanova, who wrote a moving letter in spite of Meyerhold's shabby treatment of her nearly thirty years earlier. Igor Ilinsky, Erast Garin, Lev Sverdlin, Mikhail Zharov, Nikolai Bogolyubov, Yutkevich, Okhlopkov and more wrote in support of their Master. On 26 November, the Supreme Court 'reconsidered' the case, and on 30 November published its findings laconically:

> The matter of the charge against Meyerhold-Raikh, Vsevolod Emili-evich, has been reconsidered by the Military Board of the Supreme Court of USSR on 26 November 1955.
>
> The sentence of the Military Board of 1 February 1940 in relation to V. E. Meyerhold-Raikh is rescinded, considering the absence of the commission of the crimes detailed in the charge sheet.
>
> [Signed] Deputy Chairman, Military Board of the Supreme Court of USSR, Colonel of Justiciary, V. Borisoglebsky.[76]

Meyerhold had been officially 'rehabilitated'.

In July 1956 a commission was established by the Soviet Institute for the History of the Arts to collect and publish Meyerhold's literary legacy, and in December of that year the influential *Teatr* magazine published 'Documents from the Legacy of V. E. Meyerhold'. On 14 February 1957, Erdman, Shostakovich, Ilinsky, Maxim Shtraukh, and others presented 'An Evening with Vladimir Mayakovsky and Vsevolod Meyerhold' at the State Museum of Literature. These, and gradually increasing numbers of other events, meetings, concerts, and so forth concerning Meyerhold were held in the face of strong opposition from many powerful people in the Communist Party and Soviet life, and in a culture fostered by them of fear and insecurity.

So Meyerhold's name was being whispered again. In 1967, his daughter, Maria Valentei, edited a 600-page compendium, *Vstrechi s Meierkhol'dom*

(*Meetings with Meyerhold*); the next year the two-volume *Stati, pis'ma, rechi, besedy* (*Articles, Writings, Speeches, Discussions*) appeared; and in 1969 an exhaustive study of his work was published: Konstantin Rudnitsky's monumental *Meyerhold the Director*. Finally, in 1992, the Meyerhold flat in Bryusov Lane was acquired and converted into a Meyerhold Museum, a branch of the Bakhrushin Theatre Museum of Moscow, with Maria Valentei as director.

Triumphant – or relieved – as Meyerhold's relations and supporters must have been by this series of developments, it might still have seemed to many that the creative link between his work and that of those who came after had been irrevocably broken, and in some senses this was perhaps true. Boris Ravenskikh, for instance, who had worked as Meyerhold's assistant in the 1930s, staged a dynamic and perhaps Meyerholdian production of Tolstoy's *The Power of Darkness* at the Maly Theatre in 1956, with Igor Ilinsky as Akim. According to Anatoly Smeliansky, Ravenskikh

> revealed a festive, luminous side to this atrabilious play. Into its claustrophobic world of murder, jealousy, and terror in an old woman's soul, he brought the white light of tragedy . . . [Besides this, Smeliansky also noted] Ravenskikh seemed to have musically orchestrated the whole text. It was not straightforward musical accompaniment; rather, a certain 'spirit of music' informed the whole production.[77]

This sounds like a direct descendant of Meyerhold's theatre. Unfortunately, Smeliansky continues by describing how, shortly after this, Ravenskikh became 'one of the mainstays of post-Stalin official theatre, with its saccharin idealisation of "the people"'.[78]

Some of the bigger names in the post-Stalin theatre asserted a debt to Meyerhold. Georgy Tovstonogov, for instance, sometimes employed Meyerhold's device of quoting other productions, notably in his 1972 *Government Inspector*, and Anatoly Efros invoked Meyerhold's name while attacking directors like Ravenskikh and Nikolai Okhlopkov for 'presentationalism'. More significant was Yuri Lyubimov, who had watched Meyerhold rehearse as a young man, and whose work at the Taganka Theatre frequently recalled Meyerhold. With a bust of Meyerhold on his desk, he rejected the usual Soviet repertory and created something surprisingly oppositional out of the reality of Soviet experience. His adaptation of *Ten Days That Shook the World*, for example, first performed on 2 April 1965, split the text into a montage of forty-two discrete episodes, each with its own title.[79] In this production he used Meyerhold's *Fairground Booth* device of cardboard cut-out costumes for his presentation of the US Senate. I described this production shortly after seeing it in Moscow:

The attitude to the spectator is stated from the moment he or she enters Taganka Square, for revolutionary music blares out from the lighted theatre, then tickets are torn by a 'Red Guard' who spikes the stubs on his bayonet, and in the foyer an apparently impromptu group of performers sing revolutionary songs, dance and make fun of the audience. Inside, the acting has a corresponding directness which is coupled with a wide variety of highly developed skills – acrobatics, clowning, dance, declamation and tableaux, all superbly distilled into a disciplined, fast-moving ensemble effect. The *mise-en-scène* we are presented with is an open stage, bare to the brick walls at the back, modified from time to time by the use of projections, single props or pieces of furniture, and brilliant lighting effects. The piece is governed by a sharp, jagged rhythm, and saturated with music – hardly any scene proceeds without musical accompaniment. And the whole produces a montage of attractions which forces the spectator to assess his or her attitude, first to the revolution by defying preformed prejudices and stock sentimentalities, and second – equally important – to the theatre itself. The production does not show characters or a conventional story line, in which we can and should believe, it presents an essential theatricality (despite the 'realness' of its subject), which grabs us by the lapels, teases us to know more, allures us, startles us, but above all shares with us a delight in the theatricality of theatre. This ability simultaneously to make the medium illuminate the message and the message illuminate the medium is truly dialectical and dynamic.[80]

Lyubimov, who was also a friend of Nikolai Erdman, developed a repertoire which focused on those plays Meyerhold had wanted to direct, but never did, including not only Erdman's *The Suicide*, but also *Boris Godunov*, his production of which ran into trouble with the Soviet censor, and *Hamlet*.

But, as Jonathan Pitches has reminded us, the true Meyerhold tradition resides in the bones of the practitioner. And in the early 1970s Nikolai Kustov, who had been a close collaborator of Meyerhold in his last years, and had indeed taught Biomechanics in the 1930s, was persuaded to pass on at least some of his knowledge. He taught a group from Pluchek's Theatre of Satire the rudiments of Meyerhold's system, including five of his basic exercises, Shooting from the Bow, Throwing the Stone, the Slap in the Face, the Stab with the Dagger and the Leap on the Chest. Two of those who learned the exercises then, Gennady Bogdanov and Alexei Levinsky, have continued to teach them ever since, both in Russia and abroad, and each has recorded his version of Biomechanics on video.[81]

Moreover, it has become clear to those who know Meyerhold's ideas that though his overt influence in the Soviet, and indeed world, theatre from

1940 often went unacknowledged, surprising traces of it actually remained. Ironically, some of its best features were attributed to Stanislavsky! Thus Bella Merlin's training in Moscow, described in detail in her book, *After Stanislavsky*, included an inspiring course called 'Scenic Movement', which was clearly 'after Meyerhold', not Stanislavsky. Even improvisation in the role was attributed by her teacher to Mikhail Chekhov, when it had in fact come first from Meyerhold.

Beyond Russia, too, Meyerhold's influence is hard to pin down. Yet it has been evident, if unspoken, in many of the most challenging and dynamic theatre groups of the west. The new forms of 'physical theatre', which emerged around 1980, for instance, owe an incalculable debt to Meyerhold, as does the practice of such twentieth-century directors as Ariane Mnouchkine, Peter Brook, and Jerzy Grotowski, as well as companies like Théâtre de Complicité. And the debt of Brechtian theatre to Meyerhold is also huge but unquantifiable.[82] Meyerhold's work feeds into the live theatre at all sorts of levels, his influence often unrecognised, yet increasingly pervasive. The fact that his emphases on the centrality of movement in performance, on theatre as metaphorical and playful, and on the theatricality of theatre, are now so widely accepted is testimony to the failure of Stalin to silence Meyerhold, and to the power, clarity, and originality of his ideas.

Twenty-first-century perspectives

In the last forty years, many studies have shown clearly and very effectively what productions by Meyerhold looked like, how they appeared on the stage, what costumes, music, scenery, and so on was used, and more. *The Drama Review* alone has published a series of such studies which have been invaluable in reclaiming what is not merely of antiquarian interest, but is an extremely important legacy of the age of theatrical Modernism. These include Nick Worrall's essay on *The Magnanimous Cuckold*, Llewellyn H. Hedgbeth's on *D.E.*, František Deák's on *Sister Beatrice*, and Alma Law's, also on *The Magnanimous Cuckold*.[83] Nick Worrall has also examined *The Government Inspector* elsewhere, as has Jonathan Pitches.[84] The questions we must now address include: why did Meyerhold create these works? What did they amount to? What do they hold for us? How can we best use what these essays present to us?

Meyerhold uses theatre as a self-contained language, and his work initially invites a semiotic approach, perhaps through the ideas of Ferdinand de Saussure and Charles Peirce. If theatre is a language, operating along similar principles to everyday language, it creates its own structures. These may signify *about* the 'real' world, but they do not *represent* it, nor do they depict it, nor do they express it. On the contrary, whatever exists on stage automatically acquires the status of a *theatrical* signifier, or sign, the first and perhaps most important of which is the actor himself, his physical presence, his body. This is especially clear in Meyerhold's emphasis on 'mirrorising', though it is worth noting that early in his career, when his ideas were still raw, his actors resisted the notion of merely becoming a 'sign'.[85] But in effect he came to understand that everything on the stage was a 'sign', from a costume, such as the Knight's cloak in Blok's *The Unknown Woman*, or the work-person's overalls in *The Magnanimous Cuckold*, to the very gender of the performer, as when Mikhail Zharov played the washer-woman Brandakhlystova in Sukhovo-Kobylin's *The Death of Tarelkin* or Zinaida Raikh played Hamlet in *A List of Assets* by Yuri Olesha. In a sense, the 'antics appropriate to the theatre' which he taught were a lexicon of signs.

In order to make meanings, such signs must be seen in relation to one another. Action, stage setting, music, gesture, prop all interrelate. It was Meyerhold who made this conscious, when he insisted that a performance was a performance, not reality, and that the actor should *play* (or, play-act). Thus nothing is 'real' in Meyerhold's theatre; each sign acquires meaning only because of its relationship with all the other theatrical signs he creates, that is, through the conventions of theatre. What the actor does, what the scenery looks like, and so forth, are understood because of the convention the production is adopting, and this remains true even if the performance is as close to real life as naturalism can reach. And it will be accepted by the audience as such. It follows from this that Meyerhold's theatre does not attempt to privilege a written text, and that his production does not attempt to 'realise' this text. Meyerhold's theatre uses the playwright's contribution along with those of others – actors, composers, lighting technicians, and so on – to create its own kind of theatrical 'text'.

What is doubly challenging in Meyerhold's work, and may seem extraordinarily contemporary, is that his adherence to the grotesque constantly nudges him to change conventions. How do we respond to this? By understanding each work in its own terms, as a *theatrical* text, signalled by his claim to be 'the author of the production'.

Meyerhold thus aligns himself with Russian Formalism, which arose contemporaneously, and which investigated problems such as what was 'artistic' about art. The Formalists, several of whom knew Meyerhold well, could point to the way his work defamiliarised not just its apparent subject matter, but conventions themselves, in order to show that theatre is theatre, and thus throw the responsibility for the creation of meaning onto the spectator. And Meyerhold's theatre, more than any other perhaps, 'bared its devices', using 'stage assistants' to alter the scenery, exposing the bare brick wall at the rear of the stage, and destroying the audience's 'suspension of disbelief' at crucial moments, as at the end of *The Fairground Booth* when Pierrot turns to the audience and wistfully asks: 'Are you laughing at all this?' Meyerhold's technique of 'self-admiration' simultaneously embodies theatricality, defamiliarisation, and baring the device.

Formalism

In the 1910s in Russia, the thinking of a number of intellectuals, linguists and literary critics coalesced around the idea that the artistic process itself was essentially 'artificial', and that that artificiality was the key to why art was art. Independently they formed discussion groups: the Moscow Linguistic Circle, headed by Roman Jakobson, and *Opoyaz*, the Society for the Study of Poetic Language, headed by Viktor Shklovsky, in St Petersburg. They were more interested in the form than the content of literature, and hence became known as 'Formalists', a pejorative term applied to them by their enemies after the 1917 revolution.

They argued that literature (and art generally) *signified* reality, rather than *reflecting* it. Indeed, they said that literature 'estranged' reality. Shklovsky claimed that literature could reveal the 'stoniness' of a stone. This led to the Formalists' interest in intertextuality: the way a work of literature relates to other, often earlier, literary works, forms, and conventions. In their studies of the avant-garde, especially the work of Futurists like Mayakovsky, however, they often went further than mere comparison. They argued that earlier literature could be 'defamiliarised', and thus that new works, such as those of the Futurists, fatally exposed their underlying assumptions, patterns of thought, and ideologies. This in turn pointed them towards the 'devices' of literature, and especially literature which 'bared' its own devices: that is, literature that was self-conscious and reflected overtly on its own conventions.

The Formalists as a group disintegrated in the 1920s, Shklovsky staying in Russia to write some fascinating memoirs, and Jakobson emigrating first to Prague and then to the United States.

Semiotics and Formalism sometimes seem to coalesce to form Structuralism, and Meyerhold's theatre yields something to a Structuralist investigation too. He disregarded traditional act and scene divisions, and split the drama down into what he decided were its structural components, the episodes, which balanced, contradicted, or outweighed one another. For most of his career, moreover, he also saw character as a mixture of action-function and convention, though towards the end he came to use a more psychological approach than we would expect in a Structuralist composition. But still, it is possible to detect a kind of mythology, somewhat like those Roland Barthes unearthed, beneath some of Meyerhold's theatre, though it may also seem that Meyerhold somehow wriggles away from too overt attempts to classify him. His work is elusive, and relies on intertextuality, metaphor, and the deliberate breaking of conventions to create in the spectator joy – 'life's juices' as one observer called it, or *jouissance* in Barthes' phrase.

In Meyerhold the structures break apart, and the grotesque medley of heterogeneous antics and devices takes over, for he sees the world as fragmenting, or perhaps experience as fragmentary. He takes a script and breaks it up, and the performance teases us. It debunks those who even seek coherence, like *The Fairground Booth's* Mystics or *Mystery Bouffe's* Lev Tolstoy. It throws up allusions and associations, as when the mayor believes his daughter is going to marry Khlestakov in *The Government Inspector*, and exults: 'Shout it from the housetops, ring every bell in the town, damn it, make it a real celebration!'[86] In Meyerhold's production, peals of bells rang out, evoking all sorts of associations such as the church bells rung for funerals as well as weddings, the exiled revolutionary, Herzen's magazine, *Kolokol (The Bell)*, and the bells of Matthias the Polish Jew made famous by Stanislavsky. This is a theatre which revels in implication, creates a unique mix of violence and clowning, and draws strength from metaphors like the stage setting for *The Magnanimous Cuckold*, the masquerade in *Masquerade* or the silent 'Officer in Transit' in *The Government Inspector*.

Meyerhold's is the classic example of a theatre which asks the spectator to create the meaning for himself. He abhorred a calm audience, and always attempted to stir up reactions. Indeed the 'Theatre of the Straight Line', his early formulation of how theatre should be conceived, has the spectator at the end of the line, a target towards which his theatrical arrows speed. The 'montage of attractions' can only be said to be successful when the spectator makes the connections between the diverse 'attractions', or signs, with which he is presented. But the problem for the spectator is that Meyerhold's grotesque theatre is not as easily predictable as, say, melodrama or naturalistic drama is. Meyerhold constantly and deliberately breaks expectations, creating what Jauss calls an 'aesthetic distance' between the audience's expectation and the work's demands. In Meyerhold's theatre, the actors invade the auditorium, the scenery begins to move, actors improvise, and they cavort on the forestage, not behind the proscenium. Meyerhold would have been at home in Shakespeare's Globe or at the theatre Pepys described. The popular audiences after the 1917 revolution who crowded his theatre for a few years cracked nuts, made loud comments, walked about, chatted. They loved Meyerhold's work. The culturally conservative Communist politicians hated it, basically because they never trusted 'the people'. Meyerhold made the audience complicit in the process of play-making through the actors' asides and winks delivered from the forestage. For him, the production only 'ripened' in front of an audience.[87]

The problem for those who would control others was that Meyerhold refused to provide theatre which led audiences to predetermined conclusions. He permitted the spectator the freedom to make his own meaning from the performance. Even in his most overtly propagandist pieces, such as *Mystery Bouffe* or *The World Turned Upside Down* by Sergei Tretyakov, it is arguable that the political meaning was not embedded in the work, but rather lay upon it like icing on a cake, which could be removed to allow the consumer to sample only what lay underneath. So these works can be read as much more iconoclastic, and therefore anti-Communist (at least as we now know Communism to have been), than they may have sometimes seemed, and precisely in this reading it is possible that *jouissance* is to be found. Did Meyerhold misunderstand the revolution? Is it possible that he was fighting for a kind of democratic, almost anarchistic, society which was fundamentally at odds with Lenin's ideas? Or is this reading one which is in resistance to the inscribed Communism? Could it have been made before it was plain that Communism, far from setting people free, was actually only a modern and improved way of closing them down? It seems that many of Meyerhold's 'texts' may still be deconstructed (partly thanks to the descriptions which this section began by recording), and new and unexpected meanings found. He it was who urged: 'Trust the spectator.'[88]

Meyerhold's theatre was a kind of theatrical Formalism. Inevitably, therefore, it clashed with the dominant Marxism of the 1930s, especially that promulgated by the Communist Party of the Soviet Union. The two modes of perception fought (literally) to the death. Meyerhold's project seemed doomed, an anachronism, barren. But to us, over half a century later, it opens up a cornucopia of possibilities, which the twenty-first century will use as it pleases.

Further reading

Many of Meyerhold's writings have been published in Russian collections, the most notable of which are:

Meierkhol'd, V. E., *Stati, Pis'ma, Rechi, Besedy*, Moscow: Iskusstvo, 2 vols, 1968. (Articles, writings, speeches, discussions. Volume 1 covers the period until 1917, volume 2 the period after 1917.)
Meierkhol'd, V. E., *Perepiska, 1896–1939*, Moscow: Iskusstvo, 1976. (Correspondence.)

Significant writings, and discussion of them, are also available in Russian in the following works:

Mikhailova, Alla, *Meierkhol'd i khudozhniki*, Moscow: Galart, 1995.
Sherel', A. A., *Meierkhol'dovskii Sbornik*, 2 vols, Moscow: Komissiya po tvorcheskomu naslediyu V. E. Meierkhol'da, 1992.
Sitovetskaya, M. M., *Meierkhol'd repetiruet*, 2 vols, Moscow: Artist, Rezhisser, Teatr, 1993.
Valentei, M. A., *Vstrechi s Meierkhol'dom*, Moscow: Vserossiiskoe teatral'noe obshchestvo, 1967.

His work is available in English in:

Gladkov, Aleksandr, *Meyerhold Speaks Meyerhold Rehearses*, Amsterdam: Harwood, 1997.
Meyerhold, Vsevolod, *Meyerhold on Theatre*, London: Eyre Methuen, 1969.
Schmidt, Paul (ed.), *Meyerhold at Work*, Austin, Tex.: University of Texas Press, 1980. (Many of the articles in this work are by friends and colleagues of Meyerhold.)

Critical and biographical works about Meyerhold in English include:

Braun, Edward, *Meyerhold: A Revolution in Theatre*, London: Methuen, 1995.
Eaton, Katherine B., *The Theatre of Meyerhold and Brecht*, Westport, Conn.: Greenwood, 1985.
Hoover, Marjorie L., *Meyerhold: The Art of Conscious Theatre*, Amhurst, Mass.: University of Massachusetts Press, 1974.
Kleberg, Lars, *Theatre as Action*, London: Macmillan, 1993.
Leach, Robert, *Revolutionary Theatre*, London: Routledge, 1994.
Leach, Robert, *Stanislavsky and Meyerhold*, Bern: Peter Lang, 2003.
Leach, Robert, *Vsevolod Meyerhold*, Cambridge: Cambridge University Press, 1989.
Pitches, Jonathan, *Vsevolod Meyerhold*, London: Routledge, 2003.
Rudnitsky, Konstantin, *Meyerhold the Director*, Ann Arbor, Mich.: Ardis, 1981.
Symons, James, *Meyerhold's Theatre of the Grotesque*, Cambridge: Rivers Press, 1973.

4 Bertolt Brecht

Life and work

Bertolt Brecht (or 'Bert Brecht', as he liked to style himself) was born in Augsburg, Bavaria, on 10 February 1898. He was christened Eugen Berthold Friedrich, and his father was a Catholic, while his mother was Protestant. The father, 'a typical representative of the solid and respectable

Figure 4.1 Bertolt Brecht.

bourgeoisie',[1] worked in the Haindl paper factory, and became a director there in 1914. Brecht and his father occasionally quarrelled – Brecht recorded in his diary in September 1920 that after some apples had been stolen from the family orchard he defended the thief, maintaining a tree's produce could not be private property. His father flew into a rage, accusing him of communism and shouting that his literary work amounted to nothing. But usually he took pride in his son, and supported him financially for many years. Brecht's mother, who died in 1920, dreamed of her son becoming a great poet. He in turn clearly loved her: his friend Hanns Otto Munsterer claims that the women in Brecht's later plays can only be fully appreciated when his adoration of his mother is understood. Brecht also had a younger brother, Walter, whose attitude to his famous elder brother seems to have been at best ambiguous, perhaps a mixture of jealousy, mistrust, and admiration.

When the First World War broke out, Brecht was at school. He sighed later that he had been 'lulled to sleep' for nine years there, and had therefore been unable to teach his teachers much,[2] but he had founded a school magazine, performed in his own puppet theatre and had begun to attend the theatre proper in Augsburg. When the war came, like many others he was proudly patriotic, though he later modified this attitude, and when the time came for him to join up, his father did all he could to prevent it. By 1918, however, he had become a medical orderly, a post he described with high humour later to his friend, Sergei Tretyakov:

> I bound up wounds and painted them with iodine, I administered enemas and gave blood transfusions. If a doctor had said to me: 'Brecht, amputate this leg!' I would have replied: 'As you order, Herr Staff Doctor!' and cut off the leg. If somebody had given the order: 'Brecht, trepan!' then I would have cut open the skull and poked about in the brain.[3]

From this time, too, came his *Legend of the Dead Soldier*, a poem which describes how a dead soldier is patched up and marched back to the front.

This is the work of a 'poète maudit', who 'wallowed in' Rimbaud,[4] and mourned Frank Wedekind as 'ugly, brutal [and] dangerous,' when he died in March 1918. The following summer Brecht and a friend spent weeks rambling through the Bavarian countryside, earning their board and lodging by entertaining the customers in wayside inns, as often as not hiking through the night or sleeping rough under the stars. To Arnold Zweig, Brecht was 'a descendant of the folk singers, [and] the unknown poets of the open road'.[5] For two or three summers after the end of the First World War, on hot afternoons [Brecht and his friends] would go swimming in the Hahnreibach, lie naked in the Wolfsahn meadow, or go climbing trees . . . Brecht recited funeral orations and devotions . . . so grotesque that we doubled up with laughter and rolled around in the reeds. The next day provoked philosophical musings.[6]

These probably took place in Brecht's attic room. His parents had allowed him the top floor of their house, which had its own entrance, and here the young would-be writer played host to young ladies as well as to his men friends, composed his earliest ballads, and began drafting plays and poems, usually in company with one or more of his delighted and supportive companions.

He also loved the local fairs. 'I keep on spending my evenings mooching around the *Plarrer*', he notes in his diary, 'where they hammer their nigger minstrel tunes into you till you can't get them out of the creases of your skin'.[7] Brecht also liked the ice cream parlour, where he could flirt with the waitresses and sing his ballads to his own accompaniment, the 'Lachkeller', a pub with entertainment where he met and performed with the comedian, Karl Valentin, and the Blumensale Theatre, where Valentin also appeared. Here the audience sat at tables, the more conveniently to smoke and drink during the acts, which often contained pungent political comment. In these idyllic years, Brecht also discovered love and (not quite the same thing) sex. Throughout his life, his affairs were multifarious, complex, and usually destructive. Like Shakespeare, Wagner, and many other geniuses, his treatment of his lovers was too often disgraceful, especially, as Peter Thomson has pointed out, for one who wrote so often about 'goodness' (though it should be added that *The Good Person of Szechuan*, for instance, is not about 'goodness' in people, but 'not-goodness' in society).

His first great love was Paula Banholzer, 'Bi'. 'A queen is a queen, terror is terror, and Bi is Bi', Brecht wrote, and, when she was naked, he thought her naive as a child and artful as a (film) star. In summer 1918 they became lovers, greatly to their mutual delight, but soon Bi became pregnant, and Frank, Brecht's first child, was born on 31 July 1919. He was cared for largely by foster parents, neither his father nor mother spending much time with him, and ironically when he grew up he was conscripted into Hitler's armed forces and killed in November 1943. Bi and Brecht continued as lovers, but gradually became less passionate, though he remained possessive, and even dedicated *Drums in the Night* to her in 1922. Nevertheless, by then he was involved with other women, most notably Marianne Zoff, an Austrian opera singer, with whom he was living in

Munich in March 1921. She too became pregnant, and despite his diary note – 'I can't get married. I must have elbowroom, be able to spit as I want, to sleep alone, be unscrupulous'[8] – in November 1922 they were married, four months before their daughter, Hanne, was born.

Brecht the young man was a fascinating, charismatic mass of contradictions: a shabby provincial, who yet seemed worldly wise, a wildly romantic cynic, someone who was frequently ill, yet whom many remembered as laughing with gusto, and inspiring laughter in others. He noted in his diary in August 1920: 'I'm continually forgetting my opinions, [and] can't ever make up my mind to learn them off by heart'.[9] In October 1921 he derided Wagner ('Enough to make you sick') one day, and lauded Charlie Chaplin ('The most profoundly moving thing I've ever seen in the cinema') the next.[10]

By then Brecht was working strenuously at becoming a writer. Determinedly, he sought a publisher, or publishers, for his work, which included poems and ballads, short stories, and plays, both full-length and one-act. He shoved typescripts into the hands of those higher on the ladder than himself, such as Lion Feuchtwanger, and gradually he began to make progress. He wrote theatre criticism for the local newspaper, a short story appeared in print, he was offered some directing work, and in 1922 his second play, *Drums in the Night*, was performed successfully at the Munich Kammerspiele. It was published, too, in a volume with the earlier *Baal*, and he was taken onto the staff of the theatre. In November that year Brecht was awarded the prestigious Kleist Prize: recognition that he was a significant new talent in the German theatre. The following year, *Baal* and his third play, *In the Jungle of Cities*, were both produced, and Brecht received, jointly with Lion Feuchtwanger, a commission to adapt Marlowe's *Edward II* for the Kammerspiele. Brecht himself directed it in March 1924 – his first successfully completed professional production. And six months later he moved to Berlin, to take up a post as dramaturg at Reinhardt's Deutsches Theatre.

Now was formed the persona of Brecht the Berliner: combative, sexy, and unpredictable, who was associated equally with 'new drama' and scandal. The artist Wieland Herzfelde remembered 'a very argumentative, very polished, and even sharp-tongued person. He had a passion . . . for saying things which shocked'. Arnold Bronnen described Brecht's 'bristly wan face with piercing button-eyes, and unruly bush of short dark hair . . . A pair of cheap wire spectacles dangled loosely from his remarkably delicate ears and hung across his narrow pointed nose. His mouth was peculiarly fine, and seemed to hold the dreams which others hold in their eyes.'[11]

Brecht's Berlin

Berlin enjoyed an economic boom between 1925 and 1929. The First World War years had been desperate in the city, and the immediate aftermath almost as bad, with political assassinations – from Karl Liebknecht and Rosa Luxemburg in 1918 to Walter Rathenau in 1922 – political rebellion – the Spartacists rising in 1918, the Kapp putsch in 1922 – and inflation, which saw the mark's value against the dollar spiral from 4.2 to 4.2 billion.

From 1925, rising personal incomes and comparative political stability produced a frenetic 'Babylon' of delights: six-day bicycle races, non-stop dance marathons, free body culture (which encouraged nude dancing), and cabarets with strippers and honky-tonk pianos, or, at less sleazy venues, the vicious satirical poems and songs of Erich Kastner, Walter Mehring, and Kurt Tucholsky. Duke Ellington's *Chocolate Kiddies* jazz review was the hit of 1925.

Serious music and theatre also flourished. Directors like Max Reinhardt, Leopold Jessner, and Erwin Piscator presented stunningly original productions, starring actors like Elizabeth Bergner, Tilla Durrieux, Max Pallenberg, and Alexander Moissi. They were matched by glamorous film stars – Marlene Dietrich, Pola Negri, Emil Janning, and others. In music, the batons of Wilhelm Furtwangler and Otto Klemperer conducted avant-garde music by composers like Arnold Schoenberg, Paul Hindemith, and Ernst Krenek. Some of Berlin's biggest scandals were caused by opera. Alban Berg's *Wozzeck* provoked boos, whistles, and even fist fights. At Brecht and Weill's *Rise and Fall of the City of Mahagonny* one woman fainted, and other spectators howled and jeered. From the second performance, Nazis organised claques to try to disrupt the evening. Soon they were to disrupt the carefree Babylon – Berlin – utterly.

His love affairs continued to be complex and extraordinary. By the end of 1924 Marianne Zoff had left Brecht, having found him in bed with Helene Weigel, a beautiful Jewish actress with a successful career, who married Brecht in 1928. They had two children, Stefan, born on 3 November 1924, and Barbara, born on 18 October 1930. But this should not imply that Brecht was anything like faithful to Weigel. His other lovers in the 1920s included Asja Lacis, a Latvian-born, Russian-trained actress, who informed him of some at least of the excitement of Meyerhold's revolutionary theatre; Marieluisse Fleisser, a significant playwright in her own right, and author of, for example, *Pioneers in Ingolstadt*; and, most significantly, Elisabeth Hauptmann, a would-be writer from a well-off Prussian family, whose fluency in English was to prove decisive to Brecht when she translated Gay's *The Beggar's Opera* for him.

Brecht's first Berlin-created work was *Man is Man* (though he had been toying with a play about a character called Galy Gay for years). Written in the closest collaboration with a group of sympathetic friends, including Elisabeth Hauptmann, Bernhard Reich (Asja Lacis's partner), Brecht's school friend Caspar Neher, who designed the first production at Darmstadt on 26 September 1926, and the journalist, Emil Burri, the play is a brilliant *tour de force*, that is still greatly underestimated, lyrical, cynical, theatrical, and funny. Feuchtwanger wrote: 'when the live Galy Gay holds the funeral oration for the dead Galy Gay, I know of no scene by a living author which can equal it in greatness of grotesque-tragic invention and basic grasp'.[12] It is, in fact, Brecht's first 'epic' drama, and some of its awkwardnesses, which do not detract from its dramatic power, come from the fact that Brecht was still formulating what he meant by this term. In May 1939, looking back on this work, he noted in his journal: 'I brought the epic elements "into the business" ready-made from the Karl Valentin theatre, the open-air circus, and the Augsburg Fair. Then there was film, especially the silents in the early days before the cinema began to copy drrrramatics [sic] from the theatre.'[13]

The Weimar Republic

German defeat at the end of the First World War led to chaos: the Kaiser abdicated and went into exile. The navy mutinied. Bolsheviks and anarchists, led by the Spartacists of Karl Liebknecht and Rosa Luxemburg, tried to set up a Soviet-style government, but they were brutally crushed, and in the summer of 1919 Germany signed the Treaty of Versailles.

By this, Germany lost her overseas colonies, some territory to Poland and Alsace-Lorraine to France. She was disarmed, forced to pay reparations to the victorious allies, and to admit Allied occupation of the industrial Rhineland.

In August 1919, a new republican constitution was agreed at Weimar, and accepted by plebiscite. Weimar had been Goethe's home, and the new constitution attempted to embody his democratic idealism. Its central provisions, though sometimes strengthening central government, were characterised by guarantees of democratic freedoms, including granting the vote to all men and women over the age of twenty. But its very liberal idealism appalled many reactionaries, and its freedoms allowed extremists of left and right to flourish. In the end, in 1933, they tore it down.

Equally significant was the new subject matter which so scoured life in the Weimar Republic, and which Brecht was now approaching: capitalism, the market, imperialism, and the relationship between economics and politics. Whether this signified a whole-hearted conversion to Marxism at this time is doubtful, but it does show an attempt to dramatise questions of power, and especially of the creation and workings of specific power structures. His experience of working as a member of a collective at the theatre of the Communist director, Erwin Piscator, at this time also sharpened his thinking, not only about political power, but also about the theatre itself, its function and standing as a social and intellectual institution, whose interests it served, what the role of the audience is or should be, and the place of dramatic literature within it.

Erwin Piscator

Born in 1893, Erwin Piscator was politicised by his experiences in the First World War. He flirted with Dadaism before taking over the Proletarian Theatre in 1920 in Berlin. In 1924 he became director of the Berlin Volksbühne, but his Communism, and his addiction to technology – sound recordings, projections, film, etc. – were too controversial, and he was dismissed. With backing from wealthy patrons, he established the Piscator-Buhne on Nollendorf-Platz in 1927. Here, with a collective of artists including Brecht, he strove for a new epic political theatre. The Piscator-Buhne's eventual bankruptcy was perhaps inevitable, but its director's achievements and influence were immense. After 1933 Piscator went into exile, first in the Soviet Union, then in the United States, where he taught at the New York Dramatic Workshop. He returned to West Germany after the Second World War, where he mounted a number of controversial plays. He died in 1966.

These are questions underlying the series of plays Brecht wrote in the late 1920s and early 1930s, known as *Lehrstucke*, which were deliberately created for an alternative 'theatre for instruction'. Their subject is dialectics itself. Spare in form, they use a minimum of naturalistic detail, and employ songs, direct address to the audience, and courtroom scenes where points of view can be argued. They aim to fuse content, form and function, or rather to let the contradictions between these stimulate reflection.

Alongside the *Lehrstücke*, Brecht worked with Kurt Weill to create a series of musical and operatic works, the first and most successful of which was *The Threepenny Opera*, based on Gay's *The Beggar's Opera*, which opened at the Theatre am Schiffbauerdamm in Berlin on 31 August 1928. It was a shimmering success, especially because of its caustic and sentimental ballads which still retain their allure today. Brecht and Weill followed it with the less popular, but still attractive, *Happy End*, and, in March 1930, the major opera, *The Rise and Fall of the City of Mahagonny*. Meanwhile, the rights to film *The Threepenny Opera* had been bought, and Leo Lania, Bela Belasz, and Ladislas Vajda began to adapt the original.[14] But the project went sour, with disagreements, accusations of bad faith, and finally recourse to the courts. Brecht and Weill failed to prevent the film from going ahead, though each received some monetary compensation, and the events provoked Brecht into writing his only completed novel, *Threepenny Novel*, as well as the long theoretical essay 'The Threepenny Lawsuit'.[15]

In January 1933 the work of Brecht and many other progressive or controversial artists was stopped in its tracks. Hitler became German Chancellor. In the last years of the Weimar Republic, and especially after the Wall Street crash of 1929, the quality of life in Germany rapidly deteriorated. Unemployment soared, politics became polarised, and anti-Semitism strode the street in ugly fury. Would Hitler restore sense and stability? The answer came less than a month after he took power: the Reichstag, the nation's parliament, was burned down. Within days, swathes of the country's intellectual and artistic elite had either been arrested or had fled abroad. Brecht was one of the lucky ones. He escaped.

The Third Reich
Hitler's 'Reich' counted itself the third in German history. The first Reich was the 'Holy Roman Empire of the German Nation', which lasted for 850 years, from the tenth century until 1806, when the Emperor Francis abdicated in the face of Napoleon's expansion in Europe. The second Reich was that of Bismarck and Kaiser Wilhelm

II, lasting from 1871 until the defeat in 1918. Hitler proclaimed that the third Reich would last for a thousand years. In the event, it collapsed in twelve.

Yet for a writer exile is particularly terrible, for the most basic tool of his trade, his language, is useless to him. And when his homeland is simultaneously being ravaged, as Germany was by Nazism, the loss becomes almost unendurable. Brecht and his family found a home in Denmark, on the island of Fyn, which became their base for nearly six years. It may be added that exile did not quash Brecht's sexual appetite. In Denmark he had at least two significant love affairs, first with Margarete Steffin, whom he had first met in Germany shortly before the Nazis took power and who now became a valued collaborator as well as his lover, and second with Ruth Berlau, a wealthy Danish Communist, who was both a political activist and a determined theatre worker.

The sudden severance from his home, his successful career, and its future possibilities clearly affected Brecht. He worked on a number of plays and other texts, though not with anything like the sharpness which might have been expected from his earlier works, and spent much time in travel. Sometimes this was in connection with productions of his works, sometimes for meetings or conferences of anti-Fascist writers or other progressive bodies, where he spoke, argued, and listened. Thus, in summer 1933 he was in Paris, and he returned there in the autumn. In 1934 he spent October and November in London. In the spring of 1935 he stayed with Tretyakov in Moscow; he was in Paris again in June, and in New York from October to December. He spent nearly four months of 1936 back in London, and in autumn 1937 and again in spring 1939 he was in Paris.

One of the reasons for his travels was to enable him to take part in the increasingly bitter arguments among progressive and left-wing intellectuals, writers, and artists about the nature of 'Realism', and in particular the Soviet-proclaimed 'Socialist Realism'. Brecht rejected this, and perhaps partly in a deliberate attempt to demonstrate that a much more subtle and challenging form of Marxist art was possible, he turned back to writing plays. The result was the series of dramas which made his name after the Second World War. In 1938 he completed *Fear and Misery of the Third Reich* and the first version of *Galileo*. In 1939 he began work on *The Good Person of Szechuan* (which, however, was not completed until 1941) and wrote *Mother Courage and Her Children*, which received its world premiere in Zurich in April 1941. And in 1940 he completed *Mr Puntila and His Man Matti* and *The Resistable Rise of Arturo Ui*.

Socialist Realism and Formalism; Naturalism and Realism

The 1917 Russian revolution brought new, apparently Marxist perceptions of reality, and therefore new subject matter and new priorities for the arts. At the First Congress of the Union of Soviet Writers, held in Moscow in August 1934, Andrei Zhdanov, Stalin's Culture Minister, proclaimed the doctrine of Socialist Realism as the only acceptable form of writing for genuine Socialists. (See p. 22 above.)

Soviet-supporting critics like Georg Lukács and Alfred Kurella tried to develop Zhdanov's generalisations into a workable theory. They put the emphasis on content, and scorned especially the Modernist obsession with form ('Formalism') which, they said, either offered 'old' content in continually changing, 'new' forms, or else simply 'form' without content. For Lukács, since the subject matter of art – specifically literature – was new, the actions of individual characters in a work of fiction or drama were newly significant, because their motivation revealed the submerged causes. Realism required psychological and illusionist dimensions, because those were what enabled the reader or spectator to empathise with the character, accept his motives and thereby 'go along with' his actions.

But, for Brecht, new content required new forms, and indeed form and content were two halves of the dialectic which was the *sine qua non* of all art. This, he maintained, was true Realism, and it was concerned less with *reproducing* reality than with *mastering* it. In his journal he drew up a table which set his conception of Realism against what he called 'Naturalism' (though we may suspect he meant Socialist Realism). Thus, where Naturalism highlighted the 'reaction of individuals', Realism focused on 'social causality'; where Naturalism provided 'copies', Realism provided 'stylisations'; and whereas in Naturalism society was 'regarded as a piece of nature', in Realism society was 'regarded historically'. For Brecht, therefore, form as well as content was to be historicised. History was part of what had to be mastered, not simply something which flowed inevitably on, like a river towards the sea. And the V-effect was employed not simply to see the object 'afresh' (the original Formalist conception), but rather to expose its context (historical or other), and thereby act as an enabling agent for the reader or spectator.

In the meantime, world events were again pressing in on Brecht. The increasing likelihood of war in Europe forced him and his family to leave Denmark for Sweden in April 1939, and a year later they were forced further from Europe's epicentre to Finland. Finally, in May 1941, 'changing countries oftener than their shoes', they moved via the Soviet Union to the west coast of the United States. On the way, in Moscow, Margarete Steffin's desperate illness prevented her further travel. Brecht was distraught, and telephoned her from every station along the Trans-Siberian railway, the route of his escape. She died on 4 June. It has been suggested that Brecht should have stayed with her, but he had a passage on the last ship to the west coast of America (and it was going via Manila in the Philippines). Moreover, as Eric Bentley has pointed out, had Brecht spent even a week longer in Moscow, it is likely he would have disappeared into the gulag. Though he muffled his criticism of Stalin's regime in public, he was in no doubt about its reality in the privacy of his diary: 'Literature and art are up the creek, political theory has gone to the dogs, what is left is a thin, bloodless, proletarian humanism propagated by officialdom in an official article.' Later, he noted that 'in Fascism, Socialism is confronted with a distorted mirror-image of itself'.[16] The same month Brecht left the Soviet Union, June 1941, Germany invaded.

Brecht and his family lived in Santa Monica, California, for most of the six years they were in the United States. Times were not easy, though the physical danger they had endured in Europe from the Nazis was gone. The actor Fritz Kortner referred to Brecht living an 'almost Gandhi-like ascetic existence'[17] which, however, was punctuated by visits made and received:

> Helene Weigel held open house every Sunday evening. They were very nice occasions socially, unpretentious, warm, with beer and an item or two of Weigel's cooking. Hostess was a very good role for this actress, even if Host was not something her husband could bring himself to be. He would deposit himself in a corner where people had to come and seek him out, whereas she would flit about and make sure that any who felt unwelcome changed their minds.[18]

The move from Europe to America was another destructive upheaval for Brecht, and he recorded in his diary: 'for the first time in ten years, I am not working seriously on anything'.[19] He pondered whether to become an American citizen. In 1944 Ruth Berlau became pregnant. She discovered she also had a stomach tumour which was removed, but the baby, born by caesarean section, did not survive.

Brecht obtained a little work from Hollywood, most notably with Fritz

Lang on the script of *Hangmen Also Die*, but he had little else to show for living so close to so many studios. Otherwise, besides one or two adaptations of classics, he wrote most of *The Visions of Simone Machard* with the also exiled Lion Feuchtwanger, and the following year created *Schweyk in the Second World War*, an ironic sequel to Hašek's masterpiece. Finally, in 1944, with Ruth Berlau, he wrote the brilliant *Caucasian Chalk Circle*. In 1945, Charles Laughton, a significant film star, became entranced with *Galileo*, and he and Brecht began to work to create an English version which would be acceptable to American audiences.

> The collaboration with Laughton was the classic one of our profession – playwright and actor. At certain points he saw the play collapsing, at which he built himself up like an immoveable mountain of flesh until the required change was identified and made. This stubborn sensitivity proved to be more fruitful than his factual suggestions (which he always offered with the greatest circumspection).[20]

The production opened in Hollywood on 30 July 1947.

Brecht, however, was hardly able to enjoy this before he was summoned by the House Committee on Un-American Activities to Washington. He appeared before them on 30 October and, controlling his responses by recourse to his familiar cigars, he fenced courteously with the lawyers who tried to extract a commitment to Communism from him. 'Did you write that, Mr Brecht?' the prosecutor asked, having read (badly) a translation of a poem. 'No', replied Brecht, 'I wrote a German poem, but that is very different from this.' The transcript records like a stage direction: '[*Laughter.*]' The chairman, in dismissing Brecht, assured him that he was 'a good example' to other witnesses. But within little more than twenty-four hours, despite fog almost as thick as the obfuscating cigar fumes he had exhaled in the witness-box, Brecht, with typically heroic cowardice, was flying out of the United States, back towards Europe.

House Un-American Activities Committee (HUAC)
In 1938, the House of Representatives in Washington created an Un-American Activities Committee to investigate alleged disloyalty and subversive activities.

In 1947, HUAC instituted Hearings Regarding the Communist Infiltration of the Motion Picture Industry, and after taking 'friendly' evidence from such luminaries as Ronald Reagan, summoned eleven 'unfriendly' witnesses, one of whom was Brecht. He was in fact the only one who answered the committee's questions: the remaining ten ('The Hollywood Ten') refused and all were gaoled.

A later purge of Hollywood decimated the industry by establishing a 'blacklist' for anyone suspected of 'Communist' connections: they were not to be allowed to work in films. HUAC famously posed the question: 'Are you now or have you ever been a member of the Communist Party?' They also pressurised witnesses to name other 'Communists' for the blacklist (which ran to several hundred people). Most – like the famous director, Elia Kazan – submitted to the pressure. A very few, such as the playwright Arthur Miller, refused, and suffered for their integrity.

By the late 1950s, the American people were growing sick of HUAC's 'red-baiting'. In 1969, it was renamed the House Internal Security Committee, and in 1975 it was abolished.

He landed in Switzerland where *Mother Courage and Her Children* had successfully premiered. Teo Otto, stage designer of that *Mother Courage*, noted that 'the years that followed the war were a period of hope clad in rags', a comment which in a way summarises Brecht's own attitude at this time. In Switzerland, his adaptation of *Antigone*, as well as the premiere of *Mr Puntila and His Man Matti* were staged, and he worked on both *The Days of the Commune* and the theoretical statement, *A Short Organum for the Theatre*.

By the end of 1948 he was ready to re-enter the now divided Germany. He came via Czechoslovakia to the Soviet sector of Berlin. It was the time of the Cold War. East and west could not meet. Brecht, though he retained an Austrian passport, became effectively an East (Communist) German. The attraction, above all, was the offer of his own production of *Mother Courage and Her Children*, with his wife, Helene Weigel, in the title role. This opened at the Deutsches Theatre in Berlin on 11 January 1949, and was a success comparable only with that of *The Threepenny Opera* over twenty years before. Brecht's theatrical future was then cemented with the establishment of the Berliner Ensemble, his own company, a mere month after the Communists proclaimed their sector of Germany the independent German Democratic Republic. And for the rest of its existence, East Germany supported Brecht's theatre to the hilt, through bad times and good. The subsidy was nearly three million marks per annum at the beginning, and it rose from there.

The repressive state and its theatrical jewel did not always co-exist easily. After the death of Stalin, the East Berlin workers revolted. Perhaps they were still infected with the Nazism of yesteryear, but their uprising was brutally crushed by Soviet tanks, and Brecht notoriously wrote a letter apparently supporting the repression. Was his reward the allocation to the Ensemble in March 1954 of the old Theatre am Schiffbauerdamm, where *The Threepenny Opera* had premiered in 1928, and where now his new, perhaps unsurpassed production of *The Caucasian Chalk Circle* received its first performance? Or the Stalin Peace Prize, which he was awarded in 1955? Perhaps it was permission to take his company abroad. In 1954, and again in 1955, they appeared in Paris, where in each year they won First Prize at the Théâtre des Nations. And in August 1956 they came to London.

Brecht was still an enigma. It was noticeable that his fierce rationality had become softer, and increasingly tempered by cunning. On the other hand, his position as a moralist was still contradicted by his personal immorality, at least in its sexual dimension. In these Berlin years he found time for new liaisons, most notably with Kathe Reichel and Isot Kilian. Nevertheless, he was no longer the bohemian outsider with a penchant for scandal of earlier years. Teo Otto recalled: 'For all his genius Brecht was endearingly simple; his talk was not aimed at the book of quotations, nor did he ever, in speech or gesture, flirt with posterity. He liked beer, sausages and straightforward conversation, was witty, humorous and a dead shot with words.'[21] Erwin Strittmatter, who only knew him after the war, said simply: 'Since Brecht died I have never again laughed tears.'[22]

In May 1956 Brecht was taken to hospital after a heart attack. That summer he was 'shrunken in body, swollen somewhat in the face, flaccid. And without that familiar and distinctive voice.'[23] In August he returned to rehearsals, and wrote a particularly apposite note of encouragement to the company before they left for London.[24] Any recovery, however, was an illusion. He died of a coronary thrombosis on 14 August 1956.

The key questions

German art and culture in the early decades of the twentieth century were dominated by Richard Wagner's idea of the *Gesamkunstwerk*, the total work of art which fused music, poetry, light, scenery, dance, and more into a single overwhelming whole. Beside this were more apparently progressive theatrical forms, like Naturalism and Expressionism, which also offered what was basically an intense experience. And over decades a theatre 'apparatus' had been created in Germany which was capable of 'theatring down' anything which challenged this intensity.[25]

For Brecht, however, a new age had dawned: the 'scientific age', which required thinking theatregoers, not people who were swept away by an overwhelming tide of experienced feeling. For the scientific age was characterised by fluctuating money markets and wheat distribution, the development of petroleum complexes, and so on, which humanity had to master. Artistically, this provided subject matter not easily comprehended by a form developed to enhance a mythical mystique. 'Petroleum resists the five act form',[26] Brecht proclaimed. Moreover, as a Marxist, he was fond of repeating Marx's observation: 'Philosophers have only interpreted the world in various ways; the point, however, is to change it.' Could the theatre help to 'change the world', in Marx's sense? How? How could theatre intervene in the daily affairs of humankind, unveil the commodifications inherent in bourgeois society, show how it is man-made and not eternal? Could theatre not simply interpret the world, but actually help people to change it?

This question, daunting enough in itself, was further complicated, however, by Brecht's insistence that theatre, even as it addressed this task, was to remain 'entertaining', though his concept of 'fun' was something other than Wagnerian self-forgetfulness. In 1939, in a lecture to Scandinavian students, he demanded:

> How can the theatre be both instructive and entertaining? How can it be divorced from spiritual dope traffic and turned from a home of illusions to a home of experiences? How can the unfree, ignorant man of our century, with his thirst for freedom and his hunger for knowledge; how can the tortured and heroic, abused and ingenious, changeable and world-changing man of this great and ghastly century obtain his own theatre which will help him to master the world and himself?[27]

If he could find the answer to this, he would truly create a theatre for 'the children of the scientific age'.

Brecht's answers

Brecht's answers to his key question changed over time, but there is a relentless persistence in his search for what he called 'epic theatre' for most of his working life.

Early in his career, he asserted that 'to expound the principles of the epic theatre in a few catch-phrases is not possible',[28] but even then it was clear to him that it would *report events*, and therefore be dispassionate. In addition, unlike comedy or tragedy, epic would deal with the totality of human relations. But Brecht was careful to place these relations in specific, changing, historical situations upon which they depended. Thus:

The extraction and refinement of petroleum spirit represents a new complex of subjects, and when one studies these carefully one becomes struck by quite new forms of human relationship. A particular mode of behaviour can be observed both in the individual and in the mass, and it is clearly peculiar to the petroleum complex. But it wasn't the new mode of behaviour that created this particular way of refining petrol. The petroleum complex came first, and the new relationships are secondary.[29]

By studying people and their interrelations in particular situations, epic would enable opinions to be formed, and criticisms, or judgements, to be made. Thus epic theatre aimed to be influential; it would help to change the world.

This led to an epic form of drama which, in terms of construction, does not lead to an inexorable climax, or revelation, but rather proceeds step by step. If it were a horse race, our eyes would be on the course, not on the finish. It is a montage, in which each scene has a self-contained life, and, like the segments of a worm, each is capable of life even when cut off from its neighbour. It implies, not an ending, but a continuing, for human relations do not just 'end', and opinions and judgements are formed and revised. Thus *The Good Person of Szechuan* concludes with 'A Player' addressing the audience:

> What is your answer? Nothing's been arranged.
> Should men be better? Should the world be changed?[30]

To help the spectator to a position from which to consider this question, it was necessary for the play to concentrate on *how* things happen. Lion Feuchtwanger wrote in 1928 that Brecht wanted the spectator to 'observe the mechanism of an event like the mechanism of a car'.[31] Then he would be in a position to weigh the evidence and judge it. In 1931 Tretyakov reported Brecht's proposal for a 'panopticum theatre' which would present 'the most interesting trials in human history', such as the trial of Socrates, a witchcraft trial, and so on,[32] and it is no coincidence that so many of Brecht's plays include trials. Towards the end of his life, Brecht wanted to rename epic theatre 'dialectical' theatre because it presented a situation dialectically for discussion and judgement. It also presented it as something which *had happened*. Brecht wanted his theatre to 'historicize' the events portrayed: '*Historicizing* involves judging a particular social system from another social system's point of view':[33] 'Anyone who has observed with astonishment the eating habits, the judicial processes, the love life of savage peoples will also be able to observe our own eating customs, judicial processes and love life with astonishment.'[34] Understanding one system through watching another, or the present through seeing the past, also of course suggests possible futures.

The heart of Brecht's method was the 'alienation' or V-effect. The word 'alienation' in English carries connotations of turning someone away from something, or inhibiting them. Brecht's German original, *Verfremdung*, probably derives from his stay in Moscow at the flat of Sergei Tretyakov, when he came into contact with a number of 'Formalists', most notably Viktor Shklovsky, who believed the purpose of art was to make us see the world afresh. At its most basic, this meant showing, say, the 'stoniness' of a stone. It was a process of seeing anew – what the Russians called *ostrannenie*, 'estranging' – but Brecht added to it something to do with the function of the stone. He asked, was it merely a nuisance, something to stub your toe on, or could it be used to throw at riot-controlling police, or to help build a barricade? This creates a process which involves something more than simply seeing afresh, and it therefore requires its own word, *Verfremdung*. Unfortunately, there is no agreement on an appropriate English equivalent: 'distanciation'? 'defamiliarisation'? It may be best to make do with 'V-effect'. Brecht made a number of attempts to define the V-effect. In *The Messingkauf Dialogues* he wrote: 'It consists in the reproduction of real-life incidents on the stage in such a way as to underline their causality and bring it to the spectator's attention.'[35] He saw Mei Lan-fang's Chinese players and thought their technique embodied the V-effect.[36] He even claimed it was a key to human progress: 'The man who first looked with astonishment at a swinging lantern and instead of taking it for granted found it highly remarkable that it should swing, and swing in that particular way rather than any other, was brought close to understanding the phenomenon by this observation, and so to mastering it.'[37] The theatre's brightly lit stage is particularly successful in making us 'look again'. Brecht emphasised that not 'looking again', because we think we know something, usually means that we are taking it for granted. 'Habit is a great deadener', as Beckett reminds us in *Waiting for Godot*. It is to combat 'habit' that the V-effect is useful.

Oriental theatre

There are enormous and vastly varied traditions of performance in Asia. Two which influenced Brecht were the Japanese Noh plays, especially Arthur Waley's English versions of these, and the Chinese theatre of Mei Lan-fang.

Waley published *The No Plays of Japan* in 1921, highlighting their simplicity, stylisation, and the severity of their style. One play, *Taniko*, was translated from Waley's English into German by Elisabeth Hauptmann, and used almost word for word by Brecht as the play *He Who Says Yes*.

Mei Lan-fang (1894–1961) acted in 'the Pear Garden', the highly traditional and stylised Chinese dance theatre, all his life. He was in fact the foremost performer on this stage. He appeared in Moscow in April 1935 when Brecht was staying there with Tretyakov, who acted as Mei's host. At one performance in the Actors' Club, Brecht, Meyerhold, and Eisenstein were all present, and all wrote about the experience.

It operates when you think of your mother as someone's lover, or your teacher in his underwear. You look at your watch many times every day; yet when did you last 'see' it? Without looking, can you tell what form its numerals take, or if the number of jewels it contains is written on its face? The crude historical pictures hung out at the Bavarian fairs created a V-effect for the stories they illustrated. In the theatre, the effect is obtained when a woman plays a man to point up gender differences; or when or if we saw Romeo forcing money owed to him out of one of his tenants so that he could the better entertain Juliet. The whole barrage of typical 'Brechtian' theatre effects were originally devised to produce the V-effect: the use of placards, the half-curtain, exposing the source of lighting, the direct address to the audience; and so on. Particularly effective is when a character stops speaking and begins to sing, interrupting himself, as it were.

A theatre which 'historicised' and subjected its content to V-effects was not for those who simply wanted their drama 'dished up' for them. That was what Brecht called 'culinary' theatre, where the audience can safely 'hang its brains up in the cloakroom along with its coat'.[38] Initially his alternative vision was a 'smokers' theatre', perhaps like Karl Valentin's Blumensale Theatre, for 'smoking is an attitude highly conducive to observation'.[39] The ideal spectator was one capable of 'complex seeing', who could swim with the river, but also float above it. For his 1931 production of *Man Is Man*, he said he wanted a spectator who would resemble a reader, cross-checking, referring to the equivalent of footnotes, going back and re-reading. He was delighted at one audience discussion of *Mother Courage* in 1949 when a spectator singled out the drum scene . . . and praised the fact that it was precisely 'the most helpless person who was prepared to help, the same one as had been called a "poor creature" by her brother a few scenes earlier'. What a spectator! He must have made a note of this sentence in the third scene (with annoyance) – in the eleventh he found his answer.[40]

This spectator has in fact been drawn into the productive process of the theatre. His critical response, his aesthetic judgement has been brought into play decisively, so that the play has, in a sense, produced him, just as he has produced the play. This was precisely the two-way, dialectical process Brecht sought.

Implicit in such a response, of course, is enjoyment. Throughout his career Brecht insisted that 'fun' is necessary in the theatre. In 1926 Elisabeth Hauptmann noted that 'if Brecht gets no fun out of what he has created, he immediately goes and changes it'.[41] And this remained his approach. Twenty years later, he stated: 'theatre needs no other passport than fun, but this it has got to have'.[42] Of course, for Brecht, learning was fun, dialectics was fun, and he protested 'against the suspicion that [they are] highly disagreeable, humourless, indeed strenuous affair[s].' He asserted, significantly, that 'the contrast between learning and amusing oneself is not laid down by divine rule'.[43]

Theatre practice

For Brecht, 'the proof of the pudding is in the eating'. He often seemed content to accept any theatrical practice which seemed to answer an immediate need of the 'theatre of the scientific age'.

For example, he was not very interested in actor training, and might employ any actor who was intellectually and artistically interested in the problems posed by his epic theatre. Nevertheless, he did suggest a number of acting exercises or improvisations for the epic actor, such as adopting different but typical attitudes of smokers, or developing scenes out of simple situations, like, for example, women (or men) folding linen.

Observation, Brecht maintained, was the actor's key. He should observe like the scientist who watched the swinging lantern.

> Above all other arts
> You, the actor, must conquer
> The art of observation.
> Your training must begin among
> The lives of other people. Make your first school
> The place you work in, your home,

The district to which you belong,
The shop, the street, the train.
Observe each one you set eyes upon.
Observe strangers as if they were familiar
And those whom you know as if they were strangers.[44]

But merely observing was not enough

> because the original says what it has to say with too subdued a voice. To achieve a character rather than a caricature, the actor looks at people as though they were playing him their actions, in other words as though they were advising him to give their actions careful consideration.[45]

Consequently, a Brechtian actor will perform many exercises in observation, watching and imitating others, describing for others to imitate, and so on. But the point will be in *presenting* the observed behaviour.

This is implicit in Brecht's most significant acting exercise, the 'Street Scene'. You witness an old man who is crossing the road knocked down by a lorry. Explain what you saw by demonstrating it. First, you show the old man trudging painfully along, puffing, leaning on his stick. You point out that he does not look to see if there is any traffic, but simply steps off the kerb. Then you show the lorry driver, and how he took his eyes off the road to light a cigarette at the critical moment. You demonstrate so that each participant's share of the responsibility will be clear.

You need not be a highly trained actor in order to do this. You can explain that, say, the old man leaned on a stick: you need not actually have a stick. Brecht points out that it may increase the clarity of the demonstration if the acting is not perfect, because it is important that the bystanders – police, other witnesses, etc. – should concentrate on *what happened*, and not be distracted into admiration of the witness's acting skills. Besides, there is no attempt here to create an illusion. This is a report. In no sense are you to 'experience' the action. Your characterisations depend on the events and relevant observable features – did he limp? was his hair too long so it prevented him seeing the approach of the lorry? And so on. You might indulge in a little make-up by, say, ruffling your hair, but only if it is relevant to explaining the event. Do you speak passionately? Not unless there is a particular point to be made by it, and even then you may preface your apparent increase in emotion by acknowledging that 'he got really cross'. Do you 'lose yourself' in the performance? Of course not. Finally, Brecht is eager to point out that this 'theatre of the street' is *useful*. Its purpose is to enable judgement to be made as to the responsibility for the accident. Many things might depend on it, such as the lorry driver's job, or insurance payments, or the building of a pedestrian crossing at this corner. This acting does not spring from the actor's 'soul'; it quotes other people.

One of Brecht's finest plays, *The Measures Taken*, has often been mis-interpreted as an apology for Stalinism, or an attack on individualism. In fact, it is not an apology or an attack on anything. It is a *report* of an incident, like the street scene, which then invites us to analyse and judge it. And we must judge the judgement too. The play does not endorse a particular course of action; it opens up something which has happened to questioning. It is helpful if the spectator knows the outcome of the event in advance. Then it is easier to focus on *how* it happened, and what can be done about it. Brecht's adaptation of *Hamlet* for German radio began with Horatio explaining that the listener was *going to* hear of

> carnal, bloody and unnatural acts,
> Of accidental judgements, casual slaughters,
> Of deaths put on by cunning and forc'd cause,
> And, in the upshot, purposes mistook
> Fall'n on the inventors' heads.

Then the play proceeded. In this way, Brecht's theatre provides a contrast to the *intensity* of other systems, and especially of German Expressionism, Stanislavskian naturalism, and Wagnerian feeling.

When it came to production, Brecht often seemed unable to rehearse a play unless there were plenty of people present, any of whom might make suggestions or ask questions. Carl Weber, an assistant director at the Berliner Ensemble, described how, when he appeared at his first rehearsal, he believed the coffee break was in progress so he sat waiting, until someone said: 'Well, now we're finished, let's go home.' Brecht sat in the middle of the stalls, towards the front, and responded volubly to whatever was pro-ceeding, guffawing with laughter, looking puzzled, shouting a suggestion, and occasionally – about twice per production, he calculated – losing his temper. Rehearsals were the means to explore the play. He sought solutions to problems which the play set, collaboratively and in a spirit of enquiry and intellectual adventure. It reminded some visitors of a children's nursery.

Brecht's attitude to his company was unequivocal. According to Weber, 'he truly loved actors, and they returned this love in kind'.[46] They appreciated his desire, granted at the Berliner Ensemble, for very long rehearsal periods – up to, or even longer than, a year – before he felt ready to put his productions before the public. However, his rehearsal process became increasingly formalised after his death, and if the following description seems over-schematic, it is because it draws some aspects from the later Berliner Ensemble model, to focus Brecht's practice.

At the first rehearsal it was usual for Brecht to introduce the work briefly, and make some generalised statements about the play, the story line, its central oppositions and perhaps about how rehearsals were to proceed. The work began with the first 'naive' reading. In this, parts were read round the group. When the speaker changed, the next reader took over, but there was no attempt to match actors to parts. Actors read lightly, with interest, but with no attempt at characterisation or 'drama'. Stage directions, scene headings, and so on, were also read out. The scene (or whole play) was then discussed, often in the manner of the discussion reproduced in *Brecht on Theatre*.[47] If possible it proceeded dialectically, by question and answer: 'What happens in the first scene? Brecht asks. A street is being built, leading to the town. At whose behest? At the behest of the Socialist Unity Party. Brecht says no. Silence . . . Brecht then adds, "That is revealed only in the third scene".'[48] 'What happens?' was the key question. Discussion focused on the story. 'The exposition of the story and its communication by suitable means of alienation constitute the main business of the theatre.'[49] Where? When? Who? What? All specific, concrete questions. Where does it happen? When does it happen? Who is involved? What happens?

Then the answers were evaluated. What is interesting about this play? Why are we proposing to present it? Discussion covered historical, political, social, and moral questions, and finally aesthetics. Whatever was agreed upon here would inform all the work on the play, and had to be accessible ultimately to the audience. These discussions led naturally to the first decisions about settings, costumes, music, and so on.

Brecht, who worked well with designers, especially his friend from school days Caspar Neher, preferred to begin rehearsing without preconceived designs, and encouraged his designer to make initial sketches during the naive readings. These would implicitly include suggestions about characters' postures and possible groupings. Designs begin 'with the people themselves' and 'what is happening to and through them', Brecht insisted. The designer 'provides no "decor", frames and backgrounds, but constructs the space for "people" to experience something in'.[50] Weber pointed out that Brecht wanted above all *a space* to tell his story in, and Thomson uses the German word *Bild*, which means not only picture and frame, but also includes the connotation of understanding, as in the English phrase, to 'get the picture'.[51] With this in mind Brecht's setting for, say, *Mother Courage and Her Children* was deceptively simple: the white, silky curtain at 'half height' across the stage, its draw wires constantly visible to remind us we are watching a play; the revolve built into the stage floor; the hanging military paraphernalia. No more than these. But Jones points out that the horizontal division of the space by the curtain wires, when the action beneath seems circular, is not accidental: 'Brecht, who believed that the round and round theory was an exploitative myth, presented his fiction within a frame that was horizontally bisected, as if stage reality were dialectical and capable of objectifying and particularizing human actions.'[52] The onstage buildings in this production had a chunky reality, but were incomplete, suggestive rather than real. In the earlier production of *Mother*:

> the stage was not supposed to represent any real locality: it as it were took up an attitude towards the incidents shown; it quoted, narrated, prepared and recalled. Its sparse indication of furniture, doors, etc, was limited to objects that had a part in the play, i.e. those without which the action would have been altered or halted.[53]

Mother

Mother is a realist novel in the Tolstoyan tradition by Maxim Gorky, published in 1906. Though based on fact, it tells the almost archetypal story, at least from a Socialist perspective, of the growth of a proletarian mother's revolutionary consciousness. It was adapted several times for the stage, especially after the Bolshevik revolution in Russia, and on 10 January 1926 one of the survivors of the original events, a Comrade Smirnov, was interviewed by *Pravda*.

The most famous adaptation was by Nathan Zarkhy for the film *Mother*, directed by Vsevolod Pudovkin, in 1926. But, as Zarkhy admitted, 'the course of the story and of the characters is developed independently [from Gorky's novel] – from the cause of the mother's change of heart and her unintentional treachery to her death in the demonstration'.

Brecht's adaptation was similarly free, and also rejected the 'realist' mould of the original. But he did remember from the film the sequence of the coming of spring, when the frost begins to drip off the twigs and the house roofs, and the ice on the river starts to crack. He was to use Pudovkin's imagery to unforgettable effect in *The Caucasian Chalk Circle*.

This production also used projections – pictures and texts – which referred to the great events like war and strikes going on beyond the particular story being told, but affecting its events. The settings, projections, and so on were designed not 'to help the spectator, but to block him; they prevent his complete empathy, interrupt his being automatically carried away'.[54]

During this preparatory period of rehearsal, initial casting was carried out. But it was always plain that at this stage casting was provisional. It is also worth remembering that in the finest of the *Lehrstucke*, actors actually change roles during performance. In *The Messingkauf Dialogues* Brecht warns:

> Parts are allotted wrongly and thoughtlessly. As if all cooks were fat, all peasants phlegmatic, all statesmen stately. As if all who love and are loved were beautiful. As if all good speakers had a fine voice . . . 'He has a kingly figure.' What does that mean? Do all kings have to look like *Edward VII*? 'But he lacks a commanding presence.' Are there so few ways of commanding?[55]

Once cast, further naive readings helped the actor to approach his character.

> When reading his part the actor's attitude should be one of a man who is astounded and contradicts . . . Before memorizing the words, he must memorize what he felt astounded at and where he felt impelled to contradict. For these are the dynamic forces that he must preserve in creating his performance.[56]

Then the character's 'super-task' had to be worked out. The 'super-task' referred to the character's place in the overall purpose of the play and how it contributed to its political, historical, moral, social, and aesthetic concerns. Discovering the super-task involved three steps. First, the actor had to look at his character objectively, concentrating especially on his function in the story, his concrete actions, and his status. He was actively to seek the contradictions in the part, and note objectively the choices the character made. Second, he had to see the character 'from inside', through his actions rather than his emotions: 'In phase two the actor empathises with the character and the "magic if" places the actor in the circumstances of the character. The introduction of the 'method of physical actions' is consistent with Brecht at this point since it focuses the actor on behaviour rather than feelings.'[57] Third, the actor had to 'objectify' the character and adopt a 'critical attitude' so that he could show that he was showing. This involved clarifying but not resolving the contradictions, and presenting not a 'through-line' but the sweep and rhythm of a zigzag path, inconsistent and certainly not 'inevitable'. Finally, the actor should enjoy creating this contradictory, even fragmented being, should obtain 'fun' from it and from the result, and should present it to his audience with grace and humour.

Imperceptibly we have reached the second, main phase of Brecht's

sal process. This begins with 'blocking', that is, arranging the actor's
ments and the stage groupings. Brecht never came to rehearsals with
preconceived plans of where or how movements should occur; virtually
everything was improvised. Sometimes he would have a strong idea, which
he would demonstrate (extremely convincingly, by the way), but he was
always open to alternative suggestions. Actors were actively and urgently
encouraged to make their own suggestions or, rather, they were encouraged
to show and try out variations.

The blocking was to be so clear that a spectator, unable to hear the actors'
voices, viewing the production through thick glass, would still be able to
follow the twists and turns of the story.

> Positions should be retained as long as there is no compelling reason for
> changing them – and a desire for variety is not a compelling reason. If
> one gives in to a desire for variety, the consequence is a devaluation of
> all movement on the stage; the spectator ceases to look for a specific
> meaning behind each movement, he stops taking movement seriously.
> But, especially at the crucial points in the action, the full impact of a
> change of position must not be weakened. Legitimate variety is
> obtained by ascertaining the crucial points and planning the arrange-
> ment around them.[58]

According to Eric Bentley, blocking was so important that Brecht 'would go
through every scene like a movie director noting every "frame" in a
sequence'.[59] He insisted that every movement, even a hesitation, should be
performed with conviction. 'If the actor turns to the audience it must be a
whole-hearted turn', he said[60] and Bentley called his blocking 'stylised,
almost mannered, definitely pictorial and formal'. He noted:

> [Brecht's] pet hate was actors in a straight line or symmetrically
> disposed across the stage. His preference was, for example, a solitary
> figure in one corner, and a clump of figures at a distance (a clump, not a
> row). As to movement . . . Brecht would have two things to say about
> actors' 'walks': first, don't walk a pace or two, make it a walk clear across
> the stage; second, don't walk while talking, walk in a silence, make
> a dramatic pause out of your walk, let the only sound be the sound of
> your feet.[61]

As for groupings, in 1933 Brecht asserted: 'The epic theatre uses the
simplest possible groupings, such as express the event's overall sense. No
more "casual", "lifelike", "unforced" grouping; the stage no longer reflects

the "natural" disorder of things. The opposite of natural disorder is aimed at: natural order.'[62] He artfully used the work of painters to ensure 'natural order', such as Bruegel's *Peasant Wedding* which served as the model for the wedding scene in *The Caucasian Chalk Circle*.

For blocking purposes, the text was split into 'processes'. Each process was a complete entity, an element of the scene, a particular interaction between characters. Each process might be given its own explanatory title, telling what happens in it, so that it became, virtually, a tiny playlet of its own. If the story consisted of 'one thing after another', as Brecht insisted, each process was a single 'thing', and, significantly, complete in itself. It should not appear as part of some seamless chain. When the relationship changes, or a decision is taken, the scene reaches a 'nodal point', where one process ends and the next begins. A nodal point is an interruption, a change of direction, a moment of decision. In the third, fourth, or fifth naive readings, actors were encouraged to say 'Stop!' at the nodal points, and pause, before continuing. The blocking needed to notice the nodal points, because they were often where movement occurred, and might be suitable points for silence.

In *Fear and Misery of the Third Reich*, in the scene entitled 'Charity Begins at Home', the First SA Man's line, 'What does he say, then?' creates a nodal point: at this moment he can let the Old Woman's remarks pass, or he can pursue them. He chooses to pursue them.[63] In *Mother Courage and Her Children*, a nodal point occurs in the penultimate scene when the Peasant's Wife says to Kattrin: 'Pray, poor creature, pray.' At this, Kattrin stops being a spectator and becomes involved.[64] In *Man Is Man*, a nodal point occurs when Wang asks Widow Begbick for beer 'for a white man'. Not only does Begbick change her mind here and decide to serve him, but Polly and his comrades realise where Jip is, and that they will have to do something themselves, rather than just wait for Jip's return.[65]

The junction of process and nodal point may also be thought of in terms of *gest*, an original but elusive term which Brecht used with annoying inconsistency. As early as 1920, when writing *Drums in the Night*, he desperately sought a 'gesture' that would carry complex meanings, and be 'visible from the gallery, strong enough to smell and be carried away by'.[66] John Willett, Brecht's English editor, defined *gest* as an amalgam of 'gist and gesture; an attitude, or a single aspect of an attitude, expressible in words or actions'.[67] Brecht himself wrote:

> The realm of attitudes adopted by the characters is what we call the realm of gest. Physical attitude, tone of voice and facial expression are all determined by a social gest: the characters are cursing, flattering,

instructing one another, and so on. The attitudes which people adopt towards one another include even those attitudes which would appear to be quite private, such as the utterances of physical pain in an illness, or of religious faith. These expressions of a gest are usually highly complicated, so they cannot be rendered by any single word and the actor must take care that in giving his image the necessary emphasis he does not lose anything, but emphasises the entire complex.[68]

A gest is self-contained, and may involve any or all of a process, a social relationship, and a significant gesture or movement.

A song has almost all the characteristics of a gest, and it is significant that it was in connection with *The Threepenny Opera* and *The Rise and Fall of the City of Mahagonny* that Brecht first employed the term. He referred to moments such as the tenderest, most romantic melody in *The Threepenny Opera*, when Macheath and Polly sing of how her wedding dress has been nicked, the ring stolen and 'love will or will not endure/Regardless of where we are'.[69] The song is a self-contained process which makes its own concrete contribution, functioning, according to Brecht, as 'a muck-raker, an informer, a nark'.[70] This is only successful, however, when the music is given, as it were, its own space.

> Mark off clearly the songs from the rest.
> Make it clear that this is where
> The sister art enters the play.
> Announce it by some emblem summoning music,
> By a shift of lighting
> By a caption
> By a picture.
> The actors having made themselves singers
> Will address the audience in a different tone.
> They are still characters in the drama
> But now also openly
> They are the playwright's own accomplices.[71]

Brecht called this separation of the musical items in the production of *The Threepenny Opera* a 'striking innovation', underlined by the presence *on stage* of the small orchestra. The land of Richard Wagner was amazed! Later, when Brecht sought to employ music and song less crudely, each song still retained the characteristics of a gest, no matter how well integrated into the texture of the play, because it inevitably *interrupted* the spoken dialogue and was self-contained.

Brecht's composers

Brecht worked with a number of prominent composers, among them Kurt Weill (1900–50), who composed *The Threepenny Opera*, *Happy End*, *The Rise and Fall of the City of Mahagonny*, *He Who Says Yes*, and more. Weill wrote two short Expressionist operas before he worked with Brecht in the late 1920s and early 1930s. The two collaborators were perhaps less suited to one another than their joint works might suggest. In 1933 Weill, like Brecht, was forced into exile. In 1934 he composed *The Eternal Road*, a pageant of Jewish history with a book by Franz Werfel, and the following year he emigrated to the United States with his wife, Lotte Lenya (Jenny in the original *Threepenny Opera*). In America he composed musicals with writers such as Maxwell Anderson and Ogden Nash, including *Knickerbocker Holiday*, *One Touch of Venus*, and *Down in the Valley*. He became a US citizen in 1943.

Hanns Eisler (1898–1962) was temperamentally closer to Brecht than was Weill. A student of Arnold Schoenberg, but a committed Communist (though not a Stalinist), he sought a social and political role for music, and a 'communicative' style, which is best heard in his scores for *Mother* and *The Measures Taken*. He also wrote the music for the film *Kuhle Wampe*, and set some of Brecht's and other political ballads to music. He lived in the United States between 1933 and 1948, when he returned to East Germany.

Paul Dessau (1894–1979) was a Socialist conductor who emigrated to the United States in 1933, returning after the Second World War to East Germany. He composed scores for Brecht's *Mother Courage and Her Children*, *The Good Person of Szechuan*, *The Caucasian Chalk Circle*, and *Mr Puntila and His Man Matti*, which he also made into an opera. Dessau continued to compose into his old age, including the opera *Einstein*, premiered in 1971.

Brecht also worked with, among others, Paul Hindemith (1895–1963), who composed *Lindberg's Flight* and *The Baden-Baden Lesson on Consent*; and Rudolf Wagner-Regeny (1903–69), who composed *Trumpets and Drums* for the Berliner Ensemble.

Walter Benjamin defined epic theatre as 'gestural', by which he seems to have meant something close to, if not the same as, Brecht's *gest*. The gest is something which epitomises, or typifies, the whole, he argues. It works like a quotation. Consequently, Benjamin continues, it is difficult to 'falsify', and, because it is self-contained, it is also easily interrupted. Thus, if a scholar scratches his head, as a gest this might suggest a dithering, somewhat other-worldly character. If the gest is interrupted, the import of scratching the head suddenly becomes noticeable – it is what people who do not really know what they are talking about do; they have to think; they are not so certain as might appear. Gest and interruption thus become to a degree equivalent to process and nodal point. And note, in this example, they 'inform' on the scholar's pretensions.

Walter Benjamin
Born in 1892, Walter Benjamin was not much esteemed in his life-time, but has since become recognised as a highly original Marxist critic. Best known for *The Author as Producer* and *The Work of Art in the Age of Mechanical Reproduction*, Benjamin was an independent scholar trying to live by his writing.

Among his most influential ideas is that of the art work's 'aura' – what gives it its special status. He believed that film could demolish this 'aura' in a revolutionary way because a film is composed shot by shot. He asserted of film almost precisely what Brecht asserted of theatre: that the consecutive construction of self-contained shots (*gests*) obstructs the spectator's empathy and encourages his thinking, and perhaps even action. Benjamin did not discount the power of reactionary (e.g. Nazi) films, but pointed to the fundamental lie implicit in the pretence that they were non-political. This, he affirmed, was a problem of the means of production.

In 1933 Benjamin went into exile in France, where he became increasingly lonely and desperate, and in 1940, fearful the advancing Nazis would catch him, he committed suicide.

It is possible to argue that Brecht's plays are composed of sequences of gests. In discussing Peter Lorre's performance in *Man Is Man*, Brecht notes that his 'efforts to make particular incidents seem striking . . . cause him to be represented as a short-term episodist'.[72] In *Fear and Misery of the Third Reich*, it was the interruptions to the gests which prevented it from becoming naturalistic, as some of Brecht's critics imagined it to be. He confided to his journal:

Fear and Misery of the Third Reich has now gone to press. Lukacs has already welcomed *The Spy* [one scene in the play] as if I were a sinner returned to the bosom of the Salvation Army. Here at last is something taken straight from life! He overlooks the montage of 27 scenes, and the fact that it is only actually a table of gests, the gest of keeping your mouth shut, the gest of looking about you, the gest of sudden fear, etc. The pattern of gests in a dictatorship.

And he warns: 'The actor will be well advised to study the street scene before playing one of the short scenes.'[73]

Brecht emphasised the *social* dimension of the gest. He pointed out that a man cringing from a fierce dog may be gestic, but this has no social content until it becomes clear that he is a tramp who is constantly harassed by watchdogs. The gest of uniformed and strutting Fascists only becomes social when they stride over corpses. Weigel's gest for the Governor's Wife in *The Caucasian Chalk Circle*, by which she made her servant 'make a back', which she then sat on, was of exactly this order.

These are details which are fundamental in Brechtian theatre. Indeed, his directing centred on building up details incrementally, one at a time, until the whole picture was finished. From the beginning of his career this was true of Brecht's work. When directing *Edward II* in 1924

> The demands which Brecht made on his actors were unusual and strange for them. German actors attach little importance to formal actions such as eating, drinking or fencing. They summarise them, simply indicate them casually. Brecht, however, demanded not only that they should be performed realistically and exactly, but also that they should be skilful. He explained to the actors that such actions on the stage should give the audience pleasure.[74]

In later productions he spent hours on details: how Grusha should pick up the baby, or the Recruiting Officer approach Eiliff. 'The devil is in the detail' he was fond of saying, and transcripts of his rehearsals show his painstaking attention to the 'devil'.[75]

Each detail informs a single process between nodal points. Each nodal point is marked by a change, or a possible change, in the scene's direction. Brecht's rehearsal exercise, known as 'Not . . . But . . .' was designed to elucidate this. At each nodal point the action stops and the actors play out, first, what did *not* happen, and then what *did* happen (that is, the written scene), prefacing each alternative with the spoken word – 'Not –' or 'But –'. This naturally creates a strong V-effect.

simplest sentences that apply in the (V-effect) are those with
ut': (He didn't say 'come in' but 'keep moving'. He was not
~ut amazed.) They include an expectation which is justified by
experience but, in the event, disappointed. One might have thought
that . . . but one oughtn't to have thought it. There was not just one
possibility but two; both are introduced, then the second one is
alienated, then the first as well.[76]

Thus, Shen Te did *not* send the gods away, *but* offered them a bed for the
night. Brecht notes about Grusha in his journal: 'She should be stubborn
and not rebellious, submissive and not good, long-suffering and not
incorruptible, etc, etc'.[77]

Besides the 'Not . . . But . . .' exercise, Brecht sometimes made his actors
work in the third person:

> I put in 10 minutes epic rehearsal for the first time in the eleventh
> scene. Gerda Muller and Dunskus as peasants are deciding that they
> cannot do anything against the Catholics. I ask them to add 'said the
> man', 'said the woman' after each speech. Suddenly the scene became
> clear and Muller found a realistic attitude.[78]

He also transposed scenes into simple stories, and asked the actors to act
them, keeping the existing blocking, but reading the story (told in the third
person, of course) instead of using the play's lines. Other rehearsal
techniques included rehearsing in the past tense, and saying the stage
directions as they were carried into effect. Actors swapping roles was also a
valuable means of giving the actor a new view of his own character. Where
an actor had trouble with a speech or even a song, he was asked to para-
phrase it, or to transpose it into his native dialect. For actors who had to sing
– and Brecht preferred them not to be trained singers – he asked for 'a kind
of speaking-against-the-music', so that 'if he drops into the melody it must
be an event'. He adds characteristically: 'the actor can emphasize it by
plainly showing the pleasure which the melody gives him'.[79]

It is impossible to block the play without having the settings present, and
at every stage at least rudimentary scenery was used. Costumes, too, were
worn when available, though Brecht preferred his designer not to think
about these until he had seen the actual actors. And props, too, added their
own sort of authenticity:

Weigel's props

As the man who grows millet will choose
The heaviest grain to plant in his

Experimental plot, and as the poet
Searches for words that are fit,
So too does she select with equal care
The properties her characters possess:
The pewter spoon
That hangs from the collar of
Courage's Mongolian jacket,
The bound party card of friendly Vlassova,
The other, Spanish mother's net
For fish or the metal bowl in which
Antigone gathers dust . . .
Everything is chosen
According to age
Uses
And beauty
By knowing eyes and her
Net-making bread-baking
Soup-cooking hands
At home with reality.[80]

At a certain point in rehearsals – 'when all the details had been brought to a certain point, not of completion, but of diminished possibilities'[81] – the play's overall shape was explored in a series of runs-through. The ultimate aim was to ensure that the story emerged with clarity. 'Everything hangs on the story', Brecht insisted; 'it is the heart of the theatrical performance'. Alienation in the acting and the gestic construction of the separate incidents was not forgotten, however: 'The parts of the story have to be carefully set off against one another by giving each its own structure as a play within the play.'[82] Thus was revealed the story's chain of causes and effects.

A single run-through could reveal much, especially some of the contradictions Brecht prized so highly, as he noted in his journal in December 1948: 'At the first run-through of scenes 1 to 8 [of *Mother Courage*], Ihering notices variations in Weigel's portrayal of Courage that we had not observed when we were looking at the individual scenes. The variations are therefore of the right sort, they can only be seen in long sequences.'[83] Runs-through also importantly enabled director and actors to find and fix a 'tempo' for the performance, and Brecht recommended special rehearsals for this (in costume, since costume tends to slow actors down). And, just before the first performance, Brecht insisted on a 'marking' rehearsal, that is, a complete run-through carried out extremely rapidly, perhaps at double speed, with lines spoken quietly but completely and distinctly, and moves carried through with absolute accuracy. The marking rehearsal was not only invaluable in ensuring that every actor knew precisely what he was doing, when and how, it also greatly enhanced the quality of the actors' relaxation, as well as, paradoxically, releasing new energy.

At last came the performance. Then 'whatever the actor offers in the way of gesture, verse structure, etc, must be finished and bear the hallmarks of something rehearsed and rounded-off. The impression to be given is one of ease, which is at the same time one of difficulties overcome.'[84] The concept of ease is extremely hard to define, but it is helped into existence by the marking rehearsal, and it embraces the relationship with the audience. Carl Weber wrote of *Mother* at the Berliner Ensemble:

> The set was 'quoting' an environment rather than representing it; there was extensive use of projections and scene titles; the small chorus, in its songs to the audience, commented on the fable and/or the actions shown on stage; there was an enchanting ease and, yes, elegance with which even the most serious scenes were performed.[85]

Brecht himself compared it to the ease with which flood water tears away the banks of a river, or an earthquake shakes the ground. And the final results might be photographed and preserved in a 'modelbook'.

Modelbooks

Brecht published 'modelbooks' after his productions of *Antigone* and *Mother Courage*; he also published *Aufbau einer Rolle – Galilei*, which is comparable to the modelbooks, as well as *Theaterarbeit* – detailed records of the Berliner Ensemble's first six productions.

Modelbooks consist of the playtext; several hundred photographs of the production; and copious explanatory notes and commentary on the production. Their purpose initially was to record in detail a particular production, though the *Courage Modelbook* actually recorded three productions by Brecht: the 1949 production with Helene Weigel as Courage; the 1950 production with Thérèse Giehse as Courage; and the 1951 Berliner Ensemble production, again with Weigel as Courage.

Brecht published these modelbooks when German life, culture, and theatre were in almost total ruin after the Second World War: they were in the first place an attempt to begin to rebuild. But they were also to demonstrate in great detail a new kind of performance, to offer practical solutions to problems of production, and incidentally to demonstrate in practice the validity of his anti-Socialist Realist theoretical position. The modelbooks focus on theatre practice, not writing plays. But Brecht warned against slavish copying: 'A model is not a blueprint.'

Even after the first night, however, Brecht continued to give notes and alter the production. Thus, when it was clear that audiences for *Mother Courage* were responding to the central character as a put-upon 'little person', the opening song was transposed out of Scene 1 and made into a kind of Prologue, rather like 'Mack the Knife' in *The Threepenny Opera*. This made Courage seem more predatory, and more in control of her own destiny, as she actively hunted out the war. Often, however, the changes served to invest the play with more humour. 'A theatre that can't be laughed in is a theatre to be laughed at', he insisted. His last note to his company before his death, written as they were embarking on their first tour to London, as a result of which both Brecht's plays and his company were to be hailed internationally as the most significant of their time, contained exemplary instructions:

Our playing needs to be quick, light, strong. This is not a question of hurry, but of speed, not simply of quick playing, but of quick thinking. We must keep the tempo of a run-through and infect it with quiet strength, with our own fun. In the dialogue the exchanges must not be offered reluctantly, as when offering somebody one's last pair of boots, but must be tossed like so many balls. The audience has to see that here are a number of artists working together as a collective (ensemble) in order to convey stories, ideas, virtuoso feats to the spectator by a common effort.[86]

These concerns informed Brecht's own productions throughout his career. Before the Nazis seized power, his most significant production was probably *Man Is Man* at the Berlin Staatstheater in 1931, with Peter Lorre as Galy Gay and Helene Weigel as Widow Begbick. Brecht's production aimed for the detachment of a sporting contest, with its transformations – Jip's from soldier into god, Fairchild's from terror of the regiment to civilian, Begbick's canteen into empty space, and Galy Gay's into a 'human fighting machine' – seen as music hall turns, and Galy Gay's development from packer to person, to 'blank page', to remorseless fighter, viewed as no more

Figure 4.2 Man Is Man, Berlin Staatstheater, 1931.

than a shuffling of masks. The production, in other words, was constructed as a montage, and Brecht built on this by using wildly different acting styles, a jagged rhythm which broke up the flow of the action, actors on stilts, projections above the stage, and so on.

Thus, Fairchild's transformation was marked off as a separate incident. The half-curtain was drawn, the 'Stage Manager' appeared and announced: 'Presenting an insertion: Pride and demolition of a great personality'. The sequence was then performed, but with further interruptions from the 'Stage Manager'.[87] The soldiers themselves were presented as huge grotesques, according to Sergei Tretyakov: 'Across the stage strode giant soldiers, holding on to a rope so as not to fall from the stilts concealed in their trousers. They were hung about with rifles and wore tunics smeared with lime, blood and excrement.'[88] They were proto-Fascists, apparently, yet also vital, exploited, comradely, and clown-like. And they often set – or broke – the rhythm of the performance: at the sale of the elephant, Uriah acted as a kind of master of ceremonies, announcing each 'turn' as if he were presenting the rounds of a boxing match. These interruptions not only broke up the flow of the drama, they also, paradoxically, served to ratchet up the tension. The interruption therefore had a dual function: it entertained and also, simultaneously, it made the adrenalin flow – as at a real boxing match.

Brecht's production employed the half-curtain, before which the first scene, and other interludes, were performed. Most of the scenery was extremely sketchy, and easily moved and removed. At the back were screens upon which captions were projected. Thus, for Scene 2, when the soldiers were to lose Jip, the screen read: '4 – 1 = 3'. When the soldiers enlisted Galy Gay to take Jip's place, '3 + 1 = 4' was projected. And for Scene 8, when it is demonstrated that 'man equals man', '1 = 1' was projected on the screen.

The acting was criticised for its lack of clarity and consistency. Partly this was because Brecht was attempting something new, that is, the use the gest as the basis for the presentation. Thus, the dismantling of the canteen involved a typically cool and illuminating piece of gestic acting by Helene Weigel:

> One of the more striking aspects of the dismantling of the canteen was the lowering, washing and folding of the sheets suspended as a roof above the stage. Begbick unhooked them with a long pole while delivering her first lines . . . She washed them while singing the song about the loss of her good name by lowering them into a trap in the stage. She moved them as though they were in water and then pulled up clean sheets substituted for the dirty ones beneath the stage. On the reprise of her song she folded the clean sheets with the soldier Uriah.[89]

Peter Lorre's Galy Gay structured his performance through a sequence of gests, such as his showing of fear by simply turning away from the audience, dipping his hands in whitewash, smearing it across his face, and then turning back (a trick learned from Karl Valentin). Lorre aimed to show man as inconsistent and contradictory: he tried to expose different kinds of behaviour, to illustrate 'this way' of doing various things, as opposed to other ways. The separate incidents were supposed to cohere in the spectator's imagination, as with film montage. And they led to his final memorable appearance: 'a figure with a knife between his teeth, hung with hand grenades, in a tunic stinking of the trenches – the shy and proper petty bourgeois of yesterday, now a machine for murder'.[90]

The Caucasian Chalk Circle was Brecht's last completed play before he left his American exile to return to Europe, and the last completed production of his life. The production was designed by Karl von Appen, who had been incarcerated by the Nazis for four years as a Communist. Brecht asked him for something like a traditional nativity scene, with Grusha and the peasants like Mary and Joseph, and the Fat Prince and the Governor's

Figure 4.3 The Caucasian Chalk Circle, Berliner Ensemble, 1954. Helene Weigel as the Governor's Wife.

entourage like the three kings. Von Appen created a series of backcloths, which floated from the flies and cut across the revolve stage upon which Grusha escaped to the mountains. Scenery was minimal, but aesthetically attractive. Props were selective, made to suggest, not naturalistic detail, but rather dramatic potential. And masks were used for socio-political reasons: the rulers' faces were frozen, where the faces of the lower classes were expressive.

Music played a distinctive role in this, as in so many of Brecht's productions. He suggested that the song at the end of the first act should be 'cold', so that Grusha could act 'against' it as she decided to take the child: the comparison with Charlie Chaplin's *The Kid* was thus reinforced. For the Flight to the Northern Mountains, 'the theatre needs driving music which can hold together this very epic act. However', Brecht continued, 'it should be thin and delicate.'[91] The music reinforced the tension in this chase which reached its climax in the escape over the rotten bridge. The songs in *The Caucasian Chalk Circle* were not as crudely separated as they had been in some earlier productions, like *The Threepenny Opera*, but they still performed the function of interrupting the action, even when, as now, the actors 'acted' (mimed) what the singer described, or themselves sang emotionally. The song changed the focus and the rhythm and refreshed the drama as well as the spectator.

The acting stunned many spectators. Angelica Hurwicz's Grusha had the frantic urgency of Bruegel's *Dulle Griet*, yet the patient stoicism of a peasant wife. Helene Weigel, as the Governor's Wife, sat still and barely raised her voice, yet commanded all those about her, and the stage and auditorium as well. Brecht's own careful description of the Prologue shows something of the unforced simplicity which the production achieved:

> For the members of the kolkhoz 'Galinsk', the destruction of the farm is hard to understand. Nobody disputes the fact that it was permissible, but the deed cannot be accepted happily by the owners who have now returned. There is an oppressive pause, and the group that has gathered together for the discussion now divides into two kolkhozes. The expert notices the oppressive mood and covers up the difficult situation. In a dry and businesslike manner, she begins to read the protocol. The circumstances under which the irrigation plan originated have great significance for the course of the discussion . . . There is a pregnant pause. The old farmer from the kolkhoz 'Galinsk' gets up, covers the considerable distance to the group from the kolkhoz 'Rosa Luxemburg' and shakes hands with the young tractor driver. There is applause on both sides: for the defenders of the homeland and for the farmer who acknowledged the arguments of the defenders.[92]

It was such careful, yet carefree, performance that enabled Brecht's work to make its intellectual and emotional impact.

Brecht after Brecht

In 1949 Sir John Gielgud, having just read an essay by Brecht, wondered aloud: 'Mr Brecht presumably writes his own scripts, and it might be

Figure 4.4 The Threepenny Opera, Berliner Ensemble, 1964.

interesting to see a performance of one of them.'[93] A quarter of a century later, plays by Brecht featured on the *English* Literature 'A' Level syllabus. But a quarter of a century after that, with the implosion of Communism and the world struggling in the wake of Reaganomics and Thatcherism, few playwrights stirred less enthusiasm than Brecht. It was an extraordinary switchback ride, which needs some explaining.

Initially, Brecht's legacy was left in the hands of the Berliner Ensemble, who were charged with staging his plays and proselytising his working methods. Helene Weigel retained the managership of the company, and a group of young directors, headed by Manfred Wekwerth and including Benno Besson, Peter Palitzsch, Joachim Tenschert and, later, Manfred Karge and Matthias Langhoff, together with brilliant actors like Ekkehard Schall and Wolf Kaiser, pushed the work forward.

In 1960 the company again won the First Prize at the Théâtre des Nations, Paris, and through the 1960s they were generally regarded as the world's leading theatre company. But already accusations of playing safe and becoming more museum than living theatre were being heard. In 1969, Wekwerth left after a bitter dispute, and when Helene Weigel died in 1971, Ruth Berghaus became artistic director. She brought something of a new broom, staging, for example, *Cement* by the much-banned playwright, Heiner Muller, and enlisting new directors like Einar Scleef and B. K. Tragelehn. But this was too radical for the East German Communists, and in 1977 Manfred Wekwerth, admirably acceptable and soon to become a member of the ruling Politbureau, returned. His own work, like his new version of *Mother Courage*, was often poorly received, but he employed Heiner Muller, whose 1988 production of Brecht's fragmentary *Fatzer* was widely acclaimed. It was, however, the dying fall of the old Communist-created company. To many, by the time the Berlin Wall fell in 1989, the Ensemble was bloated, stagnant and directionless.

In West Germany, indeed across Europe (and America), a not dissimilar pattern was discernable. In the twenty years after Brecht's triumphant *Mother Courage* in 1949, there were no fewer than 478 different productions of Brecht plays in West Germany, even though during this time there were at least three (incomplete) boycotts of his work – in 1953 after the East German workers' rising, 1956 after the invasion of Hungary, and 1961, when the Berlin Wall was built. *Mother Courage* alone received sixty-six different productions in this period to 1968, *Mr Puntila and His Man Matti* fifty-three and *The Good Person of Setzuan* fifty-two. As the truth about Soviet Communism came to be more clearly recognised, dissatisfactions with the post-war settlement rose to the surface, new freedoms associated with peace marches, 'flower power', and rock music were discovered, and Brecht seemed to offer a timely, refreshing, and intellectually honest form of left-wing theatre. But (to cut a complicated history short) the 1968 'revolution' in Germany and France failed, and suddenly there seemed to have been just too many Brecht productions. 'Brecht fatigue' set in. Though West German theatre was still capable of astonishing productions, such as Peter Stein's 1970 *Mother* in West Berlin, which demonstrated the effectiveness of Stein's concept of collective work, Jurgen Flimm's *Baal* in Cologne in 1981 and Manfred Karge's *Mother* at Bochum in 1982, many German practitioners stopped engaging with Brecht's ideas, and the writer Peter Handke referred contemptuously to Brecht's plays as 'fairy tales'.

Nevertheless, in West and East Germany, the Brechtian example had informed, and sometimes inspired, a generation of unusual and interesting playwrights, including, in the West, Martin Walser, Thomas Bernhardt, and Franz Xaver Kroetz, and in the East, Helmut Baierl, Volker Braun, Peter Hacks and, of course, Heiner Muller whose statement – 'to make use of Brecht without being critical of him is to betray him'[94] – showed both the problem and the potential of writing after Brecht. The problem in the East may, paradoxically, have been reduced by the Berliner Ensemble's dog-in-the-manger attitude which prevented other companies in that half-country from presenting his work. Muller was profoundly helped, too, by his collaboration with the French director, Robert Wilson.

The Berliner Ensemble visited London in 1956. Its impact was immediate and stunning. Playwrights like John Osborne and Robert Bolt, although certainly not 'left-wing', nevertheless embraced 'alienation'. Theatres of all descriptions scrambled to present the great East German. After what seemed like an age of well-made plays and drawing-room comedies, theatre suddenly became relevant to the real social and political problems of life. With gathering momentum, with much enthusiasm but somewhat less understanding, Brecht came to dominate much of British theatre in the 1960s and 1970s. Some of the best productions probably included Bernard Miles as Galileo at the Mermaid Theatre in 1960 and as Schweyk in *Schweyk in the Second World War* in 1963; the Royal Shakespeare Company's *Caucasian Chalk Circle* in 1962; and *Happy End*, directed by Michael Geliot, initially at the Edinburgh Festival, later at the Royal Court, London, in 1965. In 1969, Michael Blakemore presented a brilliant *Resistable Rise of Arturo Ui* at the Glasgow Citizens Theatre, and London's Half Moon Theatre did a similarly memorable *Mother* the following year.

Brecht was by now not only on the school syllabus, his work was performed ubiquitously, from the National Theatre to the new 'theatre-in-education' companies, to amateur and student groups, and even to school plays in new comprehensive schools. Inevitably, Brecht influenced other theatre work too. The Royal Shakespeare Company's *Wars of the Roses* sequence in 1963, and Peter Brook's production of *The Marat/Sade* the next year, were both enriched by their intertextual relations with Brecht, and the work of playwrights such as John Arden, especially in his earlier work, Edward Bond, Caryl Churchill, and Howard Brenton all benefited from their understanding of him. It was only later, in the 1980s and 1990s, when Margaret Thatcher dominated the country and leading actresses like Judi Dench and Glenda Jackson found themselves 'failing' with Mother Courage, that the reaction could be seen clearly to have set in.

In France, the Comédie-Française and the regional theatres alike staged Brecht through the 1960s and 1970s: statisticians noted that in 1972 Molière was the most frequently staged playwright in the country, followed by Shakespeare, and then Brecht, ahead of Chekhov and Marivaux. Perhaps thanks to Jean Vilar, who had directed *Mother Courage* at the Théâtre National Populaire as early as 1951, and who also created a brilliant *Arturo Ui* at the time of de Gaulle's war against Algerian independence, French theatre seemed to have discovered a lighter, perhaps more cynical, Brecht than elsewhere, with some notably adventurous productions, including *Baal*, directed by André Engel in Strasbourg in 1976, and *Mr Puntila and His Man Matti*, directed by Georges Lavaudant at Grenoble in 1978. In some ways more significant were a number of brilliant French productions of work by other playwrights who owed much to Brecht: Roger Planchon's 1957 production of *Paolo Paoli* by Arthur Adamov was an early example; Ariane Mnouchkine's 1986 production of Hélène Cixous' *L'Histoire terrible mais inachevée de Norodom Sihanouk roi du Cambodge* a later, but no less challenging one. And French film of the period, especially the work of Jean-Luc Godard and Jean Marie Straub, consistently acknowledged the depth of its debt to Brecht.

Russia embraced Brecht a little later than the rest of Europe, but by the late 1960s he was as popular there as anywhere. Two productions of note may be mentioned. In 1960, Maxim Shtraukh directed the country's first *Mother Courage* at the Mayakovsky Theatre in Moscow. The protagonist was played by the former Eisenstein protégée, Judith Glizer, who, at the end of the play, started to drag her wagon off, but fell down dead. Purists were appalled, but Shtraukh's reasoning, that Brecht's 1938 conception, pre-war and during the heyday of Hitler and Stalin, was no longer valid in 1960, could have been debated more generously. The fact was, however, that Brecht was considered too significant, perhaps too sacred, to interrogate in such a way, and this attitude of reverence pertained well beyond Russia. In 1963, Yuri Lyubimov burst onto the Moscow theatre scene with an extraordinary production of *The Good Person of Szechuan* with a student company, later to form the core of his troupe at the Taganka Theatre. Lyubimov had not seen a Brecht production before. He played the drama on a virtually bare stage, and used placards, some, with legends like 'Brecht' and 'Street Scene', permanent, and others, announcing the scenes, changing. He used music, mime and a sharply stylised approach to the acting:

> Exits and entrances were choreographed in a disciplined, military manner, often describing rectangular movements on stage, thus precluding any illusion of an accidental or naturalistic occurrence . . . Inna Ulyanova, who played the house-owner, employed a series of ironic gestures to define her role. She tried to use her female charms on Shui Ta by pulling up her skirt when seated on the table, and by indicating her silhouette when referring to her 'business affairs' with him.[95]

Most controversially, Lyubimov's gods were Soviet bureaucrats.

In Italy, Giorgio Strehler mounted a series of Brecht productions, commencing with a *Threepenny Opera* in 1951 which won Brecht's own imprimatur. In India, Badal Sircar found a way of using a Brechtian approach to Indian material, and in South America, Brecht's work was a seminal strand in Augusto Boal's 'Theatre of the Oppressed'. In the United States, where Eric Bentley, H. R. Hays, and a few others persistently advocated Brecht against a pervasive anti-Communism, Brecht was perhaps particularly noticeable in forwarding the careers of a number of women directors, including Judith Malina, who directed *He Who Says Yes* and *He Who Says No* as early as 1951, and whose highly acclaimed *Antigone*, premiered in 1967, stayed in the repertoire of the Living Theatre for over twenty years: 'Wherever we played it, it seemed to become the symbol of the struggle of that time and place – in bleeding Ireland, in Franco's Spain, in Poland a month before martial law was declared, clandestinely in Prague'.[96] Other American women who were successful with Brecht were Zelda Fichandler, who directed *The Caucasian Chalk Circle* in Washington in 1961, and Nina Vance, who presented *Galileo* in Houston, Texas, in 1962. Brecht, however, was never as omnipresent in America as he was in Europe, and by 1987 at Stratford, Ontario, *Mother Courage*, played to houses just 26 per cent full.

By then, of course, the world had had enough, not just of Communism, but of Brecht, too. It had, like Guzzler Jake in *The Rise and Fall of the City of Mahagonny*, gobbled so much of him, it simply had to spew him out, or burst. His star, like the political philosophy to which he had apparently tied himself so tightly (had not official Communism's most favoured cultural son, Georg Lukács himself, given the oration at Brecht's funeral?), fell as rapidly as it had risen. There were other factors too. The modelbooks undoubtedly inhibited experiment. The 'Brecht industry' (books, articles, televised cultural clichés, and so on, as well as productions of the plays) lent a blanket conformity to anything 'Brechtian'. The 'Brecht style', the half-curtain, the 'worn' authentic props, the pseudo-peasant pastel greys and fawns of costumes and props, created a theatrical uniformity which became excruciatingly dull, while the 'Brecht method', including hackneyed V-effects and anticipated gests, sank into a morass of orthodoxy. What was more, the whole Brecht 'enterprise' was grossly constricted by the policy of his heirs, who forbade any experimentation. For instance, anyone wanting to perform Brecht's experimental montage of scenes, *Fear and Misery of the Third Reich*, was only permitted to present the authorised scenes in the authorised order. Brecht, the embodiment of experiment, had become a cultural mausoleum. Ironically, he resembled nothing so much as the Beyreuth Wagner, when his descendants' ban on experimentation virtually killed the *Gesamkunstwerke*. The nadir was reached with a lurid and moralistic biography, in which Brecht was virtually held responsible for both the Second World War and the continuance of the gulag, which enterprises he seemed to have prosecuted while his exploited and besotted mistresses, unable to think for themselves and working to Brecht's orders, wrote the 'great plays' between them.[97]

But then some unexpected chinks began to appear, not least in a reassessment of Brecht in the light of new critical and philosophical ideas discussed in the 'Twenty-first-century perspectives' section below. But in the theatre too, despite the continuing restrictive hold of those with copyright powers, some progress was hesitantly made.

In 1992, with a much trimmed work force and under a new management team of Muller, Palitzsch, Langhoff, Fritz Marquardt, and Peter Zadek, the Berliner Ensemble was effectively privatised. Leaner and more focused, it certainly acquired a new energy, and Muller's production of *Arturo Ui*, with the brilliant Martin Wuttke in the title role, was seen and admired across the world. True, by the end of the century the Ensemble needed further reorganisation, and Claus Peymann, formerly of the Vienna Burgtheater, was appointed artistic director. A new policy directed towards contemporary work bore fruit early in 2000 when George Tabori's *Brecht-Akte*, about the CIA's pursuit of Brecht in America, was staged, but still Brecht (including a revival of Muller's *Arturo Ui*) continued to dominate. Still, the Ensemble installed a Theatre Playground for children, and a Flying Classroom, where actors and directors met the public to discuss their work. But whether it could – or should – become anything more than a house of homage to its founder is difficult to argue.

Nevertheless, by the end of the century, it was noticeable that the epic 'idiom' pervaded contemporary theatre, often unacknowledged. Most obviously it was seen in the emphasis on *what happens* to the diminishment of interest in, say, a character's past or personal psychology. Sophocles, Shakespeare, Ibsen, Tennessee Williams, Arthur Miller, all created dilemmas based on their characters' *pasts*. It is Freud's position. And Ibsen always asserted that, no matter how much he seemed to be arguing for women's rights or other progressive causes, his *primary* subject was the individual in society. Today, almost invariably, the emphasis is the other way round. As Fredric Jameson has suggested, 'Brecht's thought is present everywhere today without bearing his name and without our being aware of it.'[98]

And there are other straws in the wind. One noticed that in the summer of 2002, the hottest off-Broadway ticket in New York was for a production of *The Resistable Rise of Arturo Ui*, starring Al Pacino. And at the same time in Scotland a small-scale touring production of *The Good Person of Szechuan* was unexpectedly well attended and inaugurated eager community discussion.

Twenty-first-century perspectives

By the end of the twentieth century, Brecht seemed 'dead' to many. He had acquired the status of 'classic' and his plays, though no doubt interesting, were no more (and no less) relevant to today's politics, societies or aesthetics than were, say, Buchner's *Woyzeck* or D. H. Lawrence's *The Daughter-in-Law*. He was said to have held and presented a simplified view of life. The Marxism he had espoused all his life had disintegrated in Moscow, and his avant-garde Modernism was outdated and gauche in a time of international mass culture, global consumerism, and the world wide web.

Yet already, for those with their ears to the ground, a new kind of investigation around Brecht was beginning, and in the twenty-first century perhaps a new kind of Brecht is emerging. Note has been taken of the fact that Brecht was an inveterate experimenter – he published his works under the title *Experiments* – and after the 1960s, perhaps, it began to be noticed that his output was considerably more diverse, and more challenging, than a number of 'great plays' fit for national theatres. He wrote stories, plays (of various sorts), novels, poems, songs, diaries, theory, political analyses, cultural commentary, philosophy. His mode of production was fundamentally collaborative, and most typical of his creative work was its characteristic reworking of pre-existing material. He re-possessed older plays, and was notoriously lax about 'plagiarism', so that he affords a rich mine for diggers after intertextuality.

In addition, Brecht was never happy to consider any work of his 'finished': he wrote and re-wrote tirelessly. His extraordinary rehearsals at the Berliner Ensemble perhaps aspired to be 'endless'. His only certainty was doubt. His work on one level appears extraordinarily 'modern' in that it challenges individual conceptions of identity, and indeed asks what we mean by identity. All of which suggests that he is a remarkably suitable body for dissection by contemporary theorists.

And indeed he had seemed so to some as early as the 1950s. Roland Barthes applauded Brecht's idea of the gest, grappled with his concept of 'demystifying', and pointed out the politics of the sign. For Barthes, Brecht offered a system (a 'readerly' text) which the Structuralist could analyse, while denying the possibility of 'final' meaning (in this sense producing 'writerly' texts). Brecht's irony and his self-reflexivity were further elements Barthes enjoyed, and indeed his *Mythologies* is profoundly Brechtian in its method.

Brecht also provided a paradigm for the emerging Feminist theatre movement. Lizbeth Goodman noticed that just as Brecht's work did not fit the 'apparatus' of German theatre in the 1920s, so Feminist theatre did not fit the theatre apparatus of the western world in the last quarter of the twentieth century. Perhaps as a consequence, his collaborative method was developed most consciously, and most successfully, in women's groups. His theory, too, helped those feminists who argued that gender is a social construction: Shen Te-Shui Ta played by a man is a very different proposition to Shen Te-Shui Ta played, as is usual, by a woman. And Brechtian historicisation also proved a useful tool for Feminist theatre practice which sought to unearth and deconstruct the oppressed position of women in history. The heart of his writing sometimes seems to parallel, and be extended by, writing by women such as Hélène Cixous, with her facility in exposing contradictions. And Sue-Ellen Case pointed out that Brecht's epic form has an inherently female dimension as compared to the subliminal maleness of tragedy. Where the structure of tragedy is comparable to – even modelled on – the male sexual experience, proceeding from foreplay to arousal to ejaculation, the structure of epic is more like the female experience of multiple consecutive orgasms.[99]

Another challenging theatre project infused with the knowledge and spirit of Brecht was Augusto Boal's 'Theatre of the Oppressed'. Taking his cue from Brecht, Boal asserted the manipulative oppression of Aristotelian theatre, from the Greeks to soap operas, and proposed not just a theatre in which the audience could *think* their way out from under this hegemony, but one in which they could *act* against it, in a 'rehearsal of revolution'.[100] Boal's ground-breaking and positive work and ideas have become widely available through a series of thought-provoking books.

Meanwhile, in more academic circles, Brecht has begun to provide unexpected areas for examination. Thus, the old 'three-phase' Brecht, conjured out of a biographical reading (early anarchic works, middle-period austere Marxist *Lehrstücke*, and 'mature' great plays, all knitted up theoretically in *A Short Organum for the Theatre*) was challenged by Elizabeth Wright, who saw his fragments, revisions, and notes as often more revealing than the *Short Organum* and centred a critique in the often disregarded *Lehrstücke*. She showed how the early plays operated deliberately to disrupt and decentre, and this enabled her to deconstruct the conventional boundary between comedy and tragedy. Wright believed that, for various reasons, Brecht's more radical ideas had not fertilised his later work, and that only in the later, less 'tidy' productions of Heiner Muller and Pina Bausch had these ideas begun to bear the appropriate fruit.

Steve Giles deconstructed the *Threepenny* 'Lawsuit' and its ramifications to reveal the genesis and perhaps the significance of Brecht's Marxism, which he also related provocatively to problems associated with the mass media and to post-modern and post-structuralist theory. Fredric Jameson highlighted Brecht's 'showing of showing'. He suggested that the shape of Brechtian thought derived specifically from the acting out of stories, with a V-effect which inevitably leads to 'choosing'. Indeed, the *Lehrstücke* he characterised specifically as 'machines for choosing'. Jameson's Brecht has something in common with the traditional Buddha, who said:

> My teaching is a method to experience reality and not reality itself, just as a finger pointing at the moon is not the moon itself. An intelligent person makes use of the finger to see the moon. A person who only looks at the finger and mistakes it for the moon will never see the real moon.[101]

Sarah Bryant-Bertail attempted a contemporary assessment of 'the Brechtian legacy' which widened the scope of enquiry to include Piscator's 1920s work and also some post-Brechtian stagings by Stein, Mnouchkine, and others. Her work complemented Steve Giles's in its deconstructing of the mass media, especially representations of war and capitalism, and suggested that theatre is perhaps uniquely placed to act as a forum for the critiquing of contemporary crises.

Inevitably, these comments provide only the tiniest peephole into some contemporary philosophical and critical approaches to Brecht. But it is instructive that at last his whole oeuvre is being interrogated, and through it new and fruitful ways of thinking about identity, culture, politics, and society are being found.

Further reading

Brecht's works are published in Berlin and Frankfurt, in Germany, in a series so far stretching to thirty volumes: *Bertolt Brecht Grosse kommentierte*

Berliner und Frankfurter Ausgabe, Berlin and Frankfurt: Aufbau and Suhrkamp.

Methuen has published almost all Brecht's plays in English translation, in a series of eight volumes of the Collected Plays. A ninth volume, containing adaptations, was published in the United States in 1973, but has not yet appeared in Britain. In addition, various single volumes and other translations of the plays have been published.

Methuen are also responsible for the ongoing publication of Brecht's 'Plays, Poetry and Prose', of which the Collected Plays are a part. This series, originally edited by John Willett and Ralph Manheim, and now by Tom Kuhn, includes four volumes of poetry, one volume of short stories, *Diaries 1920–1922*, *Journals 1934–1955*, and *Letters 1913–1956*. Brecht's *The Threepenny Novel* was published in England by Penguin in 1961, though the translation first appeared in the United States as *A Penny for the Poor* in 1937.

Methuen have also published significant selections from Brecht's theoretical writings, most notably in:

Kuhn, Tom, and Giles, Steve, *Brecht on Art and Politics* (first published 2003).
Silberman, Marc, *Brecht on Film and Radio* (first published 2000).
Willett, John, *Brecht on Theatre, the Development of an Aesthetic* (first published 1964; reprinted many times).

Methuen also published *The Messingkauf Dialogues* originally in 1965, and it has been reprinted several times since.

Critical analysis and discussion about Brecht is carried on in the annual publication of the International Brecht Society, *The Brecht Yearbook*.

Critical books about Brecht are too many to enumerate, even if one were to confine oneself to books written in English only. Notoriously, there has been something of a 'Brecht industry' in the half century since Brecht himself died. What follows is one reader's selection of the most interesting of these works from the last fifteen years or so:

Brooker, Peter, *Bertolt Brecht: Dialectics, Poetry, Politics*, London: Croom Helm, 1988.
Bryant-Bertail, Sarah, *Space and Time in Epic Theatre*, Woodbridge: Camden House, 2000.
Giles, Steve, *Bertolt Brecht and Critical Theory: Marxism, Modernity and the 'Threepenny Lawsuit'*, Bern: Peter Lang, 1998.
Giles, Steve, and Livingstone, Rodney (eds), *Bertolt Brecht: Centenary Essays*, Amsterdam: Rodopi, 1998.
Jameson, Fredric, *Brecht and Method*, London: Verso, 1998.
Kleber, Pia, and Visser, Colin, *Re-interpreting Brecht: His Influence on Contemporary Drama and Film*, Cambridge: Cambridge University Press, 1990.

Martin, Carol, and Bial, Henry (eds), *Brecht Sourcebook*, London: Routledge, 2000.

Suvin, Darko, *To Brecht and Beyond: Soundings in Modern Dramaturgy*, Brighton: Harvester, 1984.

Thomson, Peter, and Sacks, Glendyr (eds), *The Cambridge Companion to Brecht*, Cambridge: Cambridge University Press, 1994.

Wright, Elizabeth, *Postmodern Brecht: A Re-presentation*, London: Routledge, 1989.

5   Antonin Artaud

Life and work

Antonin Artaud was a 'prophet' who 'raised his voice in the desert', according to Peter Brook.[1] His work was visionary, iconoclastic, daring; yet his life has been described by one of his admirers as indicating 'failure and misery'.[2]

Born on 4 September 1896, Artaud grew up in the cosmopolitan Mediterranean port of Marseilles, where his father, Antoine-Roi Artaud, was a shipping agent. He was a cold man, disliked by his son, who had a much more emotional, if erratic, relationship with his Levantine Greek mother, Euphrasie-Marie-Louise Nalpas. The family were intense, inward-looking, and religious.

At the age of four, the boy Antonin was taken gravely ill with what he believed to be meningitis. He recovered, but this seems to have set the pattern for a sickly childhood, further embarrassed by the development of a stutter. He had frequent debilitating headaches, which were to afflict him all his life, and which were to drive him to drugs as the only solution he could find for the racking pains. At the age of ten he almost drowned, and by the time he was twenty he had spent time in sanatoria. His father was able to have him invalided out of the French army in the First World War, and in autumn 1918 he was sent to Le Chanet sanatorium near Neuchatel, Switzerland.

Meanwhile, at the age of fourteen he had begun to publish poems in a little magazine he created with his friends. In 1920 he was under the care of Dr Edouard Toulouse in an asylum at Villejuif, where he assisted with Toulouse's magazine, *Demain*. Toulouse's special interest was the mentality of genius, and he had already studied the minds of Zola, Poincaré, Daudet, and others. In 1923 Artaud was entrusted with the task of editing a collection of his writings. But by then Artaud was developing his own literary career with work that was jagged, unsatisfactory, but studded with

Figure 5.1 Antonin Artaud.

brilliance. He himself was intensely dissatisfied with it, believing it failed to capture the truth of his experience of life. Yet it was the best he could manage, and to many readers poems like the following, written in the early 1920s, seemed extraordinarily powerful and original.

Dark poet

Dark poet, a maid's breast
Haunts you,
Embittered poet, life seethes
And life burns,

And the sky reabsorbs itself in rain,
Your pen scratches at the heart of life.

Forest, forest, alive with eyes,
On multiple pinions;
With storm-bound hair,
The poets mount horses, dogs.

Eyes fume, tongues stir,
The heavens surge into our senses
Like blue mother's milk;
Women, harsh vinegar hearts,
I hang suspended from your mouths.[3]

This poem may suggest why Artaud has often been called the true heir to
the 'poètes maudits' of French literature, especially Baudelaire and
Rimbaud. Such angry defiance, coupled with the insistence on the
conjunction of life and art, puzzled the better-connected reviewers and
editors, such as Jacques Rivière of *La Nouvelle Revue Française*, who rejected
some poems Artaud sent him, but entered into a probing, and sometimes
frighteningly honest, correspondence with him:

> Dear Mr Rivière,
> My mental life is all shot through with petty doubts and unalterable
> certainties expressed in clear, coherent language. My weaknesses are
> more tremulous in texture, themselves larval and ill-formed. They bear
> living, anguished roots reaching down into the heart of life. But they do
> not bear life's turmoil, since in them we do not feel the cosmic afflatus
> of a soul shaken to its foundations. They come from a mind which has
> not considered its weakness. Otherwise it would spell it out in terse,
> forceful words. There, my dear Sir, lies the whole problem. To have the
> inalienable reality, the tangible clarity of feeling within one's self, to
> have them so deeply they cannot help expressing themselves in
> richness of language, memorised constructions which could come into
> play, or be of some use. The moment the soul proposes to coordinate its
> riches, its discoveries, its revelations, unknowingly at the very minute
> the thing is about to emanate, a higher vicious will attacks the soul like
> vitriol, attacks the mass of words and imagery, attacks the mass of our
> feelings and leaves me as it were panting at the gates of life.[4]

The whole correspondence, published in 1927, indicates the root of
Artaud's artistic problem. Words – the usual weapons of the poet – will not
suffice to express the intense truths of his life. He could write: 'I have a

headache', but the screwing pain in the cranium is not in the words. He could write: 'My heart beats faster', but this in no way articulates the physical truth of love. So Artaud felt himself to be a poet without words, an artist without a medium.

Artaud's Paris

Paris in the 1920s was at its height as the world's intellectual, artistic and fashionable capital. Writers such as Proust and Gide, Cocteau and Breton, met in Left Bank cafés like La Coupole, La Flore and Les Deux Magots, where they rubbed shoulders with composers such as Ravel, Satie, Milhaud and Poulenc. Many of the greatest masters of twentieth-century painting, including Picasso, Braque, and Matisse, had studios in Paris, and some at least were involved with Diaghilev's brilliant Ballet Russe. In the conventional theatre Lugné-Poë was still active, and alongside him such outstanding directors as Charles Dullin, Jacques Copeau, Louis Jouvet, Georges Pitoeff, and Gaston Baty.

Paris was the capital of the social whirl too: the world of high fashion and the long cigarette-holder, the brittle world of the 'flapper', of champagne and jazz, and of revues, nightclubs, and cabarets featuring popular singers like Yvette Guilbert, Mistinguett, Josephine Baker, and Maurice Chevalier.

A premium was put on the novel and the bizarre, as one fashionable dance followed another – the foxtrot, the cakewalk, the shimmy and finally the charleston. Legs flying, music racing, Paris in the 1920s danced through the night.

In 1925 two works of poetry and prose poems had been published, *Umbilical Limbo* and *Nerve Scales*, and in 1929 *Art and Death* was published. Many have felt that some of the pieces in these collections, describing Artaud's drug-induced hallucinations, in their use of language and in the intensity of their felt experience, leave Coleridge or de Quincey far behind. But for Artaud they were profoundly unsatisfactory, merely nibbling the edge of the reality of his experience. Later, Artaud adapted Lewis's *The Monk* in 1931, and Lewisohn's *Crime Passionel* in 1932, and these too, and the more subtle work of horror, *Heliogabale*, about the Roman boy emperor whose sadism and sexual perversity were legendary, are powerful books. But for Artaud, they represented hack-work – something to earn a few francs while his real ambitions took him elsewhere.

They were more nearly represented by his first published playtext, the brief and sometimes baffling *Spurt of Blood*, which had appeared in *Umbilical Limbo* in 1925. In this, a Young Man and a Girl repeat clichéd love expressions in different tones until a hurricane blows, stars collide, and scorpions and other reptiles appear. A knight obtains 'his papers' from a Wet Nurse, whose enormous breasts he wants to gaze at. It is night, and God seizes a naked Whore by the wrist. She bites Him, and 'a spurt of blood slashes across the stage'. All die, except the Whore and the Young Man, who ogle one another. The Wet Nurse, now flat-chested, brings in the Girl, now dead, and the Knight demands his cheese from the Wet Nurse. The Young Man begs him not to hurt his 'Mummy' as scorpions crawl from under her dress and swarm in her vagina. She and the Young Man flee, and the Girl gets up, realising that the Young Man was seeking the Virgin.

A series of 'intimate' scenes in the play alternate with more or less apocalyptic events. Whether the spurt of blood itself represents God creating the world, or – somehow – the Young Man's orgasm, does not perhaps matter. The play seems to conjure up the emotional life of the Young Man, with his absurdly ineffectual father and his massive-mammaried mother, his clichéd girl friend and glitzy whore, who are all related in his imagination to colossal, universe-shattering happenings. Is this what being young is like? Attempts to pin meaning on this early work by Artaud invite intellectual disaster.

By the time he wrote *The Spurt of Blood*, Artaud was already quite an experienced professional actor, and he was discovering that the physical reality of theatrical performance provided a more visceral, more immediate, doorway to the expression of violent truth for him than poetry ever had. He had begun this career in February 1921 at the Théâtre de l'Oeuvre under Aurélian François Lugné-Poë, who had been a leading opponent of theatrical Naturalism since the 1890s. The following season he became a member of the Atelier – part drama school, part performing company – of Charles Dullin, a younger but perhaps more brilliant director than Lugné-Poë. Here Artaud played an impressive series of parts, including in Calderon's *Life Is a Dream*, for which he also designed sets and costumes, and Tiresias in Cocteau's adaptation of Sophocles' *Antigone*. Nevertheless, his unpredictability did not always please Dullin. At one rehearsal he entered the stage as the Emperor Charlemagne on his hands and knees, and crawled towards the throne, animal-fashion. When Dullin stopped him, with the mild suggestion that Charlemagne was unlikely to enter his throne room in such a manner, Artaud petulantly responded: 'Oh well, if you want *realism!*'

In 1923 he joined Georges Pitoeff's company at the Comédie des Champs-Elysées. Pitoeff had worked with Meyerhold in St Petersburg. His repertoire included Blok's *The Fairground Booth* and Andreyev's *He Who*

Gets Slapped, in both of which Artaud appeared, as well as in *Six Characters in Search of an Author* by Pirandello and *R.U.R.* by Karel Čapek. However, the individuality of his talent, and the extremism of his ideals, probably made him a difficult employee, and his season with Pitoeff was virtually the end of his acting career in the theatre. One audience member remembered him in Dullin's company: 'He had a thin, sarcastic bony face, a deep voice that sounded as if he were deaf it was so unmodulated, his stage presence non-existent. He seemed to lack physical talent because of his conviction . . . that any physical imitation of reality would have seemed bogus to him.'[5] Calling the revered Comédie-Française 'a brothel', as he did in 1924, probably did little to help his theatrical career.[6]

At Dullin's theatre he had met a young actress, Genica Athanasiou. She had, in fact, played the title role in *Antigone* and was beautiful as well as talented. Artaud himself was strikingly good-looking at this time, his beauty apparently enhanced by his purple (laudanum-stained) lips. Leaving a rehearsal one day, he had slipped into Genica's hand a poem he had composed to her: romantically enough, their relationship grew from this. Twelve months later, he wrote to her of their 'year of total, absolute love. It's beautiful. I'm happy and it's through you.'[7] The relationship lasted until the late 1920s, and was probably the most significant of Artaud's life. There were other lovers later, but his attitudes, especially towards sex, became increasingly difficult, not least for himself.

In 1924 his father died and his mother came to live with him in Paris. By then his acting career had gravitated to film, where perhaps there was more money, and certainly less pressure on him to conform to the demands of an ongoing troupe. His first film that year was Claude Autant-Lara's *Fait Divers*. Later he was to play, among other parts, Marat in Abel Gance's *Napoleon Bonaparte* (1925), Frère Massieu in Carl Dreyer's *The Passion of Joan of Arc* (1927), in which he was, according to Anaïs Nin, 'beautiful' having 'the deep-set eyes of a mystic, as if shining from caverns . . . shadowy, mysterious',[8] a beggar in the French version of G. W. Pabst's *The Threepenny Opera* (1931), and Savonarola in Gance's *Lucretia Borgia* (1935).

More significant than his acting parts were Artaud's attempts at creating film scenarios of his own. Only one of these was realised, when Germaine Dulac produced *The Seashell and the Clergyman* in 1927. Artaud had hoped to be involved in this work, and indeed had wanted to play the leading role, but this proved impossible, and though it has been quite widely admired, the finished film did not please Artaud. He had, he said, been searching 'for the sombre truth of the mind in images which emerge exclusively from themselves, and do not draw their meaning from the situation in which they develop but from a sort of powerful inner necessity which projects them into the light of a merciless evidence.'[9] At the premiere on 7 February 1928, Artaud disrupted the showing, accusing Dulac of distorting his idea, and calling her a 'cow'. Nevertheless, the film is a fascinating beginning, and one can only regret that more of his scenarios were not turned into films.

The Seashell and the Clergyman has been described as the first Surrealist film, and this, of course, was the period of the ascendancy of the Surrealists in French artistic life. The baffling *Spurt of Blood* is also perhaps best thought of as a product of Surrealism. Artaud had joined Andre Breton's artistic movement in October 1924, and he immediately became involved in the work of producing the journal *La Révolution surréaliste*. Indeed he edited and wrote most of the third issue, which appeared in April 1925.

Surrealism

'When man resolved to imitate walking, he invented the wheel, which does not look like a leg. In doing this he was practicing surrealism without knowing it.' So wrote Guillaume Apollinaire in the Preface to his 1917 play, *The Breasts of Tiresias*. However, it was not until after the First World War that Surrealism as a self-conscious artistic movement was established. It aimed to address man's 'destiny' through subjective fantasy: it argued that 'classical standards' are imposed by a cultural/economic elite, and it upheld the value of personal experience, the life of the subconscious, childishness, savagery, the capricious and the unpredictable.

Surrealist poetry therefore often seemed nonsensical, though sometimes it achieved a haunting beauty, as in André Breton's *Hotel of Sparks*, with its opening lines:

The philosophic butterfly
Rests on the rose star
And that makes a window of hell
The masked man is always standing in front of the nude
   woman
Whose hair glides as light does in the morning on a street
   lamp they have forgotten to put out

(Wallace Fowler (ed.), *Mid-Century French Poets*,
New York: Grove Press, 1955, p. 155)

However, his naturally dark mentality and instinct for self-absorption chimed ill with the progressive, even optimistic, outlook of the Surrealists, and he soon drifted away from them, being expelled formally in December 1926. A significant cause of the rift was the Surrealists' increasingly serious flirtation with Communism and the Soviet Union. Artaud was angrily non-political, which has led at least one responsible critic to speculate about his relations with Fascism.[10] However that may be, in 1926 he was cursing 'these bog-paper revolutionaries' whose 'taboos' he rejected:

> I personally feel there are several ways of looking at the Revolution and among these Communism seems to me much the worst, the most restricting. A lazy man's revolution . . . Bombs need to be thrown, but they need to be thrown at the root of the majority of present-day habits of thought.[11]

By the time he wrote this in November 1926, Artaud, with another former Surrealist, Roger Vitrac, and Robert Aron, had founded the Alfred Jarry Theatre, named after the scandalous playwright of the 1890s. Their First Manifesto was published in November 1926, and despite continual struggles to find actors and a theatre, to obtain funding, not to mention an

Figure 5.2 Illustration from the brochure for the Alfred Jarry Theatre, 1926.

audience, and to defeat the censors, the police and even Surrealist hecklers, the Alfred Jarry Theatre existed for three years and produced four different programmes. Artaud wrote that 'Each new play constituted a feat of willpower, a miracle of perseverance. Not to mention the positive outbursts of hatred and envy these performances unleashed.'[12] Nevertheless, the press were often impressed. *La Monde* noted:

> The Alfred Jarry Theatre, whose dramatic ambitions are gratifying, has just given the first performance in Paris of Strindberg's *A Dream Play*. The very least one can say of Antonin Artaud's production is that he uses it as a strikingly sensitive, intelligent, careful illustration of the subtlest meanings in the text.

while *La Gazette du Franc* commented: 'The universe M. Artaud succeeds in conjuring up is one where everything assumes a meaning, a secret, a soul. It is difficult to describe and even more so to analyse the effects achieved, but they are really striking. A true reintegration of magic, of poetry in the world.' *Le Gaulois* added: 'it was very strange . . . the scenery was very imaginatively devised, as well as the acting.'[13] By 1930, however, the Alfred Jarry Theatre had run its course. The obstacles to its work were too exhausting, and besides Artaud's relations with Vitrac had become extremely strained. Vitrac's ambitions for a more commercial career no longer chimed with Artaud's intensity and serious purpose. They parted company.

Roger Vitrac

Born in 1899 in Pinsac, France, Vitrac was one of the signatories of André Breton's *First Surrealist Manifesto* of 1924, but he was expelled from the group with Artaud the following year. These two, together with Robert Aron, went on to establish the Alfred Jarry Theatre in 1927, which presented two of Vitrac's plays, *The Mysteries of Love* and *Victor*, both directed by Artaud. *The Mysteries of Love* is widely recognised as among the most successful Surrealist plays, and has been staged several times since the 1920s: an English translation is published in Bert Cardullo and Robert Knopf (eds), *Theater of the Avant-Garde, 1890–1950*, New Haven, Conn.: Yale University Press, 2001. Though Vitrac probably influenced the writers of the post-war Theatre of the Absurd, his own later plays were less successful, and he died in 1952.

Artaud was now virtually poverty-stricken, and his artistic prospects had dimmed almost to nothing. It was at this low ebb that on 1 August 1931 he visited the Paris Colonial Exhibition, where he watched the performance of an ethnic Balinese theatre troupe with growing amazement. These eastern dancer–actors offered him a vision of the kind of theatre he had been seeking, but had only been half able to articulate. Suddenly his most profound ideas and his most outrageous demands seemed to have found expression. The show liberated him spiritually and artistically. The following month, looking at the painting *Lot and His Daughters* by Lucas van Leyden in the Louvre, Artaud was struck by the work's extreme theatricality and pathos. In his mind, the implicit incest in the relationships between the main characters, especially in the context painted, triggered a 'tremendously important mental drama'.[14] The painting, with others, like Bruegel's *Dulle Griet*, became almost as important for him as the Balinese theatre performance. In a sense they combined to form an image of what was to become 'the Theatre of Cruelty'.

> **Balinese theatre**
> The Balinese theatre performance which so inspired Artaud was a *barong* dance, featuring the *barong*, a lion-like dragon figure who aids people by opposing the evil Rangda. By putting those who depend on it into a trance, the *barong* shows its power, which is further demonstrated spectacularly when those entranced turn their swords and knives on themselves, but do no harm.

Over the next few years he wrote a number of essays trying to clarify for himself as much as for his readers this concept of a Theatre of Cruelty. The essays were finally collected and published under the title *The Theatre and Its Double*, in 1938. One of the most famous, 'Theatre and the Plague', formed the basis of a lecture which Artaud delivered at the Sorbonne in Paris on 6 April 1933. In the audience was his admirer, Anaïs Nin, who recorded what turned out to be less a lecture than a full-blooded Theatre of Cruelty performance by Artaud:

> Imperceptibly almost, [Artaud] let go of the thread we were following and began to act out dying by the plague . . .
>   His face was contorted with anguish, one could see the perspiration dampening his hair. His eyes dilated, his muscles became cramped, his fingers struggled to retain their flexibility. He made one feel the

parched and burning throat, the fever, the fire in the guts. He was in agony. He was screaming. He was delirious. He was enacting his own death, his own crucifixion.[15]

His audience, expecting an academic discussion, did not appreciate the performance and left in high dudgeon. Yet as an example of what Artaud was seeking in theatre, this performance was surely remarkable, and even the audience's disapproval was not without significance.

The Theatre of Cruelty's only production took place in May 1935. Artaud adapted *The Cenci* largely from Shelley's Romantic unstageable masterpiece into a curious, fitfully melodramatic piece. It was much more wordy than might have been expected, and the central action, the rape of Beatrice, surprisingly happened off-stage. The only theatre Artaud could find for the performance was a small music hall, the Folies-Wagram, and the production was financed largely by two untalented but ambitious women who wished to act – Iya Abdy, the Russian former wife of Sir Robert Abdy, and Cécile Bressant, the wife of the publisher, Robert Denoël, who had commissioned Artaud's adaptations of *The Monk* and *Crime Passionel*. They played Beatrice and Lucretia respectively, and their presence diluted the intensity of the rehearsal process as their performances helped to deflate the finished performance.

The Cenci – Shelley and Artaud

Percy Byssche Shelley's tragedy, *The Cenci*, attempts to dramatise the apparently true story of Count Cenci, who was murdered by his daughter in 1599.

The play opens with Cenci unwillingly agreeing to forfeit a third of his estates to the Pope so that his latest murder will be overlooked. His heartlessness extends to publicly rejoicing at a banquet because two of his sons have been killed, humiliating Lucretia, his wife, and – finally – raping his daughter Beatrice. She, Lucretia, and other of his victims plot his murder, and though the hired assassins at first bungle the job, Cenci is finally killed. The Pope's legate uncovers the crime, and Beatrice and her co-conspirators are sentenced to death.

Artaud follows this outline closely, though he curtails the dialogue and often re-writes it. However, he also introduces a number of authentically exciting theatrical effects, including a finale in which the Pope's treatment of his Catholic flock is implicitly compared to

Cenci's treatment of his children, social injustice is indicted, and the denial of individual fulfilment deplored. Afterwards, the cast marches to the execution block, accompanied by crescendoing, seven-beat Inca music.

But the fault was certainly not all theirs. Artaud, having written the script, took it upon himself not only to direct, but also to act the leading role of Cenci himself. Apart from a tiny part in his own production of *A Dream Play* in 1928, Artaud had not acted on the professional stage for ten years. To undertake such a huge role was itself, perhaps, tempting fate; to try also to direct the piece which would be not just another performance, but which would introduce the world to a wholly new concept of theatre, the Theatre of Cruelty, was to invite catastrophe. And a catastrophe it turned out to be. According to *La Revue de Paris*, 'it was an offence to dramatic art, to the actor's profession, to all that we venerate'.[16] The actors found Artaud's demands almost impossible, the Russian accent of Iya Abdy was virtually impenetrable, and Artaud himself was too exhausted to give of anything like his best to his own performance. Roger Blin, a fervent supporter of Artaud, who took part in the production, explained:

> Most of the actors understood his ideas, but they couldn't carry them out, but then Artaud hadn't taken the trouble to explain himself. He was so completely inside his subject and tended to have faith, perhaps too much faith, in their abilities to comprehend him. He needed more time for rehearsal, and especially to find parallels, to find simple images to help the actors understand. It was rather abstract, but then it had to be, for it was the true, the great theatre that Artaud wanted to show them.[17]

Financially as well as artistically *The Cenci* was a failure. After seventeen performances it was laid to rest. But not all the comments about the production were negative. The critic of *Comoedia*, for instance, remarked that the entire final scene was 'done in an intelligent way, offering real grandeur, and an indisputable plastic beauty', while Fortunat Strowski, in *Paris-Midi* suggested – correctly – that the play would 'count in theatre history'.[18]

Perhaps fleeing from the evident disaster of *The Cenci*, perhaps genuinely seeking the inspiration of another primal theatre to match the Balinese performances he had witnessed four years earlier, Artaud embarked for Mexico in January 1936. His experiences there were vivid, painful, and to him unforgettable. Mexico in the 1930s was a unique mix of the ancient and the modern. Politically, the country was split between the conservative Catholics and a Soviet-inspired Communist Party. Neither of them were much inclined to support the ancient native Mexican peoples, who were consequently repressed when they were not persecuted. And if the country was politically unstable, it was intellectually fevered. Sergei Eisenstein and D. H. Lawrence (separately) had recently visited and taken inspiration from its landscapes and its peoples; Diego Rivera and Frida Kahlo were living and working there; soon Lev Trotsky's flight from Stalin would bring him too to Mexico.

Artaud delivered a series of lectures, which appealed to the intelligentsia of the country (whose interest and approval he hugely enjoyed) and waited to acquire the government's permission, as well as enough money, to enable him to visit the Tarahumara people in the north of the country. In August his problems were solved and he set off for the north. The journey was searing. His supply of heroin had become exhausted, and without drugs he suffered both his headaches and horrible withdrawal symptoms. The weather was debilitatingly sultry. And near his destination he saw local men masturbating in what he (wrongly) took to be a subliminal attempt to keep him away. Finally he reached the land of the Tarahumara people, whose confidence he worked to obtain during his five-week stay, at the end of which he was able to participate in the peyote ritual.

Sick in body as well as in mind, and personally exhausted, the experience was both terrifying and enlightening. The key moment in the ritual arrived when he had to drink the hallucinatory drug, which he did, but apparently to little effect. Suddenly he felt isolated from the other participants and bombarded by the noise, the shouts and screams, the stamping feet, and the tintinnabulations of the drums in his ears. The shaman slashed his own flesh and dragged a horseshoe through the bleeding wound. Yet Artaud was simultaneously exhilarated: though he was not really a part of Tarahumara culture, he had left the false world, the world which had rejected *The Cenci*, behind. The peyote ritual perhaps answered his need for a new theatrical cauterisation.

What effect it had on the delicate balance of his mind is more debatable. He returned to France in November 1936 and desperately tried to break his drug addiction. He became engaged briefly to Cécile Schramm, perhaps trying to adopt a more balanced lifestyle. But in the spring of 1937 he discovered tarot cards and became fascinated and absorbed by them. He also published *A New Revelation of Being*, a strange, though extremely lucid, prophecy of doom. In August he travelled to Ireland, perhaps to find another primitive theatrical culture, though ostensibly to return St Patrick's cane, which he believed he had obtained. The visit was a disaster, as his deteriorating mental state led him into increasingly impossible situations, and in September he was arrested and deported back to France. While on the ship, he became involved in a fracas with two maintenance workers and was ignominiously forced into a straitjacket. When he arrived in his native land, he was hurried away to Quatremarre Sanatorium, and he spent the following nine years in institutions for the mentally disabled. His head was shaved, he was dressed in shabby institution clothes, and he was humiliated as a drug addict. He almost starved. The artist–poet was silenced.

In 1943, Artaud was 'discovered' in a horrifying institution in Ville-Evrard by the Surrealist poet, Robert Desnos, who managed to arrange for his transfer to Rodez. Here, he was put in the care of Dr Gaston Ferdière, and he began, slowly, to write again and even to sketch and communicate. What made him improve? According to Ferdière, it was the electro-convulsive treatment which he administered to Artaud. Artaud said the effect the therapy had on him was to 'make me despair, take my memory away, numb my thinking and my heart, make me absent and aware of myself as absent . . . like a dead man at the side of a living man.'[19] He received up to sixty shock treatments, and the controversy over what happened to Artaud at Rodez continues.

Electro-convulsive therapy (ECT)
This treatment is used in cases of severe depression, especially related to schizophrenia. It attempts to reproduce the effects of an epileptic fit, since epilepsy seems to be incompatible with schizophrenia. The patient is strapped to the table and electrodes are attached to his temples. An electric current is passed through the brain and causes in the patient, first, a continuous muscular contraction lasting up to fifteen seconds, then a series of violent spasms, and finally a deep sleep. The patient is usually conscious throughout the shock convulsions, which may be – but are not necessarily – extremely painful, and usually result in short-term memory loss.

ECT is still practised today, though it remains an extremely controversial form of treatment.

On 26 May 1946 he was adjudged fit for release, and a large number of Parisian intellectuals and artists joined the effort to find sufficient funds to enable him to live independently. The list of these financial supporters reads almost like a compendium of significant twentieth-century French artists, and includes André Gide, Paul Eluard, Jean-Paul Sartre, Pablo Picasso, Jean-Louis Barrault, Jean Dubuffet, Tristan Tzara, Marcel Duchamp, Alberto Giacometti, Georges Braque, and many others. Thanks to their efforts, Artaud was able to move to a small apartment in Ivry, on the outskirts of Paris, where he lived freely, though under unobtrusive supervision. It enabled him still sometimes to wander back to his old haunts on the Left Bank of the Seine, and partake of the artistic discussion, as well as the drugs, available there. Was he unhappy? Not according to the playwright, Arthur Adamov, who knew him then: 'He had an immense and unpredictable sense of humour, and the best way to pay homage to Artaud . . . is not to say how sad everything was for him but to laugh uproariously as one recalls the way he used to laugh at almost everything.'[20]

Yet much of what he wrote in his last two years, brilliant and terrifying, or even opaque, as it often was, was imbued with a furious despair, like the verse letter to Paule Thévenin, composed just over a week before his death:

> Paule, I am very sad and desperate,
> my body hurts all over, but in particular I get the feeling that people have been disappointed by my radio broadcast.
> . . .
> I will devote myself from now on
> exclusively
> to the theatre
> as I conceive it,
> a theatre of blood,
> a theatre which at each performance will stir
> something
> *in the body*
> of the performer as well as the spectator of the play,
> but actually
> the actor does not perform,
> he creates.
> Theatre is in reality the *genesis* of creation:
> It will come about.
> I had a vision this afternoon – I saw those who will come after me and who don't quite have a body yet because swine like those at the restaurant last night eat too much. There are those who eat too much and others who, like me, can no longer eat without *spitting*.
> Yours,
>
> Antonin Artaud[21]

Figure 5.3 Antonin Artaud in 1946.

There were failures too. He tried to give a public lecture (entitled 'The Return of Artaud the Fool') which would explain his life's problems and inspirations, but when he reached the platform, and in front of a distinguished audience, he dropped his notes, began to improvise a rambling attack on the medical people who administered his electric shock treatment, and finally fled from the stage. On the other hand, his visit to the popular van Gogh exhibition in Paris inspired him to write *Van Gogh: The Man Suicided by Society*, which won the Sainte-Beuve Prize in 1947. And he received a radio commission, for which he wrote the strangely compelling *In Order to Finish With the Judgement of God*, which was recorded, but then banned the day before it was due to be transmitted, 2 February 1948. (This is 'my radio broadcast' referred to in the poem above.) Artaud's despair at yet another crass and apparently insuperable obstacle in his artistic path is understandable. He was in any case in the advanced stages of cancer. On 4 March 1948 he was discovered dead in his bed in Ivry.

The key questions

'Life consists of burning up questions',[22] Artaud declared in 1925. Other translators have rendered the central image differently: 'Life is a conflagration of questions'; or, 'Life means burning up with questions'.[23]

The central question for Artaud was how to make theatre that would cauterise the fiercest experiences of life. This had not been possible through poetry, nor through the ephemeral excitement of the Surrealist movement. The nearest he had come to it was when he was acting. The theatre therefore seemed to Artaud to be the art form from which could be demanded what he sought. Through the theatre's physical reality he believed he could create with such physical intensity and force that he could reach the spiritual, metaphysical plane, and thus achieve a kind of purgation. In the physicality of theatre, pain or exaltation might be realised, erected, squeezed, without the full consequences which real life would inevitably extract. Yet the performance's influence on real life would be significant.

The key question therefore also involved the relationship between the stage and the audience. How could that vividness of experience, which infused the theatre performance, equally saturate the spectator's apprehension, his or her being and awareness? How could performer and spectator simultaneously experience the most harrowing sensations, how could they together burn with the plague and emerge from the experience purified, metamorphosed, new?

The likeness of this to ritual needs no stressing. In ritual, the shaman, or witch doctor, or priest, leads the initiate through a searing process, which he too simultaneously experiences, and they emerge from it with the initiate initiated. A change has been effected.

Thus Artaud sought a theatre which would be like 'an open door leading [the audience] where they never would have consented to go'.[24] He wanted a theatre in which he could 'feel the bodies of men and women – and I mean their *bodies* – throb and quiver in harmony with mine'. Such an audience would gain 'the impression that they are *running the risk* of something, by coming to our plays, [which would] make them responsive to a new concept of *Danger*'.[25]

Artaud asked: is such a theatre possible?

How could he make it?

Late in his life, he cried out in terrible poetry for the theatre he was still desperately seeking:

> The theatre is not this scenic display where a myth is developed
> virtually and symbolically

but a crucible of fire and true meat where anatomically,
by trampling bones, limbs and syllables,
bodies are remade . . .
The human body dies only because we have forgotten how to transform
   and change it.[26]

Artaud's answers

Nietzsche justified physical existence as 'an aesthetic phenomenon',
and went on to suggest that the 'aesthetic' as sensation was closely related
to the 'aesthetic' as art. For art, he believed, was ultimately a heightening of
sensation. Perhaps this notion lies somewhere behind Artaud's approach.

Nietzsche may also help to explain Artaud's self-belief. In spite of rebuffs
and ridicule, Artaud's Nietzschean 'will' seemed to license him as an artist
to flout bourgeois conformism. His mission became to penetrate the dark,
erotic ferocity of Dionysian ecstasy, such as Nietzsche described, which was
at its height when Dionysus and his bacchantes, a sort of audience, were
drunk with destructive and soul-scouring frenzy. Here perhaps were the first
buds of catharsis. Late in his life, in a fragment of poetry, he wrote that 'the
theatre of cruelty wants to make the eyelids dance in pairs with the elbows,
the kneecaps, the thighbones and the toes', adding that it also 'wants to be
seen'.[27] The physicality of the experience, and the sharing of it between
performer and spectator, are the heart and lungs of Artaud's thinking. In
1934, describing the effect he sought in his adaptation of Seneca's *Thyestes*,
he wrote: 'Moved by this paroxysm of violent physical action which no
sensibility can resist, the spectator's nervous system grows more sensitive;
he becomes more receptive to more rarefied emotional vibrations, to
sublime ideas of Greek myths that will try to reach him in this show by their
physical, combustive power.'[28] The catharsis, in other words, though its aim
is spiritual, is experienced as a physical sensation.

Hence Artaud's theatre was a 'Theatre of Cruelty'. To begin with,
'cruelty' referred to the physical impact of the work. In 1926 he compared
his ideal theatre to a police raid on a brothel:

> What could be more despicable or perniciously terrible than the sight
> of police going into action? Society recognises itself in these produc-
> tions, based on the equanimity with which it disposes of life and liberty.
> A police raid suggests the steps of a ballet. The policemen come and go.
> Mournful whistles rend the air. All their movements give rise to a kind
> of distressing solemnity. Little by little the noose tightens. We see the
> point of these movements, at first seemingly pointless; little by little

they take shape, and we also see the point in space about which they pivot. The door of an ordinary looking house suddenly opens and a gaggle of women come out of the house, filing along as though going to the slaughter-house. The plot thickens; the police net was not meant for a gang of shady characters but merely for a pack of women. We are keyed right up with astonishment. Never was a more elaborate setting followed by such a denouement. We are surely as guilty as these women, as cruel as these policemen. This is really total theatre. Well, this total theatre is the ideal. This anxiety, this guilt feeling, this victoriousness, this satisfaction, set the tone, feelings and state of mind in which the audience should leave our theatre, shaken and irritated by the inner dynamism of the show. This dynamism bears a direct relation to the anxieties and pre-occupations of their whole lives.[29]

There is some straining after effect here: the involvement of the 'audience' actually seems wholly unnecessary. Two years later, his attempt to conjure up a theatre which would answer the questions he posed was sharper, more persuasive: 'Everything which stems from the mind's *fertile* delusions, its sensory illusions, encounters between things and sensations which strike us primarily by their physical density, will be shown from an extraordinary angle, with the stench and the excreta of unadulterated cruelty, just as they appear to the mind.'[30] The physical aspect of the cruelty will be like Hamlet's mirror held up to the audience; but Artaud has noticed that only the physical appears in the mirror.

By the 1930s cruelty in Artaud's thought had taken on metaphysical and cosmic dimensions. Like Nietzsche, he wished to return to language's 'etymological origins', so that he could define cruelty as 'strictness, diligence, unrelenting decisiveness, irreversible and absolute determination'. Cruelty was both conscious and lucid, he asserted: it was 'hungering after life, cosmic strictness, relentless necessity, in the Gnostic sense of a living vortex engulfing darkness, in the sense of the inescapably necessary pain without which life could not continue.'[31] The cruelty, then, refuses to let up; it takes things as far as they will go, physically, and in this sense is inescapably merged into life. Consciousness and anguish for Artaud are one. Life exercises 'blind severity', or else it is not life. 'Cruelty is this severity and this life . . . and is practised in torture, trampling everything down, that pure inexorable feeling.'[32] Finally, Artaud declared in his Second Manifesto for the Theatre of Cruelty:

The Theatre of Cruelty was created in order to restore an impassioned convulsive concept of life to theatre . . . This cruelty will be bloody if need be, but not systematically so, and will therefore merge with the idea of a kind of severe mental purity, not afraid to pay the cost one must pay in life.[33]

The physical cruelty, the blood and gore which is perhaps too often associated with Artaud's theatre, should therefore be seen as a kind of image for metaphysical cruelty which Artaud fights to define. For him, Cenci was not simply a morally repugnant, physically violent father, he was to be seen as an image of cosmic cruelty. Near the end of the play, he cries out:

> Repent! Why? Repentance is in God's hands. It is up to him to rue my actions. Why did he make me the father of a being whom I desire so utterly? Before anyone condemns my crime, let them accuse fate. Are we free? Who can maintain we are free when the heavens are ready to fall on us? . . . I have opened the floodgates so as not to be engulfed. There is a devil within me destined to avenge the world's sins. No fate can prevent me carrying out my dreams now.[34]

Yet even this brief quotation suggests that Artaud cannot escape the link between cruelty and forbidden sexuality, the sadistic and sexual elements of cruelty. This is rarely mentioned by Artaud, yet his theatre also undoubtedly plays out common fantasies of rape and murder. *The Cenci*, as well as other plays he admired, such as *'Tis Pity She's a Whore*, explore this theme relentlessly.

Artaud's emphasis on the path *through* physicality to spirituality, however, is crucial in this regard. The process of performing the story takes us, actors and audience, to a new plane.

> My heroes . . . dwell in the realm of cruelty and must be judged outside of good and evil. They are incestuous and sacrilegious, they are adulterers, rebels, insurgents, and blasphemers. And that cruelty in which the entire work is bathed does not only result from the bloody story of the Cenci family, since it is not a purely corporal cruelty but a moral one; it goes to the extremity of instinct and forces the actor to plunge right to the roots of his being so that he leaves the stage exhausted. A cruelty which acts as well upon the spectator and should not allow him to leave the theatre intact, but exhausted, involved, perhaps transformed![35]

In other words, Artaud's Theatre of Cruelty is to embrace everyone, and 'myself first of all'.[36] The fierceness of its action, its cruelty, shatters the defences of performer and spectator alike, shatters the solitude of the self, and brings communion and personal metamorphosis. Such was Artaud's idea at least.

To express such a vision was not easy, and Artaud used a number of images to try to convey what he felt to be its urgency. Foremost among these, perhaps, was his likening of the theatre to the plague. The plague provided an experience for its victims which was physical, excruciatingly painful, socially and personally disruptive, and morally unbalancing. It was, as Artaud says, a 'kind of psychic entity' ('No one can say why the plague strikes a fleeing coward and spares a rake taking his pleasure with the corpses of the dead'),[37] which at the same time causes social institutions and social order to collapse. The medieval people who suffered the outbreaks of plague commonly saw it as a scourge sent from God to make them, through extreme physical and mental suffering, change their ways. Theatre, said Artaud, should do the same. Catharsis, like the plague, should be a physical experience, not one confined to the imagination. 'It seems', he says, 'as though a colossal abscess, ethical as much as social, is drained by the plague. And like the plague, theatre is collectively made to drain abscesses'.[38]

The unexpectedness of the plague, its sudden savageness, was also what Artaud wanted from theatre:

> Just like the plague, it reforges the links between what does and does not exist, between the virtual nature of the possible and the material nature of existence. It rediscovers the idea of figures and archetypal symbols which act like sudden silences, fermata, heart stops, adrenalin calls, incendiary images surging into our abruptly woken minds.[39]

Thus theatre disturbs our peace of mind, giving a new sense of freedom to our repressed subconscious, which also, of course, allows sexual fantasies a new freedom. In this belief, Artaud concurred with Freud, that the problems of twentieth-century society could often be traced to the repressions which individuals performed, voluntarily or involuntarily, and that human beings needed to let their true fears, desires, and wants see the light of day. This is where the perverse eroticism of *The Cenci*, for instance, derives its force, and why, in the plague itself, Artaud finds something sexually arousing: 'How are we to explain that upsurge of erotic fever among the recovered victims who, instead of escaping, stay behind, seeking out and snatching sinful pleasure from the dying or even the dead, half crushed under the pile of corpses where chance had lodged them?'[40]

Artaud likens his actor to the plague victim, for both are shaken by the paroxysms of the disease. Indeed, his own attempt to live the parallel created an appalled reaction from people who attended his 'lecture' on the subject at the Sorbonne in April 1933. As a revelation (he believed that performance, 'like the plague, is a revelation, urging forward the exterior-isation of a latent undercurrent of cruelty') the performance failed, but he insisted that the laughter and jeers of the audience sprang from the fact that they were dead to experience, and could only accept abstract explanations. The use of the word 'dead' was not a mistake: for Artaud's final assertion of the comparison between theatre and the plague was that both either kill their victims or purify them. For those who are purified,

> the effect of the theatre is as beneficial as the plague, impelling us to see ourselves as we are, making the masks fall and divulging our world's lies, aimlessness, meanness, and even two-facedness. It shakes off stifling material dullness which even overcomes the senses' clearest testimony, and collectively reveals their dark powers and hidden strength to men, urging them to take a nobler, more heroic stand in the face of destiny than they would have assumed without it.[41]

Artaud uses other images besides that of the plague to try to convey his idea of a theatre of magic, which would to transform its audience. He wanted spectators to come to his theatre 'as they would to a surgeon or dentist . . . knowing, of course, that they will not die, but . . . thoroughly convinced that we can make them cry out'.[42] He suggested theatre could affect spectators like a snake charmer's music which makes the serpent, willy-nilly, rise from the earth, and he dreamed of 'theatre bringing on trances just as the whirling Dervishes or the Assouas induce trances'.[43] Finally, Artaud compared theatre to alchemy, for both attempt to turn base matter into gold, and moreover, Artaud pointed out, both were 'virtual arts' – that is, neither contained their object within themselves. Each therefore could be regarded as a 'double' of life, and each seemed to reach for the sublime.

More potently than Artaud's other images, this seems to suggest the kinship of theatre to ritual. 'I conceive theatre as . . . a magical ceremony and I will make every effort to restore to it, by the latest up-to-date means, its ritualistic and primitive character in a manner which is understandable to all.'[44] The Dionysian rout was essentially a riotous ritual, and the appeal of ancient, or apparently 'primitive', performances was their ability to figure symbolically social or personal conflicts or tensions, to experience them intensely, and thus to exorcise them. Violent images on stage similarly might take on a symbolic form and thereby be nullified.

The Theatre and Its Double

This book contains Artaud's most profound and stimulating thoughts about the theatre. It was first published in 1938 by Gallimard, Paris, in an edition of only 400 copies, but was reissued in 1944, and has been in print virtually ever since.

The essays in it were almost all written between 1932 and 1935. They do not develop anything like a logical thesis, but form what might be thought of as a series of variations on Artaud's major theme – the Theatre of Cruelty.

The title of the book was the last thing to be decided, in 1936. From the ship which was taking him to Mexico, Artaud wrote to his editor: 'I believe I've found the right title for my book. It will be: THE THEATRE AND ITS DOUBLE since if theatre doubles life, life doubles the true theatre . . . and the Double of theatre is the real, which is not used by people today.'

The theatrical image is therefore a kind of 'double' of reality, a shadow, or an embodiment of the essence, just as the actor is a kind of 'double' of the human being. The underside of what we know, the subtext of what is spoken, are 'doubles' in Artaudian terminology, and also conjure magical elements, uncatchable, perhaps 'divine'. Man, made in the image of God, is in a sense His double; and theatre, made in the essential image of life, is life's double, just as life is theatre's double. Each is the *doppelganger* of the other. And for Artaud, *true* theatre was when the theatre merged with its double, life – the moment which could be described as 'the transfiguration of theatre'. It is of course impossible for life and theatre truly to coalesce, yet the notion of ritual suggests at least the *process* of unification, suggests that perhaps a momentary merging is possible.

If so, it must be *in the present*. Of all the arts, theatre is the one which most clearly exists *only* in the present. There is nothing to carry away from a theatre performance, it is only itself. Because of this, Artaud denounced the masterpieces of the past, and urged that we should have 'no more masterpieces'! In discussing Sophocles' *Oedipus Rex*, which might be thought ideal for a 'theatre of cruelty', he acknowledged that the subject is almost pedantically appropriate for the Theatre of Cruelty: there is 'the incest theme and the idea that nature does not give a rap for morality. And there are wayward powers at large we would do well to be aware of, call them *fate* or what you will. In addition there is the presence of a plague epidemic which is the physical incarnation of these powers.'[45] Yet Sophocles' play is not acceptable, because the rhythm of the piece is that of ancient Greece. Nowhere does its pulse beat to the time of contemporary life. It may be a 'masterpiece', but it is not 'in the present' – at least, not in the shape of the text we have, translated from Sophocles. This does not mean it could not be adapted of course.

Artaud's search was for a theatre which was burningly present, so that it could give his spectators a new sense of their fragile, fiery selves. It would operate somewhat like a dream, though 'theatre is like heightened waking' too.[46] Dreams, and waking too, happen only *in the present*. Like theatre, they only exist *now*.

Theatre practice

'One can be inspired by Artaud', commented Susan Sontag. 'One can be scorched, changed by Artaud. But there is no way of applying Artaud.'[47] And Roger Blin, who was very close to Artaud during the production of *The Cenci*, argued: 'No one can cite Artaud as their authority unless they have conducted a struggle similar to that which Artaud conducted on behalf of the body against thought and against God'.[48] The paradox which con-fronted Artaud was that, on the one hand, only in live theatre can the sweat and smell, the physical reality, of the performer be *directly* apprehended by the spectator; yet only in the live theatre is the repetition of rehearsal and performance which murders immediacy absolutely requisite.

Any investigation into the application of Artaud's ideas to a real con-crete theatre situation is therefore perhaps bound to stumble. It is further hindered because he himself never had adequate time or space in which to develop them through practical application and adaptation. Any attempt to suggest a comprehensive 'theatre practice' with Artaud's name stamped on it is therefore singularly fruitless. Yet there are enough practical ideas in his writings, as well as in the unsatisfactory attempts he did make at production, to be worth gathering together. When this is done, one finds a surprising amount which can be applied in actual theatre work, and if these do not make for a 'system' in Stanislavsky's sense, they at least point towards an unexpectedly coherent approach to theatre practice.

At base, these share fundamental features with what Artaud regarded as the 'primitive' theatre of Bali, 'with gestures and mime to suit all occasions in life'.[49] The Balinese theatre was one of direct experience, however highly choreographed it may have been, and it provided, in Artaud's perception, a physical experience which addressed the senses, not the intellect. The theatre space was a physical space, and it was to be filled in a theatrical, that is, a physical, way. Thus the theatrical 'sign' was stripped of its received content and reconstituted as a kind of 'birth'. Artaud's was 'what we might loosely call a *phenomenological theatre* (as opposed to semiological) in that it seeks to retrieve a naive perception of the thing – its "objective aspect" – before it was defined out of sight by language'.[50]

Text itself was perhaps the largest barrier for Artaud, which illuminates the problem of discussing his theatre practice, for descriptions, prescriptions, arguments all tend to form in words, as do the scripts of plays, even when they are scenarios without dialogue. One of the most surprising features of his version of *The Cenci* is its extreme 'wordiness'. Perhaps *The Cenci* was a mistake, the text somehow not what he intended, so that though we can draw some possible practical ideas from it, we must be careful how we treat it. The language he advocated was 'the language of theatre': 'This difficult, complex poetry assumes many guises; first of all it assumes those expressive means usable on stage such as music, dance, plastic art, mimicry, mime, gesture, voice inflection, architecture, lighting and decor.'[51] In other theatres, Artaud opined, these elements were under-valued, and it was assumed the text carried the meaning, but for the Theatre of Cruelty he proposed that:

> Every show will contain physical, objective elements perceptible to all. Shouts, groans, apparitions, surprise, dramatic moments of all kinds, the magic beauty of the costumes modelled on certain ritualistic patterns, brilliant lighting, vocal, incantational beauty, attractive harmonies, rare musical notes, object colours, the physical rhythm of the moves whose build and fall will be wedded to the beat of moves familiar to all, the tangible appearance of new, surprising objects, masks, puppets many feet high, abrupt lighting changes, the physical action of lighting stimulating heat and cold, and so on.[52]

Such a theatre requires, first, a large performance space which Artaud came to imagine as a sort of flexible theatre-in-the-round, but with the audience in the centre, and the action pitched around them. The seats would swivel and turn, following the action, which would take place as much in the vertical plane, on raised scaffold stages, or galleries running round the performance space high on the whitewashed walls, as in the horizontal. Artaud suggests an aircraft hangar for his theatre, but with features reminiscent of Tibetan temples. This suggests a potentially dynamic physical setting for the drama, and indeed even in the disappointing *Cenci* script there are directions implying this:

> *The scene resembles* The Marriage Feast at Cana *by Veronese, but is much more savage. Purple drapes flap in the breeze and fall back in heavy folds.*

> *Suddenly, as one of the drapes is lifted, a violent orgy furiously bursting into*
> *action is revealed behind it in perspective. All the bells of Rome ring out, but*
> *muted and in time with the banquet's spinning rhythm.*[53]

The spectator was to be overwhelmed.

Costume too was to be active. Artaud had been excited by the costumes in the Balinese performance, which he referred to as 'dazzling', and suggested that their hieroglyph-like lines 'united' the actors 'with unknown natural perspectives', encircling 'their abstract sliding walk' and emphasising 'the strange criss-crossing of their feet'. Moreover, he went on, 'the folds of these robes curving above their buttocks', held the performers 'as if suspended in the air, as if pinned onto the backdrop, prolonging each of their leaps into flight'.[54] Whether such robes were to be taken 'in an immediate sense', or as something more evocative, may not perhaps have been entirely clear in Artaud's mind, and the costumes for the production of *The Cenci* were disappointingly conventional. They were like much historical drama, though Cenci himself (in Hamlet black) and some of the other men had their nerves or the muscles on their pectorals and diaphragm outlined on their costumes in grey stitching.

Artaud's *ideas* about costume were more stimulating than his actual practice, and relate closely to his ideas about masks and, indeed, puppet substitutes for people. The costume is a kind of double of the actor, and

Figure 5.4 The Cenci, Theatre des Folies-Wagram, Paris, 1935. Antonin Artaud as
     Cenci, in black, centre.

perhaps the role, or the conception of the role, is to be found somewhere in the interface between the two. Or in the way they split apart. In his 1934 scenario, *The Conquest of Mexico*, at the climax of the drama,

> Montezuma himself seems to split in two, appears double; with some pieces of him half-lit; others dazzling with light, with manifold hands sticking out of his costume, with faces painted on his body like a multiple meeting point of consciousness, but from within Montezuma's conscience all the questions are transmitted to the crowd.[55]

Practically, this is perhaps unrealisable, but it reminds one of the idea Artaud proposed to Louis Jouvet, when he assisted with the latter's production of Alfred Savoir's *The Village Baker* in 1932:

> What would you say to using about twenty dummies five metres high, of which six would represent the most typical characters of the play, with their prominent features, suddenly appearing and trudging along solemnly to the tune of a military march, which would be bizarre, full of Oriental consonances, in the midst of light signals and flares. Each of these personages could have a badge and one of them could carry the arch of triumph on his shoulders.
>
> The whole crowned by a halo of rags, stuffed to bursting point, with podgy limbs, and floating the traditional laurel leaf over the heads of the heroes. They would march enveloped in gigantic flags which would hang from the sky. I see them crossing the stage diagonally from the back right hand corner to the front left hand corner, but marching at a certain height, as though they were crossing a bridge . . . I would boldly rig out the better or less known faces with superb moustaches and fine black beards.[56]

Jouvet did not take up Artaud's idea, but we can see here, as well as in the strange dismemberment of Montezuma, developments of ideas first propounded in the cruel little Surrealist drama, *The Spurt of Blood*.

Puppets, especially puppets greater than life size, became a favourite device in Artaud's theatrical imagination, particularly after seeing the *barong* of the Balinese theatre.

> To visualise the Barong one has to think of a sort of Oriental dragon. Speaking generally his back is at the level of a man's head. His flanks are made of very rich swags of hair or cut strips of material. On his back are plates of cut leather. He has a splendid arched tail. But his most remarkable feature is his vast, elaborate carved mask, with its

lavish leather surroundings, all worn in front of the wearer's breast, so giving a characteristic hunched-shoulder quality. He has human legs showing below this completely inhuman and fantastic upper part. Most Barongs are four-legged, and are animated like a pantomime animal by two men whose bodies are concealed inside the Barong and whose legs – in horizontally-striped trousers – and bare feet appear below.[57]

In the Theatre of Cruelty, 'puppets, huge masks, [and] objects of strange proportions' are included prominently in the theatre's proposed armoury and, significantly, they 'appear by the same right as verbal imagery'.[58] Indeed, in the proposed new theatrical configuration with the audience in the centre of the performance space, and the action happening around them, puppets and masks are significant parts of the overwhelming whole:

> By eliminating the stage, shows . . . will extend over the whole audi-
> torium and will scale the walls from the ground up along slender
> catwalks, physically enveloping the audience, constantly immersing
> them in light, imagery, movements and sound. The set will consist of
> the characters themselves, grown as tall as gigantic puppets, landscapes
> of moving lights playing on objects, or continually shifting masks.[59]

The effectiveness of puppets and masks was partly conditional on how they were lit. Alfred Jarry pointed out how light helps the expressiveness of the mask: a mask lit from below communicates a different message from that which is obtained if a beam is directed from, say, one side. Artaud described the different *quality* of light in a cave from that on a windy hilltop, and went on to point out that light contains its own force, influence, and suggestive-ness. In his notes to Jouvet about *The Village Baker*, he suggests a lighting effect probably impossible at the time – a 'winged flickering'.[60] By the time he came to write the First Manifesto for the Theatre of Cruelty, he was seeking 'oscillating light effects, new ways of diffusing lighting in waves, sheet lighting like a flight of fire arrows', and he was determined that light should be an effective tool in the proposed theatre: 'Fineness, density and opacity factors must be reintroduced into lighting, so as to produce special tonal properties, sensations of heat, cold, anger, fear and so on.'[61] Colour, especially blood red, seems to have appealed to Artaud almost for its own sake, but he also looked for colour changes, sometimes imperceptible, sometimes violent, as well as flashing and dimming lights, directional spots, and more. He thought about a new sort of projector to achieve effects impossible in the 1930s, and only now becoming achievable, and effects which would attain hallucinatory qualities. Practically speaking, the best he was able to manage was his idea of slide projections on Jouvet's stage, which actors could walk through to unsettle the spectator.

For it is the actor in Artaud's theatre who is the crux and crossroads. 'The actor is both a prime factor, since the show's success depends on the effectiveness of his acting, as well as a kind of neutral, pliant factor, since he is rigorously denied any individual initiative.'[62] Sardonically Artaud adds, 'this is a field where there are no exact rules'. Nevertheless, in the Artaudian theatre, the actor is he who *is* the pain, exaltation, fear, lust, as well as the one who expresses it. The secrets of the soul are made material in the actor, who, in another metaphor much favoured by Artaud, is the 'hieroglyph' used to evoke abstract meaning, or mood, or inklings of things, images of what cannot have corporeal reality. If the world is the theatre's double, the human being is the double of the actor.

Artaud's own performances showed him capable of sublime heights, though frequently his intensity and awkwardness seem to have impeded his abilities. As a young man in Dullin's theatre, he seems to have been a bold, original, and intense actor, too stiff physically perhaps, but with plenty of potential. One contemporary described him sweeping up the steps to Charlemagne's throne in *Huon de Bordeaux*, and suddenly standing up 'in an imposing attitude which impressed everyone',[63] while Dullin himself recalled Artaud 'playing a sort of incarnation of the spirit of evil, with the name Urdemalas. I can still hear him pronouncing this name as he brandishes his whip.'[64] His physical stiffness, combined perhaps with the intensity of his fiery eyes, led him to be nicknamed 'the barbed wire actor' at this period. Films show him to have an unexpected and powerful stillness, and as Marat in *Napoleon*, he possessed 'an extraordinary command of facial distortion. When Marat is murdered in his bath, this power is dispelled, and Artaud's face becomes a startlingly composed deathmask.'[65] Most commentators seemed to think that his last stage performance, in the ill-fated *Cenci*, was at best miscalculated, since it emphasised many of his faults and lost his best qualities, though Raymond Latour in *Paris-Midi* praised 'Antonin Artaud's impeccable diction, impetuosity, brutality [and] ardour' which hit the audience 'in the face with the most searing words and passionate phrases, like slaps or battle-cries'.[66] In his final radio broadcast, the last time he appeared in any form before the public, and made only months before his death, he uttered

> his weird and violent words and . . . his wild, piercing, inarticulate cries – outbursts of such a deep intensity of anguish beyond speech that they freeze the blood: it is as though all human suffering, mankind's sum-total of dammed-up, frustrated rage, torment and pain had been compressed into these tortured, primal shrieks.[67]

Artaud himself perhaps never – or rarely – managed what his mentor Jarry advocated, and what the Balinese theatre exemplified – acting with the whole self. The Balinese performers, he said, looked like 'moving hieroglyphs',[68] and he wrote to André Gide about the same time that in the Theatre of Cruelty, 'movements, poses, bodies of characters will form or dissolve like hieroglyphs'.[69] His direction achieved something of this in *The Cenci*: in the storm scene, the actors spun like tops across the stage, and later the fearful Beatrice slid away, slowly, terrified, her back to the wall. This may remind us of the Balinese theatre, in which warriors entered 'the mental forest, slithering in fear'.[70] Movement was regarded by Artaud as the visible sign of an invisible language, and he experimented with it as much as his limited opportunities permitted. He liked group movement: actors moving in unison, as well as symbolic, artificial groupings, and the freezing of specific poses. In his unproduced scenario, *The Philosopher's Stone*, while

> The doctor [is] all tensed in a grotesque attitude of scientific curiosity, like a giraffe or heron, his chin exaggeratedly craning forward . . . Isabelle, who is dazzled by the appearance of Harlequin, assumes the form and pose of a weeping willow: she mimes a sort of dance of ecstasy and astonishment, sits, brings her hands together, holds them in front of her with timidly charming and moving gestures.[71]

The following moments provide an almost classic opportunity for finding the essence of movement as hieroglyph:

> This scene could be played in slow motion with a sudden lighting change. Harlequin, monstrous and bandy-legged, trembles (slowly) in all his limbs, the doctor advances (slowly) towards him, mad with joy and scientific curiosity, seizes Harlequin by the scruff of the neck and pushes him into the wings towards his experimental laboratory – while Isabelle, who, with sudden rapture, has felt all the wonders of true love, slowly faints.[72]

For all its problems, some audience members at *The Cenci* noticed that the movement sometimes had some of the qualities of dance.

As significant as movement in Artaud's new theatre language was its close relation, gesture. 'Gesture' was the new theatre language's 'substance and mind or, if you like, its alpha and omega'.[73] The Balinese theatre had a well-defined kind of gesture: angular, unexpected, and jerky, though often also highly conventional, which to Artaud was intensely suggestive and penetrative. At the time of the Alfred Jarry Theatre, he suggested that gesture should be infused with 'the fatality of life' and 'the mysterious happenings that occur in dreams',[74] and writing about *The Cenci* nearly three years later he asserted that 'gesture for me is just as important as what we call language, because gesture is a language in its own right'.[75] Artaud conceived therefore that gesture could embody ideas and attitudes; indeed that gestures were hieroglyphic in quality, even though it was the whole actor which formed the hieroglyph. But gesture was always distinguished from mime as imitation: it made its own distinctive contribution.

In practical terms, the epitome of theatrical gesture was provided for Artaud by a performance by Jean-Louis Barrault of a horse in an entertainment entitled *Around A Mother* in June 1935. As so often, and infuriatingly, Artaud's description is not particularly precise, but he gives us something of its 'magic':

> Great, youthful love, youthful vigour, spontaneous, lively ebullience flows among the exact moves, the stylised, calculated gesticulation like the warbling of song birds through colonnades of trees in a magically arranged forest.
>
> Here, in this religious atmosphere, Jean-Louis Barrault improvises a wild horse's movements, and we suddenly see he has turned into a horse.
>
> His show proves the irresistible operations of gesture, it triumphantly demonstrates the importance of gesture and spatial movement. Stage perspective is restored to a position of importance it should never have lost. Finally he turns the stage into a living, moving place . . . What Jean-Louis Barrault has accomplished is theatre.[76]

After the performance, Artaud and Barrault left the theatre together and galloped down the boulevard, each an imaginary horse, intoxicated by the power of gesture!

If gesture was language, words were replaced by noise, or screams. Artaud's only sustained attempt to codify training exercises was directed towards vocalisation. He emphasised the use of the diaphragm, the chest, and the head, first in a series of breathing exercises, then as the springboard for utterance. By mastering breathing, he suggested, the actor developed the means to master emotion, and his exercises moved from breathing to shouts and on to rhythm. As a young actor, Artaud had apparently revelled in many of the exercises Dullin had set his youthful company, including animal impersonations (which he later employed with actors himself), as well as exercises in the imagination, such as being a wind or a fire, to re-enact a dream, or even a simple everyday occurrence. For Artaud, such work was valuable because it forced the actor to delve into his own sensibility, and to find ways to embody secret, unformulated feelings, and to do so without premeditation.

Uncovering the most intense, deepest self was part of the problem, and the necessity, of acting. In *The Philosopher's Stone*, he writes:

> The actress must show a mixture of disgust and resignation in the impulse of her movement towards him (the doctor). Behind her coaxings, her flirtations, she shows silent rage, her caresses end in slaps, in scratches. She pulls his moustache with sudden, unexpected movements – rains blows on his stomach, steps on his toes as she stands to kiss his lips.[77]

To manage such transitions, such double actions, requires acting which is not based in psychology. Artaud noted that the Balinese actors strove for the essence of the character, not for any sort of realism, and they tended towards stock types. In *The Philosopher's Stone* the main characters are the Doctor, Harlequin, and Isabelle and, as we have noted, Cenci appealed to Artaud because he seemed to suggest some greater evil than a single bad man. Jarry, too, had worked from stock figures, and like Artaud had been interested not just in wicked types but in clown figures too.

Clowns and comedy provide a sometimes forgotten, but vital, element in Artaud's theatre. 'In spite of all his illness, he always retained an extraordinary sense of humour; one of the people with whom you laughed most', according to Arthur Adamov. For Artaud humour was a disruptive, destructive, liberating force, childish and unexpected. 'In one of the Marx Brothers' films', he recalled, 'a man, thinking he is about to take a woman in his arms, ends up with a cow which moos'.[78] The Marx Brothers' humour embodied one form of anarchy for Artaud, a revolt against convention and decorum, which yet possessed a kind of 'fatalism' which 'slipped in … like the revelation of a dreadful illness across a face of absolute beauty'.[79] One thinks of Groucho's version of the classic clown dance in *Animal Crackers* (probably Artaud's favourite Marx Brothers' film) or Harpo suddenly standing on his head in the same film, his unexpected leap onto the maid's back, his plonking his leg in someone else's hand. The effect is, in Artaud's words, 'a kind of fiery anarchy'.[80]

The Marx Brothers

The five Marx Brothers – Chico, Harpo, Groucho, Gummo, and Zeppo – were born in the late nineteenth century, and were pushed into show business by their ambitious mother. They toured vaudeville theatres across America, and in 1915 their act triumphed at the Palace Vaudeville Theatre, New York.

In May 1924 they appeared again in New York, this time with a full-length musical, *I'll Say She Is*, and followed this with *The Cocoanuts* in 1925 and *Animal Crackers* in 1928.

These last two became the first films they made, and were followed by nine more, the last (*Love Happy*) being completed in 1949. Long before this, Zeppo and Gummo had dropped out of the troupe, but the other three – Chico, Harpo, and Groucho – remain among cinema's most loved and admired comic performers.

The Spurt of Blood can be seen on one level as a sort of horrific farce, and the scenario for *The Philosopher's Stone* uses characters from the *commedia dell'arte* for scenes of clownish dismemberment and childbirth. The 1929 prospectus for the Alfred Jarry Theatre lays particular emphasis on the intention to use humour:

> Humour will be the only red or green signal to light the plays and to indicate to the audience if the road is clear, whether they can shout out or shut up, laugh out loud or on the quiet. The Alfred Jarry Theatre reckons to become a theatre for all sorts of humour.
>
> To sum up, we intend our subject matter to be: *actuality* in every sense of the word. Our means: humour in all forms. Our aims: *total laughter*, laughter extending from paralysed slavering to convulsed, side-holding sobbing.[81]

One product of humour – as the Marx Brothers consistently demonstrated, and as Alfred Jarry's *Ubu Roi* makes plain – is the destruction of sober sense. Interestingly enough, in Balinese theatre, while the priests and heroes use an archaic form of speech, which the local spectators can barely understand, the clowns speak in contemporary colloquialisms. One of Artaud's most cherished ambitions was to destroy the power of words in the theatre. He insisted that the art of theatre should not depend on words or language, which makes the script of *The Cenci* doubly surprising, since it is so wordy. He advocates actors voicing other sounds – barks, screams, screeches, growls and howls, humming, buzzing, snoring, and whistling. In *The Philosopher's Stone*, Isabelle's 'desires [and] unconscious yearnings are conveyed by vague sighs, whimpers and moans',[82] and he specifically commended the Balinese 'syncopated inflections formed at the back of the throat'.[83] In a performance he arranged in July 1947, while Marthe Robert read some of his texts about the Tarahumaras of Mexico, Artaud himself, invisible to the audience, gave vent to a medley of screams and wild noises.

Alfred Jarry

Alfred Jarry was born in 1873. At school he and his friend, Henri Morin, created an absurd marionette show satirising their teacher, M. Hebert. This was to develop into *Ubu Roi*. It created an unprecedented scandal. After the first word ('Shittr!'), the performance was stalled for twenty minutes, and the audience's catcalling and boos continued throughout the evening. But it made Jarry famous, and by liberating the French theatre from Zola-esque naturalism, it irrevocably altered the course of French drama.

Jarry himself went on to create 'Pataphysics', the 'science of imaginary solutions', and tried to live as Ubu, but, alcoholic and poverty-stricken, he left Paris in 1906 and died in 1907, aged thirty-four.

He abhorred the utilitarian use of words and the voice, and proposed instead 'incantation'. He believed the voice could best be used as an instrument to produce new sounds, harmonies, and rhythms. Thus *The Spurt of Blood* opens:

Young man:	I love you and everything is fine.
Girl [in a quickened, throbbing voice]:	You love me and everything is fine.
Young man [lower]:	I love you and everything is fine.
Girl [lower still]:	You love me and everything is fine.[84]

In *The Philosopher's Stone*, we find:

> Harlequin says the following words when he introduces himself:
> 'I HAVE COME TO HAVE THE PHILOSOPHER'S STONE TAKEN OUT OF ME.'
> *Increasing the length of pause after each part of the sentence, in a quavering, accented voice.*
> *A short pause after 'I have come'; long after 'stone'; longer still and indicated by a stop in movement on 'of me'.*
> *In a hoarse tone of voice, delivered from the back of the throat but at the same time high-pitched: the voice of a hoarse eunuch.*[85]

Artaud saw the voice simply as one weapon in the dramatic armoury, one instrument in the theatrical orchestra. It was no more and no less than an independent concrete element in its own right.

To augment the human voice, Artaud suggested new musical or other instruments, perhaps ancient or forgotten ones, surges of sound, diminuendos, tom-toms, percussion, gongs, throbbing sounds in hypnotic rhythms, whistles, and more. In *The Cenci*, besides employing an electronic keyboard (probably one of the first times this recently invented instrument was so used), Artaud included sound effects for footsteps, rhythmic stamping, a thunderstorm, crashing waves, a ticking clock, random bangs, an organ, chiming bells, and factory noises.

It is obvious that a theatre such as this has little time for conventional playwrights. Yet each time he founded, or tried to found, a theatre, Artaud was confronted with the need for a repertoire. He shouted his desire for 'no more masterpieces', yet sought certain types of play which, if treated as examples of the Theatre of Cruelty, might act on the spectator 'in the same way our dreams react on us, and reality reacts on our dreams'.[86] Among the classics, Artaud liked the work of Seneca, and especially the bloody *Thyestes*. A number of Elizabethan and Jacobean plays appealed to him, such as the comic and macabre *Arden of Feversham*. He wondered about Shakespeare, stripped of his language, but using theatrical images to create his situations, characters, and action, and the revenge tragedies of Webster, Tourneur, Middleton, and especially Ford's *'Tis Pity She's a Whore*. Buchner's *Woyzeck*, *A Dream Play* and *The Ghost Sonata* by Strindberg, and plays by Apollinaire and Maeterlinck also interested him at various times. He was of course particularly associated with Alfred Jarry and *Ubu Roi*, and the plays of his contemporary and fellow Surrealist, Roger Vitrac, and he also contemplated making plays himself using stories like that of Rabbi Simeon and of Bluebeard, to say nothing of stories from de Sade. His own works were disappointingly few. There is the early *Spurt of Blood*, and *Acid Belly* which he produced at the Alfred Jarry Theatre. His unfinished scenarios also include *The Philosopher's Stone*, *There Is No More Firmament*, and *The Conquest of Mexico*. *The Cenci*, of course, was finished, and there may be a few others which have been lost, including *The Torture of Tantalus*, apparently dealing not only with Tantalus, but also with Atreus and Thyestes, and perhaps incorporating Mexican ritual.

But the Artaudian theatre revolved around the director, or theatre artist. 'In this programme there will be no plays . . . So the director here becomes author, i.e. creator.'[87] And in terms of his own practice he insisted on being the sole director, the only creative artist in the production. When Jean-Louis Barrault suggested that they work together, Artaud politely but firmly declined: 'I do not believe that a collaboration between us is possible . . . I DON'T WANT the show, directed by myself, to have the slightest nudge or wink which doesn't belong to me.'[88]

As a director Artaud was imaginative and original. His staging of Vitrac's plays at the Alfred Jarry Theatre was generally commended as fluid and arresting, and his *A Dream Play* unexpectedly comic. In these productions he did not plan the 'blocking' in advance, nor did he fix in his own mind how the lines were to be spoken. On the other hand, one actor recalled,

> At the first rehearsal, Artaud rolled around on the stage, assumed a falsetto voice, contorted himself, howled, and fought against logic, order, and the 'well-made' approach. He forbade anyone to pay too close attention to the 'story' at the expense of its spiritual significance. He sought desperately to translate the 'truth' of the text, and not the words. It was only after he felt that he had found the truth, which his interior voyage had disclosed to him, that he fixed it meticulously, often with amazing profundity.[89]

However, his understanding of the Balinese theatre led him to develop a more dictatorial role for the director (or producer, as the position used to be called): the Balinese theatre, he wrote, 'triumphantly demonstrate[s] the absolute superiority of the producer whose creative ability *does away with words*', and 'This theatre does away with the playwright to the advantage of what in Western theatre jargon we call the producer. But the latter becomes a kind of organiser of magic, a master of holy ceremonies.'[90] It was after this that Artaud began to demand 'A company of actors . . . who will interpret *meticulously* the directions I will give them; for, of course, we will only be able to reach the mathematical precision we are attempting in these productions if the actors are prepared to follow scrupulously the directions I will give them.'[91] This suggests the dictatorial methods Artaud was to employ for the production of *The Cenci*. According to Roger Blin, who was his assistant on the production, he

> used to hold a large notebook in his lap and have some coloured crayons nearby – one colour for each member of the cast – and he used to say to me: 'Make a note of everything I say' and opposite the text I had to draw diagrams of the movements which he indicated for each character.[92]

Now, the notebook seems to resemble nothing so much as Stanislavsky's production plan for *The Seagull*.[93] At any rate, the practice seems to have led to what Artaud called 'a clockwork precision' in the production, and 'a spatial geometry' on stage. It may also account for the fact that the production was, at a significant level, sadly lifeless.

It seems that in this, his final stagework, Artaud's extreme anxiety to put into practice all the ideas and principles he had formulated during the previous barren period when he had no stage to work on, had dammed up his genuine theatrical creativity, and brought the Theatre of Cruelty apparently to a sorry end.

Artaud after Artaud

It might have been expected that after his death, the fiery – if apparently impractical – visions of Antonin Artaud would be confined to history's more fascinating might-have-beens. In fact, since 1948, Artaud's ideas seem to have chimed with something theatre practitioners of all kinds have sought, and many later developments in the theatre plainly carry his stamp.

His influence was perhaps first discerned in play-writing. Samuel Beckett, Eugène Ionesco, and Jean Genet all denied Artaud's influence, and perhaps they were telling the truth; but Charles Marowitz's passionate exclamation – 'If Jean Genet had not come along, the manifestos of Antonin Artaud might have seemed like so much metaphysical bosh'[94] – still carries more conviction than wishful thinking. It is perhaps ironic that literary texts like *The Lesson* or *Deathwatch* or *Offending the Audience* by Peter Handke should seem to exemplify the anti-literary theories of Antonin Artaud, but it is as much in the stage imagery developed by these 'Absurdist' dramatists – the room with the tiny windows and the dustbins and the wheelchair in Beckett's *Endgame* or the ever-growing corpse in Ionesco's *Amédée* – and as much in the dangerous games in Genet's *The Maids* or the Surrealist eroticism of Arrabal's *Fando and Lis*, that Artaud's influence is felt. At the other end of the scale from these tense, intense Absurdist microcosms, Peter Shaffer's epic *The Royal Hunt of the Sun* includes fierce and grating Artaudian moments as the proto-Tarahumarian lord of the sun, Atahualpa, is crushed by the Spanish conquistador, Pizarro. This play, like most of the others mentioned, also possesses something of Artaud's anarchic and subversive humour. Later plays, such as some by Edward Bond, Caryl Churchill, and Sarah Kane, probably owe much to Artaud too, though other influences are at work in these plays as well.

The most influential theatre director to explore Artaud's ideas practically is Peter Brook. According to Sellin, Brook 'misinterpreted' Artaud's ideas,[95] a claim occasionally repeated since. But it is based on a misunderstanding of Brook's work. As Charles Marowitz, his partner in the 'Theatre of Cruelty' season at the Royal Shakespeare Company in 1964, pointed out at the time, 'we are not trying to recreate the theatre of Artaud . . . we're just using him as a springboard into new areas'.[96]

Peter Brook

Peter Brook was born in London in 1925 of Russian descent. In the 1940s and 1950s he staged a series of highly acclaimed productions in Birmingham, Stratford, London, and New York.

When the Royal Shakespeare Company (RSC) was formed in 1961, Brook became an associate director, and his restless, iconoclastic searching for new theatrical means led the company to an eminent position in world theatre. In particular, his exploration of Artaud's ideas led to a number of widely admired productions, and informed his book, *The Empty Space*, where he developed his idea of the Artaudian 'holy theatre'. By the 1970s, Brook had left the RSC in order to run his own experimental International Centre for Theatrical Research at Les Bouffes du Nord, Paris, where he worked constantly to push forward the boundaries of what Artaud called 'the language of theatre'.

This Theatre of Cruelty season consisted of twelve weeks' work with a group of a dozen actors, with an average age of twenty-four, who were asked to improvise, play, and disrupt their own certainties. In contrast to Artaud, Brook as a director was instinctively non-tyrannical, and the work was not always 'successful' in conventional terms. It also left Brook open to attack from theatrical practitioners with less daring, and less humility. After twelve weeks, the group 'showed' some of the work done in January and February 1964. This included what was probably the first production ever of Artaud's *The Spurt of Blood*, which, however interesting as a piece of theatrical archaeology, was not particularly well received. (It has been done comparatively frequently since, by college and similar groups, and most of his other extant scenarios, and even *The Cenci*, have also been staged several times in the last thirty or forty years.) More significant in the season was the presentation of John Arden and Margaretta D'Arcy's brilliant fantasy on education, sexuality, and militarism, *Ars Longa, Vita Brevis*. But the deepest effect was probably created by Glenda Jackson's performance in Brook's own *Public Bath*.

To the accompaniment of whistles, cries and seedy night club jazz, a girl (Christine Keeler figure) enters and performs a striptease, while behind her a judge intones her sentence, and in front a succession of distinguished gentlemen are introduced to her for purposes of fun and flagellation. The striptease over, she descends to the forestage, is bathed in a hip-bath under the stern supervision of three wardresses, hair inspected for lice, and re-clothed in prison garb. As she enters her cell, humiliated and deprived of her human dignity, the tone changes, and we slide imperceptibly into a realization that we are watching an eager public revel in a private grief. She becomes Jackie Kennedy, and the same distinguished gentlemen are introduced, now offering condolences. As she kneels before the coffin (the bath) before it is slowly borne away, the effect is shattering.[97]

Despite some negative comments – 'The performance that I saw was a vast disappointment', remarked one academic critic[98] – the work was to inform all Brook's best productions over the next thirty or more years.

Immediately afterwards, at the Royal Shakespeare Company, he directed Peter Weiss's Artaud-influenced play, known as *The Marat-Sade*, which used actors from the 'Theatre of Cruelty' season to create an agonising and unforgettable impression, with a suavely threatening de Sade, a pedantic despot, Marat, intellectualising in his bath, unpredictable, comic, and horrifying lunatics, the whipping of de Sade with the actress's hair, the use of bright paint for blood, incantation and song, strident music and jangling percussion. Complementing this was the 1966 anti-Vietnam War play, *US*, developed as Artaud had advocated from a scenario not a script. In 1968 Brook followed another Artaud dream by choosing to direct Seneca's *Oedipus* at the National Theatre in London, in a version by Ted Hughes, and starring John Gielgud and Irene Worth. Later, he created *Orghast* (1971) with an international company in Iran, and *The Ik* (1975), both of which were created through the development of Artaudian images, stripped of discursive language. What may have been the most significant single achievement in Peter Brook's career was the 1985 production of *The Mahabharata*, a three-part, twelve-hour version of the epic which had formed the content of the Balinese Theatre performance seen in 1931 by Antonin Artaud in Paris. Any description of Brook's *Mahabharata* reveals the Artaudian theatricality that was everywhere apparent.

A scarlet-faced figure of death, a Kathakali/martial-art hybrid, dances around the thrusts of an opponent in slow-motion, then floats off into darkness with tiny steps, his propulsion apparently generated by the hissing blades of a spring sword he whirls around his head. Arjuna's unwitting confrontation with Shiva is both disturbing and comic (the division between the two is often blurred in Brook's work). The young warrior's arrows are no match for the deity's own prodigious and elemental powers – he manipulates two tiny flags whose movement through the air shatters the silence like the muffled echo of a distant thunderclap. During the frenzied, stylised battle scenes of [Part Three] while actors openly toss handfuls of ochre powder into the air (the dust and smoke of battle) a percussive score improvised by musicians visible to one side underlines the starkly disciplined ensemble manoeuvres and sudden freezes. Our perspective is multi-directional, continually evolving, as in a film.[99]

It must be emphasised that this is not Artaud's theatre, it is Brook's. But it is questionable whether such brilliance would have been possible – at least quite like this – without Artaud.

The other internationally renowned director usually associated with Artaud's ideas is the Pole, Jerzy Grotowski. His 'Poor Theatre' was a theatre of ceremony in which the actors' physicality, as well as their spirit and behaviour, was intended to impact directly on the spectator's psyche. Setting the action all round the deliberately small, privileged audience, Grotowski aimed to reduced the importance of words and to bridge the usual 'body/think' divide. Thus, in his famous production of *The Constant Prince* (1966), he stripped the text down as Artaud had proposed to do with Elizabethan tragedies, and his leading actor, Ryszard Cieslak, was genuinely humiliated, put in danger, made to feel the pain of the staged flagellation.

In France, Artaud's influence was probably mediated by two practitioners who worked with him in the 1930s, Roger Blin and Jean-Louis Barrault. Barrault declared *The Theatre and Its Double* to be the most important theatre book of the twentieth century, and though he was no slavish imitator, and indeed had other theatrical tastes and influences, several of his productions, such as his 1974 *Le Bourgeois Gentilhomme* at the Comédie-Française, bore the marks of Artaud's ideas, as did his more experimental work at the Gare d'Orsay. Blin probably became best known for his work with the 1950s avant-garde writers: he directed many of the first productions of Beckett's plays, as well as work by Adamov and Genet. Jean Vilar was another influenced by Artaud, as was Ariane Mnouchkine, whose *1789* at the Théâtre du Soleil set the audience in the centre of a series of stages, with the action flitting from one to another round the hall. Victor Garcia did something similar in his production of Arrabal's *Cemetery for Abandoned Cars*, while Jérôme Savary developed *Le Grand Magic Circus* with its spectacular effects, its ritualistic intensity, and its high-voltage energy along consciously Artaudian lines. Less visible, but certainly no less influential, was Jacques Lecoq, whose International Theatre School explored the body in space in many ways which can be seen to be consciously Artaudian. Henri Chopin too, in his development of 'sound poetry', acknowledged Artaud's influence, especially the last radio piece, *In Order to Finish with the Judgment of God*.

Jean-Louis Barrault

Born in 1910, Jean-Louis Barrault first came to prominence when Artaud hailed his performance in *Around a Mother* in 1935.

During the Second World War, Barrault joined the Comédie-Française, where he established his pre-eminence in French theatre, acting in and directing major classics. After the war he formed his own company with his wife, Madeleine Renaud, and developed a more adventurous and modern repertoire of plays by writers such as Eugène Ionesco.

After *les événements* of 1968, Barrault lost his theatre, and though he did some further brilliant experimental work, notably his production of *Rabelais* in a wrestling hall in Montmartre, he leaned more and more on a classical repertoire, becoming effectively France's leading classical theatre actor. His performance as Deburau in Marcel Carne's film, *Les Enfants du Paradis*, still has the power to astonish.

In Britain, besides the internationalist Peter Brook, a number of 'fringe' theatre groups adapted techniques and suggestions from Artaud. Most overt was Charles Marowitz, whose Open Space Theatre was dedicated to exploring Artaud's legacy. Marowitz worked out a number of montaged Shakespeare shows, in which the text was heavily cut and reordered, to create disturbing and sometimes enlightening juxtapositions. His *Artaud at Rodez* (1975) attempted to recreate Artaud's experience in the last hospital to hold him. Mention might also be made of the People Show, the Cartoon Archetypal Slogan Theatre (CAST), the Kartoon Klowns, and Ed Berman. Even some of Spike Milligan's work, especially in collaboration with John Antrobus, might be described as Artaudian. More provocative, perhaps, was the Pip Simmons Theatre Group, who staged, for instance, *The George Jackson Black and White Minstrel Show*, in which spectators were encouraged to 'buy' blacked-up white actors as 'slaves', and to whom they were then chained; and *An die Musik*, about Jewish musicians in concentration camps being forced to play beautiful music by Mozart, Beethoven, and others at the command of their whip-wielding German masters. Also as Artaudian, though less intense, was the Welfare State International group, which – perhaps significantly – grew out of work being done at Bradford Art College. 'Their performances were not plays, but epic poems, visual and aural, though virtually without words', and the group became 'dream-weavers, purveyors of images, sculptors of visual poetry, civic magicians and engineers of the imagination'.[100] Somewhat comparable to Welfare State in its use of fantasy, though perhaps more politically engaged, was Tim Etchells' Forced Entertainment group, also initially based in Yorkshire.

Europe, too, has seen plenty of Artaudian theatre in the half-century since he died. Perhaps most influential has been the work of Tadeusz Kantor, a Polish painter and scenic designer, who created avant-garde settings at the Old Theatre, Cracow, before forming his own group, Cricot II, in 1956. This group specialised in pseudo-Surrealist performances, which toured extensively. Later Kantor founded the Theatre of Death, and worked in Italy, Germany, and elsewhere. His macabre and frightening *The Death Class* (1975) was a typical product of his Artaudian imagination. In Italy, besides the ubiquitous Dario Fo, who has employed some deliberately Artaudian methods, Luca Ronconi won extravagant praise with his *Orlando Furioso*. It was presented in a huge specially created hall with two set stages, one at either end, and the audience milled about between them. Many scenes also appeared on specially constructed carts, while strange fabricated monsters flew through the air, and giant puppets stomped the floor. For at least one spectator it was 'this most thrilling of theatrical events'.[101] Meanwhile, in Spain, Antonio Buero-Vallejo acknowledged that he owed a considerable debt to Artaud in his series of outstanding plays, including *Today's a Holiday, The Sleep of Reason*, and *The Concert at Saint Ovide*.[102]

In America, Joseph Chaikin's Open Theatre explored Artaud's ideas directly and indirectly, perhaps most notably in *The Serpent*, based on the biblical book of Genesis, and using ritual and documentary material to question the interface between actor and role. Other notably Artaudian work by this company included *America Hurrah*, like *The Serpent* by Jean-Claude van Itallie, Megan Terry's *Viet Rock* and, in an interesting echo of Artaud's repertoire at the Alfred Jarry Theatre, *A Dream Play* by August Strindberg. Beyond Chaikin and the Open Theatre, the list of American groups and individuals who have developed Artaud's work in new and sometimes unexpected directions is long and impressive. Among its best-known names are Julian Beck and Judith Malina's Living Theatre, Richard Schechner's Performance Group, the Bread and Puppet Theatre, and La Mama Troupe. Their often disparate and individual work, scintillating as it often was, is too well documented to need further description here. The same is true of the Canadian Robert Lepage, whose use of technology has some interestingly Artaudian resonances.

Artaud's influence, indeed, has spread well beyond the walls of the theatre. 'Happenings' are widely regarded as being descended from his work, artists as different as Maurice Bejart and Pierre Boulez have acknowledged him, and Pina Bausch's *Bluebeard* seems on some levels to have embodied what he only wrote about. In 2003, Peter Sellers staged an updated version of *In Order to Finish with the Judgement of God* at Tate Modern in London.

Happenings

One performance art form usually believed to have grown directly from Artaud's thought is the Happening. Happenings date from John Cage's 1952 event staged at Black Mountain College, in the United States, and the form developed largely in New York in the 1950s and 1960s. It was seen as a means of exploring the relationship between the viewer or audience and the art work, and was usually made by an artist specialising in action painting or junk sculpture.

Happenings were visual, auditory, even occasionally odorous, but usually non-verbal in any recognisable sense. They had no plot line or story, but were structured as a series of more or less self-contained actions ('happenings') which acquired resonance from the resulting montage effect.

Rock music also owes Artaud a debt (see Jim Morrison's acknowledgement, for instance) and rock and pop concerts and videos are often quintessentially Artaudian. So too are some forms of documentary, including television documentary, and some films – Godard, Antonioni, and Fassbinder, who dedicated his *Despair* to Artaud, are just some of the film-makers influenced by Artaud.

Perhaps Boulez best summarised Artaud's significance for contemporary artists: 'To have seen him and heard him speaking his own texts, accompanying them with cries, noises, rhythms, showed us how to contrive a fusion of sound and word, how to make the phoneme spurt out when the word no longer can, in short, how to organise delirium.'[103]

Twenty-first-century perspectives

Artaud's profound distrust of language ('We have to vanquish French without leaving it, / For fifty years it has held me in its tongue'[104]) chimes particularly well with the ideas of many theorists and critics of the late twentieth and early twenty-first centuries, whose retreat from trusting the word as such is well known and well documented. Derrida fastened on an apparent neologism of Artaud's when he referred to the 'subjectile' of a drawing, and suggested that Artaud's aim was 'to unsense the subjectile': but 'a subjectile is not a subject, still less the subjective, nor is it the object of either'.[105] Artaud's correspondence with Jacques Rivière may be one of the earliest texts which hammers home the inadequacy of language, and the act of publishing that correspondence might be called 'post-modernist'.

Consequently it is no surprise to find that Artaud's uneasy, fragmented work has provoked and stimulated psychologists and literary theorists alike. Artaud's texts are virtually always partial, and when performed they are accompanied by inarticulate shrieks and grunts, and by physical violence. They suggest a new kind of understanding, based on something other than just language. To Julia Kristeva, Artaud's splintered and fractured texts reveal multiplicity, and become expressive precisely because they are elusive and compressed.

What might perhaps be called his 'textuality of physical experience' may promise a distinct way of comprehending the self. This can be detected, for instance, in Artaud's *The Cenci*, which uses incest and murder to investigate the self, and even to create the biography of a fantasy. It certainly relates to Gilles Deleuze and Felix Guattari's idea of continuous 'becoming', which is as relevant to Artaud's person and his personality as to his ambivalent and contradictory ideas of community and individuality. Others as disparate as Michel Foucault and R. D. Laing were also stimulated by Artaud's 'case'. For Foucault, it indicated the 'triumph of madness: the world that thought to measure and justify madness through psychology must justify itself before madness'.[106] For Laing, Artaud's insistence that society, in the shape of police, doctors, bureaucrats, friends, family, the church, and so on, was guilty of the repression of his self, was a striking illumination. Did the confinement of Artaud to mental institutions suggest that it was society or Artaud who was mad? Isadore Isou's aggressive anti-psychiatry was also stimulated by Artaud.

For Artaud, if the theatre was the double of life, fantasy was the double of reality, and both had an equal validity. It was perhaps this which led Roland Barthes to call what Artaud created a 'paradoxical discourse' – one in which individual and communal fantasies were equally permissible. Philip Auslander, however, queried whether Artaud's theatre was communal or individualistic: did Artaud aim to create community in his theatre, or to purge or cure the individual? These may seem mutually exclusive aims, even if each was held by Artaud at different times. Artaud's new theatre language was one where the 'signs' would be recognisable, as he believed was the case with the Balinese theatre, whose performers were well understood by non-Balinese people like himself. But as Ferdinand de Saussure pointed out, the recognition of signs actually depends on the pre-existence of some kind of community, without which they are incomprehensible. What is interesting is that Artaud looked mainly to the east for his community, and in this sense was a pioneer of interculturalism, though he may also have thereby laid himself open to charges of exoticism or exploitation.

The unresolved paradox between individual and community in Artaud's thinking was also noticed by Jacques Derrida, whose extensive critique of

Artaud, most notably in the two essays 'La Parole Soufflée' and 'The Theater of Cruelty and the Closure of Representation' which both appear in his collection *Writing and Difference*,[107] perhaps provides the twenty-first century with its most significant perspective. As Derrida laments, live theatre, as practised today, is a dislocated process in two senses: first, it relies on a previously written text, and then on rehearsals; and, second, the words, the props, and so on, are separate elements in the presentation. This is the apparatus of theatre, which conceals the Saussurian community of signification which theatre seeks.

Artaud's attempts to reunite the elements require him to remove the artificiality which resides in 'representation'. Props, scenery, musical instruments, and so on are therefore in Artaud's theatre to be what they are, and the divide between the stage and the auditorium will be abolished, to be replaced by 'a kind of single, undivided locale without any partitions of any kind and this will be the very scene of the action'.[108] This 'pure' theatre is, on one level, the key to Artaud's project: it is the theatre without illusion in which there is no representation of one thing by another, no impersonation of one person (character) by another (actor), but only the truth of reality, the visceral pain of genuine experience, not the pretence of its enactment. 'Cruelty' then comes to mean 'freedom from representation'.

This suggests to Derrida the concept of 'festival', in which nothing is theatricalised, nothing is 'represented'. In other words, it is 'the theatre of cruelty'. And it is worth remarking that festival creates its own community, because it can only exist once, here and now. Thus, Derrida continues, Artaud abolishes 'repetition', which denies human spontaneity, and representation which relies on repetition. This theatre only exists in the present; it is only of and for itself. Moreover, it involves a fusion of all the elements of theatre even as it creates community.

However, Derrida points out that to unify the elements – language, thought, props, stage, and so on – creates a new kind of 'text', written in what Artaud sometimes called the 'new theatre language'. We return to the dislocation which we began by trying to annihilate. Moreover, Derrida notes, the creation of community inevitably involves dislocation, because it cannot but *exclude* those not included in it, while for those enclosed it denies differences, and therefore identity. Indeed, it may be thought to harbour Fascistic undertones. Derrida implies that Artaud's project is 'impossible', though he clearly admires Artaud for attempting it.

It may be that the problems and contradictions inherent in what Artaud was seeking to achieve make it richer and more worthy of our attention: it certainly affords us space to explore and experiment, and to find what there is in Artaud's 'Theatre of Cruelty' which offers us possibilities for the future.

Further reading

Artaud's work is published in France by Gallimard, Paris. At least twenty-five volumes of his Collected Works have appeared, as well as various collections of his drawings and specific collections of letters to particular correspondents.

The English student of Artaud is not so well provided for. Four volumes of Artaud's Collected Works have appeared, and are kept in print by John Calder Publishers, London:

Volume 1 contains: *Correspondence with Jacques Rivière*, *Umbilical Limbo*, *Nerve Scales*, *Art and Death*, unpublished prose and poetry, *Cup and Ball*, seven letters and an Appendix.
Volume 2 contains: *The Alfred Jarry Theatre*, a mime play and a stage synopsis, two production plans, notes on 'The Tricksters' by Steve Passeur, reviews, *About a Lost Play*, *On Literature and the Plastic Arts*.
Volume 3 contains: Scenarios, *On the Cinema*, interviews, letters.
Volume 4 contains: *The Theatre and Its Double*, *Seraphim's Theatre*, *The Cenci*, and an Appendix.

Individual works have also been published by John Calder, London, including *The Theatre and Its Double*, *The Cenci*, and *The Death of Satan*. Selections from Artaud's writings are also available in other collections, including:

Hirschmann, Jack (ed.), *Artaud Anthology*, San Francisco, Calif.: City Lights, 1965.
Schumacher, Claude, and Singleton, Brian, *Artaud on Theatre*, London: Methuen, 2001.
Sontag, Susan (ed.), *Antonin Artaud: Selected Writings*, New York: Farrar, Straus & Giroux, 1976.

Studies of Artaud's work in English include:

Barber, Stephen, *Antonin Artaud, Blows and Bombs*, London: Faber & Faber, 1994.
Bermel, Albert, *Artaud's Theatre of Cruelty*, London: Methuen, 2001.
Derrida, Jacques, and Thévenin, Paule, *The Secret Art of Antonin Artaud*, Cambridge, Mass.: MIT Press, 1998.
Esslin, Martin, *Antonin Artaud, the Man and his Work*, London: John Calder, 1976.
Goodall, Jane, *Artaud and the Gnostic Drama*, Oxford: Oxford University Press, 1994.
Greene, Naomi, *Antonin Artaud: Poet Without Words*, New York: Simon & Schuster, 1970.
Hayman, Ronald, *Artaud and After*, Oxford: Oxford University Press, 1977.
Knapp, Bettina, *Antonin Artaud, Man of Vision*, New York: Discus Books, 1971.

Plunka, Gene A. (ed.), *Antonin Artaud and the Modern Theatre*, Rutherford, NJ: Fairleigh Dickinson University Press, 1994.

Sellin, Eric, *The Dramatic Concepts of Antonin Artaud*, Chicago, Ill.: University of Chicago Press, 1968.

Stout, John C., *Antonin Artaud's Alternate Genealogies*, Waterloo, Ontario: Wilfrid Laurier University Press, 1996.

Significant material is also collected in:

Marowitz, Charles, *Artaud at Rodez*, London: Marion Boyars, 1977.

6   Afterwards . . . after words

In the last pages of this book, I want to take a rather different and less conventional approach to my subject: an approach which uses four works of dramatic fiction. They are:

- *Mikhail Bulgakov's* Black Snow, *the exasperated account of a creative playwright caught in the tangled net of Soviet bureaucracy which was strangling the Moscow Art Theatre and, apparently, Stanislavsky ('Ivan Vassilievich') in the 1930s;*
- *Günter Grass's* The Plebeians Rehearse the Uprising, *the expression of a progressive West German view of the behaviour of Brecht ('the Boss') during the workers' uprising in East Berlin in 1953;*
- *Charles Marowitz's* Artaud at Rodez, *a dramatisation of Artaud's mental and physical life, his memories and his hopes, during his confinement at Rodez;*
- *Mark Rozovsky's* Triumphal Square, *a 'fantasy' on the life of Meyerhold ('the Master') which contrasts his mercurial theatre life with the heavy-booted tyranny of Stalin.*

The following pages propose a response to my four 'makers of modern theatre' based on theatregoing and the validity of the imagination.

Much of Triumphal Square *was written in my house in England when Mark Rozovsky stayed with me in the summer of 1991. Later that year I went to Moscow to attend the premiere at his Nikitsky Gate Theatre. What follows are some reflections and resonances prompted by that experience.[1]*

November 1991. A few wandering snowflakes waltz in the lamplight. Cold Moscow, and Communism is collapsing.

The Nikitsky Gate Theatre's stone foyer and broad staircase is white lit. The theatre to which we are headed is on the first floor, carved out of two

Figure 6.1 Triumphal Square, Nikitsky Gate Theatre, Moscow, 1991.

flats. The auditorium was perhaps the living room, the stage the dining room. The wall between them (the fourth wall?) has been removed. Lights dim. It is the premiere of Mark Rozovsky's *Triumphal Square*, a theatrical fantasy to the memory of Vsevolod Emilievich Meyerhold.

Lights down. A bureaucratic Stalin lookalike appears, nervously peering into the auditorium. He speaks the words of Gogol's Mayor:

'Gentlemen, I've asked you here today because I've got some rather unpleasant news for you. A Government Inspector is to visit . . .'

Actors, wide-eyed, floppy-costumed, startled, poke their heads out of the wings, fingers to lips. 'Shh! Shh!' they hiss.

Stalin tries again: 'Gentlemen, I've asked you here today . . .'

The actors whisper among themselves: 'Visited . . . A Government Inspector . . . We're to be visited . . . Inspector . . . He's arrived . . .'

Inspector Stalin has looked round. Now he singles out Harlequin: 'Listen, I've got to talk to you.'

Harlequin: 'I don't talk when I'm on stage.' He leaps from the wings. 'My specialty's pantomime.'

The Inspector: 'Pantomime? That old business. It's silent.'

'Yes. I'm a mask. I'm Harlequin.'

'Well, take off your mask', Stalin says urgently, 'and then what are you?'

'An actor.'

'A jester.'

Harlequin turns to the audience, whispers: 'Yes. And proud of it.'

Enter Columbine. She dances. The stage is flooded with light. The heavy hand of bureaucratic officialdom is blown away as the Master creates his cloud-light carnival. Harlequin capers, Columbine sports on a playground swing, there's music, light. Drama is play, play is carnival.

And so the themes begin to dance – movement and gesture, silence and dialogue. They merge and mirror, counteract and counterpoint. One play calls up another, *Triumphal Square* awakes *The Fairground Booth* and *The Government Inspector*. But Rozovsky's Master, I think, is also pre-figured in Günter Grass's Boss who dictates to his boss:

> To Ulbricht: whom the people mostly
> Call Billygoat. Colon. Comrade Secretary,
> No bloodshed. Kindly tell your soldiers that
> A carnival is not worth shooting at.

Harlequin and Columbine combine, the Master is Pierrot, and Stalin watches them through a snowstorm of light flickers. I remember Charles Marowitz's Barker summoning his audience to *The Cenci*:

> Ladies and gentlemen, roll up, roll up – for the event of the century, 'The Cenci!' A play so barbaric, so harrowing that at all times, a doctor and clinical psychiatrist will be in attendance to minister the faint-of-heart.
>
> THE CENCI, ladies and gentlemen, ripped from the soul of Shelley, excavated from the heart of Stendhal and transformed by the mind of Antonin Artaud into the first and unforgettable example of the Theatre of Cruelty.
>
> See the lovely and noble Iya Abdy as Beatrice – suspended on a wheel of torture – by her hair.
>
> See Antonin Artaud as the corrupt Italian nobleman commit the most unspeakable crime known to humanity.
>
> Hear sounds like you've never heard before. A stereo-phonic tempest that splits the heavens. The great bell of Amiens Cathedral reproduced on four separate loudspeakers.
>
> Get your tickets now, ladies and gentlemen, for a theatrical work that will give an entirely new meaning to the word tragedy.

And now on the Nikitsky Gate stage all the actors are gazing at the Master. 'Tonight we will present' – and he pauses dramatically – 'a tragedy!' The actors shrug and grumble. 'We don't want tragedy, we're sick and tired of tragedy.' 'We can always play any farce we like', the Master argues naively, 'but tragedy . . . happens by itself.'

The actors begin to try to improvise, and I am reminded of Mikhail Bulgakov's Ivan Vasilievich, when he called for the props bicycle for an improvisation in the rehearsal of a love scene.

'Now please take a ride on that bicycle for your beloved.'

Patrikeyev clambered on to the machine, the actress playing the beloved sat down in a chair, clutching an enormous patent-leather handbag to her stomach. Patrikeyev pedalled off and described a wobbly course round the chair, squinting with one eye at the prompter's box, which he was afraid of hitting, and with the other eye at the actress.

'Quite wrong,' said Ivan Vasilievich when Patrikeyev had stopped. 'Why were you staring at the prop man? Were you riding for him?'

Figure 6.2 Triumphal Square, Nikitsky Gate Theatre, Moscow, 1991. The mask of Meyerhold.

Patrikeyev rode round again, this time squinting with both eyes at the actress. He failed to turn the corner and pedalled off into the wings. When they had brought him back, pushing the bicycle by the handle-bars, Ivan Vasilievich was still not satisfied and Patrikeyev set off for a third time. He circled round once, leaning over sideways and staring longingly at his paramour. Steering with one hand, he made a sharp turn, bore down on the actress and smeared her skirt with his dirty front tyre.

On stage in front of me, a new intensity. Rozovsky's Master remembers what he wrote to Chekhov: 'I want to burn with the spirit of our times!' He snatches the mask of himself.

> MASTER (*takes the mask in his hands*): What makes the plot of a tragedy? (*The aria of the Holy Fool is heard, then bells start ringing.*) What is its aim? A man and the people. 'The fate of a man, the fate of the people' – these words of Pushkin we'll have to learn by heart. Do you hear me, Columbine? (*A trumpet sounds.*) The spirit of our time requires changes in the theatre as well! 'As well' – what does it mean, 'as well'?
> The earth turned upside down! The dawn! Dawn in the theatre, and in life!
> In the theatre – rehearsal; in the street – revolution!
> PEOPLE'S COMMISSAR'S COMRADE: You will have to be the drummer for our new Red culture!
> ASSISTANT DIRECTOR: Drum-sticks for the Master! From now on, he is our drummer!

And the theatre will drum in the revolution. Even Marowitz's Artaud had cried: 'One has to play along with the times in order to be revolutionary!' But Stalin's double is harassing the Master: 'The comedy of life! The tragedy of love! The dance of death!' His voice drips contempt. Then straight into his face: 'Russia expects a different art from you!'

And I recall the plebeians rehearsing the uprising:

> We've had enough playacting. Does it make sense
> To put on puppet shows for his amusement
> While out in front they're marching ten abreast,
> Arms locked and shouting: Comrades,
>   Comrades, join us!
> We want to be free men!

Gross's plebeians tipped the Billygoat's sycophant into the dustbin of history, then eagerly returned to their play:

PODULLA (*provocatively*): What material! Enough for three plays and an adaptation. You were dead right, Boss. Your theory has been confirmed. All we have to do is work, rehearse, modify, and above all preserve our God-damned serenity.

LITTHENNER: People have been killed, Boss.

PODULLA: Incidentals! Let's start digesting this new material. Can tanks be used on stage? What do you think, Boss?

LITTHENNER: They were Soviet tanks.

PODULLA (*cynically*): Why, so they were. The question is: Can we have a scene – or maybe even a whole play – taking place in a cross-section of a Soviet tank?

Street battles go on outside. The Boss goes on adapting Shakespeare's *Coriolanus*: 'I don't know if you're interested, but thanks to you I've seen the light. I've changed the whole scene. Rome. A street. But I'm making the tribunes enter before the plebeians.'

On stage, now, the Master admits to his tormentors that he has mutilated the classics. 'It was an act of sabotage', he concedes. But actually nothing is so easy as altering the script of a play. As Bulgakov's Maxudov discovered when he read his play to Ivan Vasilievich:

Bakhtin (To Petrov): Farewell. You will be following me soon . . .
Petrov: What are you doing?
Bakhtin shoots himself in the temple, falls. From afar comes the sound of an accordion . . .'
'That won't do at all!' exclaimed Ivan Vasilievich. 'Why did you write that? You must cross it out without a second's delay. Why, pray, must there be a shooting?'
'But he has to die by committing suicide,' I replied with a cough.
'Very well – let him die and let him stab himself with a dagger.'
'But you see the action takes place during the civil war . . . nobody used daggers by then . . .'
'No, they were used,' objected Ivan Vasilievich, 'I was told it by . . . what was his name . . . I've forgotten . . . what they used . . . You must cross out that shot!'
I was temporarily silenced by having made such an awful mistake and then read on:
'. . . accordion and isolated shots. A man carrying a rifle appears on the bridge. The moon . . .'
'My God!' cried Ivan Vasilievich. 'Shots! More shots! What a disaster! Look here, Leo . . . Look here, you must cut that scene, it's superfluous.'
'I thought,' I said, trying to speak as calmly as possible, 'that this scene was the main one . . .'

He thought he knew his 'main scene'. So could it not be altered? 'We can't change Shakespeare unless we change ourselves.' Thus spake the Boss in Günter Grass's play.

Change the play? change the theatre? change the world? change your self? At the Nikitsky Gate the interval has been and gone. Now a spotlight pins the Master, who tries to explain his change from being German to being Russian.

> I come from Penza. My parents were Russified Germans. My name is Karl. The name of Vsevolod was taken by me in honour of my favourite writer, Vsevolod Garshin, when I was eighteen . . . Incidentally, do you happen to know how Garshin died? He committed suicide while in a lunatic asylum.

In the asylum at Rodez Artaud fought to save his selfhood, his 'inner frenzy', after electro-convulsion therapy:

> FERDIÈRE: It is quite common for you to have such feelings. You should feel no guilt about them.
>
> ARTAUD: It is not guilt that I have begun to feel, but . . . violation. In my long, drugged sleep, I came to realize that unless I held firm to what it was you were trying to uproot, I would lose something far more precious than my sanity.
>
> FERDIÈRE: In illnesses such as yours, a certain amount of paranoid delusion cannot help but . . .
>
> ARTAUD: Tell me, Doctor, for I know you are a kind man and have my welfare at heart, I do believe that: do you not at certain moments in our meetings, or afterwards as you trudge into the sanctuary of your private apartments, do you not wish you could take away with you some of the inner frenzy which has brought me here to Rodez?
>
> FERDIÈRE: Thoughts of this kind, I can assure you, are entirely normal for someone at your stage of treatment. The main thing is not . . .
>
> ARTAUD (*slowly hotting up*): Confess, Doctor, for something of this truth has mixed itself with the fumes steaming from my charred brains . . .
>
> FERDIÈRE: You are exciting yourself, my friend, and that cannot help to . . .
>
> ARTAUD: Confess, that in the underground dungeon where you stoke your own darkest thoughts, you crave one flicker of that very con-flagration you are trying to quell . . .
>
> FERDIÈRE: M'sieur Artaud, I had hoped we could talk calmly about matters which . . .
>
> ARTAUD: Confess it . . . confess it.

FERDIÈRE: It is understandable that you should believe . . .
ARTAUD: Confess it!
FERDIÈRE: . . . that such fantasies should occur during . . .
ARTAUD: CONFESS IT!
FERDIÈRE (*after a beat*): ITS TRUE! (*Eyes averted*) It is true.

'I don't believe you!' the Master recalls his Master calling. Confession, admission. Carnival, cruelty. Change, constancy. Power and play. To enumerate themes is easy. But simply to do so denies the theatre's power to evoke, to conjure, to remind.

Triumphal Square is ending. The Stalin-double Inspector and the Master face the audience:

INSPECTOR: It's the end. Now it really is the end. The Master was shot on the first of February . . .
MASTER: On the second of February . . .
INSPECTOR: February the second? So sorry. February the second, 1940. That means on February the first somebody else was shot. On the second it was the Master, on the third somebody else, then came February the fourth, the fifth, the tenth . . . Where's his grave?
MASTER: Nobody knows that for sure.
INSPECTOR (*to the audience*): Why do they keep silent?
MASTER: The people are silent. A dumb show.
INSPECTOR: A dumb show – the end of the tragedy.
MASTER: Yes, this tragedy'll come to an end, and tomorrow there'll be another one. The show goes on!
(*Cello music is heard.*)
INSPECTOR: Suddenly the buffoon hangs over the footlights, and cries:
MASTER: 'Help! I'm bleeding cranberry juice!'
     My head is made of flannel cloth,
       My helmet's only card;
    And what I brandish in my hand
       Is just a wooden sword.
INSPECTOR: Boy and girl
       Now shed a tear –
MASTER and INSPECTOR (*together*): *Finito la Commedia!*
(*They put their arms around each other and walk off together.*)

Theatre walks into the backstage blackness, its arm round its double, life. A dialectical progress.

Inner truth, outer theatricality.

Outside, a few shards of snow drift about in the night, and the world order is changing.

Notes

Abbreviations

The following abbreviations are used in these notes for the specified editions.

For Stanislavsky

AAP: *An Actor Prepares*, London: Geoffrey Bles, 1962.
BAC: *Building a Character*, London: Methuen, 1986.
MLIA: *My Life in Art*, London: Geoffrey Bles, 1962.

For Meyerhold

MonT: *Meyerhold on Theatre*, London: Eyre Methuen, 1977.
MSMR: *Meyerhold Speaks, Meyerhold Rehearses*, Amsterdam: Harwood, 1997.

For Brecht

BonT: *Brecht on Theatre*, London: Eyre Methuen, 1973.
Diaries: *Diaries 1920–1922*, London: Eyre Methuen, 1979.
Journals: *Journals 1934–1955*, London: Methuen, 1993.

For Artaud

CW1: *Collected Works*, vol. 1, London: John Calder, 1978.
CW2: *Collected Works*, vol. 2, London: John Calder, 1999.
CW3: *Collected Works*, vol. 3, London: John Calder, 1999.
CW4: *Collected Works*, vol. 4, London: John Calder, 1999.

1 Modern theatre . . . Modernist theatre

1 Marvin Carlson, *Theories of the Theatre: A Historical and Critical Survey from the Greeks to the Present*, Ithaca, NY: Cornell University Press, 1993.
2 Bertolt Brecht, *Poems 1913–1956*, London: Eyre Methuen, 1976, p. 320.
3 Robert Leach, *Stanislavsky and Meyerhold*, Bern: Peter Lang, 2003.
4 Peter Brook, *The Shifting Point*, London: Methuen, 1988, p. 43.

2 Konstantin Stanislavsky

1 *MLIA*, p. 22.
2 *MLIA*, p. 27.
3 *MLIA*, p. 39.
4 *MLIA*, pp. 55–6.
5 *MLIA*, p. 52.
6 *MLIA*, p. 44.
7 Quoted in Jean Benedetti, *Stanislavski, a Biography*, London: Methuen, 1988, p. 52.
8 *Ibid.*, p. 58.
9 Quoted in David Magarshack, *Stanislavsky: A Life*, London: Faber & Faber, 1986, p. 122.
10 Vladimir Nemirovitch-Dantchenko, *My Life in the Russian Theatre*, London: Geoffrey Bles, 1937, p. 79.
11 S. D. Balukhaty (ed.), *'The Seagull' Produced by Stanislavsky*, New York: Theatre Arts, 1952, p. 124.
12 Claude Schumacher (ed.), *Naturalism and Symbolism in European Theatre, 1850–1918*, Cambridge: Cambridge University Press, 1996, p. 240.
13 *MLIA*, pp. 539–40.
14 See Rebecca B. Gauss, *Lear's Daughters*, New York: Peter Lang, 1999.
15 See Bella Merlin, *Konstantin Stanislavsky*, London: Routledge, 2003.
16 See below, p. 68.
17 Vasily Osipovich Toporkov, *Stanislavsky in Rehearsal*, London: Routledge, 1998.
18 *MLIA*, p. 88.
19 Émile Zola, 'Naturalism on the Stage', reprinted in Toby Cole, *Playwrights on Playwriting*, London: MacGibbon and Kee, 1960, p. 6.
20 Quoted in Toby Cole, and Helen Krich Chinoy, *Actors on Acting*, New York: Crown, 1970, pp. 486, 487.
21 Quoted in Sharon M. Carnicke, *Stanislavsky in Focus*, Amsterdam: Harwood, 1998, p. 25.
22 Nikolai M. Gorchakov, *Stanislavsky Directs*, New York: Funk & Wagnall's, 1954, p. 119.
23 *AAP*, p. 75.
24 *AAP*, p. 54.
25 Constantin Stanislavski, *An Actor's Handbook*, London: Methuen, 1990, p. 94.
26 *AAP*, p. 164.
27 Stanislavski, *An Actor's Handbook*, pp. 53–4.
28 *AAP*, p. 166.
29 Stanislavski, *An Actor's Handbook*, p. 56.
30 *AAP*, p. 177.
31 *AAP*, p. 46.
32 Balukhaty, *'The Seagull' Produced by Stanislavsky*.
33 *Ibid.*, p. 90.
34 *AAP*, p. 97.
35 *BAC*, p. 83.
36 *BAC*, p. 110.
37 *BAC*, p. 88.
38 *BAC*, pp. 89–90.
39 *BAC*, p. 140.

40 *AAP*, p. 47.
41 *AAP*, p. 185.
42 *AAP*, p. 192.
43 See Benedetti, *Stanislavski, a Biography*, pp. 214, 216.
44 *Ibid.*, p. 187.
45 See *AAP*, pp. 118–19.
46 Constantin Stanislavski, and Pavel Rumyantsev, *Stanislavski on Opera*, London: Routledge, 1998, p. 105.
47 *BAC*, p. 113.
48 Carnicke, *Stanislavsky in Focus*, p. 148.
49 Bella Merlin, *Beyond Stanislavsky*, London: Nick Hern Books, 2001, p. 17.
50 Balukhaty, '*The Seagull*', p. 108.
51 *Ibid.*, p. 109.
52 Nemirovitch-Dantchenko, *My Life*, p. 187.
53 *MLIA*, p. 354.
54 *MLIA*, p. 540.
55 Gauss, *Lear's Daughters*, p. 43.
56 Robert Russell, *Russian Drama of the Revolutionary Period*, London: Macmillan, 1988, p. 63.
57 Peter Brook, *The Empty Space*, Harmondsworth: Penguin, 1972, p. 131.
58 Michael Chekhov, *To the Actor*, London: Routledge, 2002; Michael Chekhov, *On the Technique of Acting*, New York: HarperCollins, 1991.
59 Quoted in Sonia Moore, *Stanislavski Revealed*, New York: Applause, 1991, epigraph.
60 See Merlin, *Beyond Stanislavsky*, pp. 152–63.
61 James Agate, *The Sunday Times*, 15 April 1928, quoted in Laurence Senelick (ed.), *Wandering Stars*, Iowa City, Ia.: University of Iowa Press, 1992, p. 98.
62 See Peter Brook, *There Are No Secrets*, London: Methuen, 1993, p. 7.
63 Brook, *The Empty Space*, p. 157.
64 Richard Boleslavsky, *Acting: The First Six Lessons*, New York: Theatre Arts, 1933.
65 Harold Clurman, *The Fervent Years*, London: Dennis Dobson, 1946, pp. 44–5.
66 Denis Diderot, 'The Paradox of Acting', in Cole and Chinoy, *Actors on Acting*, p. 162.
67 Merlin, *Konstantin Stanislavsky*.

3 Vsevolod Emilievich Meyerhold

 1 *MSMR*, p. 91.
 2 Nick Worrall, *The Moscow Art Theatre*, London: Routledge, 1996, p. 45.
 3 *MSMR*, p. 102.
 4 *MLIA*, p. 303.
 5 *MSMR*, p. 145.
 6 *MSMR*, p. 70.
 7 Jean Benedetti, *The Moscow Art Theatre Letters*, London: Methuen, 1991, p. 123.
 8 *MonT*, p. 41.
 9 Paul Schmidt, *Meyerhold at Work*, Austin, Tex.: University of Texas Press, 1980, p. 158.
10 For a detailed description of the political–theatrical manoeuvrings in early Soviet Russia, see Robert Leach, *Revolutionary Theatre*, London: Routledge, 1994.

11 Leach, *Stanislavsky and Meyerhold*, p. 139.
12 Leach, *Vsevolod Meyerhold*, Cambridge: Cambridge University Press, p. 17.
13 MSMR, p. 55.
14 MSMR, p. 74.
15 MSMR, p. 147.
16 MSMR, p. 95.
17 MSMR, p. 96.
18 MSMR, p. 81.
19 Schmidt, *Meyerhold at Work*, p. 214.
20 Benedetti, *Stanislavski, a Biography*, p. 345.
21 V. E. Meierkhol'd, *Perepiska 1896–1939*, Moscow: Iskusstvo, 1976, p. 350.
22 Edward Braun, 'Vsevolod Meyerhold: the Final Act', in Katherine Bliss Eaton (ed.), *Enemies of the People*, Evanston, Ill.: Northwestern University Press, 2002, pp. 154–5.
23 Balukhaty, *'The Seagull'*, p. 72.
24 Meierkhol'd, *Perepiska*, p. 45.
25 MonT, p. 138.
26 Germain Bazin, *Baroque and Rococo*, London: Thames & Hudson, 1964, pp. 6–7.
27 Laurence Senelick, *Cabaret Performance*, vol. 1, New York: PAJ Publications, 1989, p. 67.
28 MonT, pp. 138–9.
29 Quoted in Edward Braun, *Meyerhold, a Revolution in Theatre*, London: Methuen, 1995, p. 209.
30 MSMR, pp. 128, 142.
31 MonT, p. 137.
32 MonT, p. 104.
33 Cole and Chinoy, *Actors on Acting*, p. 505.
34 Yuri Yurev, *Zapiski*, Leningrad and Moscow: Iskusstvo, 1963, vol. 1, pp. 188–9.
35 MSMR, p. 165.
36 MSMR, p. 131. For a detailed analysis of Meyerhold's work on *The Death of Tintagiles*, see Leach, *Stanislavsky and Meyerhold*, pp. 52–7.
37 MonT, p. 129.
38 MSMR, p. 108.
39 MSMR, p. 104.
40 František Deák, 'Meyerhold's Staging of *Sister Beatrice*', *The Drama Review*, vol. 26, no. 1, Spring 1982, p. 50.
41 MSMR, pp. 114–15.
42 MSMR, p. 111.
43 MSMR, p. 115.
44 BonT, pp. 91–2.
45 Anthony Frost and Ralph Yarrow, *Improvisation in Drama*, London: Macmillan, 1990, p. 19.
46 MonT, p. 150.
47 MonT, pp. 122, 123.
48 MSMR, p. 103.
49 *Ibid.*
50 Benedetti, *Stanislavski, a Biography*, p. 105.
51 Deák, 'Meyerhold's Staging of *Sister Beatrice*', p. 50.
52 Schmidt, *Meyerhold at Work*, p. 184.

53 Cole and Chinoy, *Actors on Acting*, p. 504.
54 C. Coquelin, *The Art of the Actor*, London: George Allen & Unwin, 1932, p. 31.
55 Cole and Chinoy, *Actors on Acting*, p. 506.
56 MSMR, p. 96
57 Cole and Chinoy, *Actors on Acting*, pp. 504–5.
58 Jonathan Pitches, 'The Actor's Perspective', in Anthony Shrubsall and Jonathan Pitches, 'Two Perspectives on the Phenomenon of Biomechanics in Contemporary Performance', *Studies in Theatre Production*, no. 16, December 1997, p. 101.
59 MSMR, p. 194.
60 MSMR, pp. 175–6.
61 Schmidt, *Meyerhold at Work*, p. 202.
62 MSMR, p. 124.
63 MSMR, p. 160.
64 MonT, p. 56.
65 MSMR, p. 104.
66 MSMR, p. 108.
67 Schmidt, *Meyerhold at Work*, p. 207.
68 MonT, p. 62.
69 MSMR, p. 206.
70 Schmidt, *Meyerhold at Work*, p. 204.
71 See S. M. Eisenstein, *Selected Works*, vol. 1, London: B.F.I. Publishing, 1988, pp. 33–8.
72 André van Gysegham, *Theatre in Soviet Russia*, London: Faber & Faber, 1943, p. 31.
73 Nikolai A. Gorchakov, *The Theater in Soviet Russia*, Oxford: Oxford University Press, 1957, p. 204.
74 Norris Houghton, *Moscow Rehearsals*, New York: Harcourt Brace, 1936, pp. 103–4.
75 Braun, *Meyerhold, a Revolution in Theatre*, p. 278.
76 A. A. Sherel' (ed.), *Meierkhol'dovskii Sbornik*, vol. 1, Moscow: Komissiya po tvorcheskomu naslediyu V. E. Meierkhol'da, 1992, p. 40.
77 Anatoly Smeliansky, *The Russian Theatre after Stalin*, Cambridge: Cambridge University Press, 1999, pp. 10, 11.
78 *Ibid.*, p. 11.
79 Birgit Beumers, *Yuri Lyubimov at the Taganka Theatre, 1964–1994*, Amsterdam: Harwood, 1997, p. 26.
80 Leach, *Vsevolod Meyerhold*, pp. 173–4.
81 Arts Archives: *Meyerhold's Biomechanics and Rhythm*, Gennadi Bogdanov, six 3-hour tapes; *Meyerhold's Biomechanics: A Workshop*, Alexei Levinsky, 90-minute video. Both available from Arts Documentation Unit, 6A Devonshire Place, Exeter, EX4 6JA, United Kingdom.
82 See Leach, *Vsevolod Meyerhold*, chapter entitled 'Legacy'.
83 *Drama Review*, vol. 17, no. 1; vol. 19, no. 2; vol. 26, no. 1.
84 *Theatre Quarterly*, no. 2, 1972; Jonathan Pitches, *Vsevolod Meyerhold*, London: Routledge, 2003.
85 See Deák, 'Meyerhold's Staging of *Sister Beatrice*', p. 50.
86 Nikolai Gogol, *The Government Inspector*, trans. Edward O. Marsh and Jeremy Brooks, London: Methuen, 1968, p. 92.

87 MSMR, p. 110.
88 MSMR, p. 103.

4 Bertolt Brecht

1 Hanns Otto Munsterer, *The Young Brecht*, London: Libris, 1992, p. 17.
2 See Reinhold Grimm, 'Brecht's Beginnings', *Drama Review*, vol. 12, no. 1, Fall 1967, p. 22.
3 Sergei Tretyakov, 'Bert Brecht', in Hubert Witt, *Brecht as They Knew Him*, London: Lawrence & Wishart, 1975, p. 71.
4 *Diaries*, p. 132.
5 Arnold Zweig, 'Brecht Summary', in Witt, *Brecht as They Knew Him*, p. 84.
6 Munsterer, *The Young Brecht*, pp. 66–7.
7 *Diaries*, p. 21.
8 *Diaries*, p. 62.
9 *Diaries*, p. 21.
10 *Diaries*, pp. 140–1.
11 Quoted in Munsterer, *The Young Brecht*, p. 170.
12 Witt, *Brecht as They Knew Him*, p. 22.
13 *Journals*, p. 29.
14 *The Threepenny Opera, Directed by G.W. Pabst*, Classic Film Scripts, London: Lorrimer Publishing, 1984.
15 Included as part of 'The *Threepenny* Material', in Marc Silberman (ed.), *Brecht on Film and Radio*, London: Methuen, 2000, pp. 131ff. See also Steve Giles, *Bertolt Brecht and Critical Theory*, Bern: Peter Lang, 1997.
16 *Journals*, pp. 20, 285.
17 See Frederic Ewen, *Bertolt Brecht, His Life, His Art, and His Times*, New York: Citadel Press, 1992, p. 382.
18 Eric Bentley, *The Brecht Memoir*, New York: PAJ Publications, 1985, p. 32.
19 *Journals*, p. 223.
20 *Journals*, pp. 358–9.
21 Catalogue, *Bertolt Brecht on Stage*, Frankfurt-am-Main: Erich Imbescheidt, 1968, p. 17.
22 Witt, *Brecht as They Knew Him*, p. 167.
23 Bentley, *The Brecht Memoir*, p. 76.
24 See below, p. 135.
25 BonT, p. 43.
26 BonT, p. 30.
27 BonT, p. 135.
28 BonT, p. 23.
29 BonT, p. 29.
30 Bertolt Brecht, *The Good Person of Szechuan*, London: Eyre Methuen, 1965, p. 109.
31 Witt, *Brecht as They Knew Him*, p. 20.
32 *Ibid.*, p. 74.
33 Bertolt Brecht, *The Messingkauf Dialogues*, London: Methuen, 1965, p. 103.
34 *Ibid.*, p. 48.
35 *Ibid.*, p. 102.
36 See above, p. 77.
37 BonT, p. 96.

38 *BonT*, p. 27.
39 Brecht, *Messingkauf Dialogues*, p. 19.
40 *Journals*, p. 417.
41 *BonT*, p. 9.
42 *BonT*, p. 180.
43 *BonT*, p. 80.
44 Bertolt Brecht, *Poems on the Theatre*, Northwood: Scorpion Press, 1961, p. 17.
45 *BonT*, p. 196.
46 Peter Thomson and Glendyr Sacks (eds), *The Cambridge Companion to Brecht*, Cambridge: Cambridge University Press, p. 182.
47 See *BonT*, pp. 252–65.
48 Ewen, *Bertolt Brecht*, p. 472.
49 *BonT*, p. 202.
50 Brecht, *Messingkauf Dialogues*, pp. 85–6.
51 Peter Thomson, *Brecht: Mother Courage*, Cambridge: Cambridge University Press, 1997, p. 66.
52 David Richard Jones, *Great Directors at Work*, Los Angeles, Calif.: University of California Press, 1986, p. 97.
53 *BonT*, p. 57.
54 *BonT*, p. 58.
55 Brecht, *Messingkauf Dialogues*, p. 87.
56 *BonT*, p. 137.
57 James H. McTeague, *Playwrights and Acting*, Westport, Conn.: Greenwood Press, 1994, p. 49. For the Method of Physical Actions, see above, pp. 38–9.
58 See Bertolt Brecht, *Mother Courage and Her Children*, London: Eyre Methuen, 1980, p. 106.
59 Bentley, *The Brecht Memoir*, p. 61.
60 *Ibid.*, p. 139.
61 *Ibid.*, p. 61.
62 *BonT*, p. 58.
63 Bertolt Brecht, *Fear and Misery of the Third Reich*, London: Methuen, 1983, p. 75.
64 Brecht, *Mother Courage*, p. 83.
65 Bertolt Brecht, *Man Equals Man*, London: Eyre Methuen, 1979, p. 30.
66 *Diaries*, p. 34.
67 *BonT*, p. 42.
68 *BonT*, p. 198.
69 Bertolt Brecht, *The Threepenny Opera*, London: Eyre Methuen, 1979, p. 26.
70 *BonT*, p. 86.
71 Brecht, *Poems on the Theatre*, p. 13.
72 *Ibid.*, p. 56.
73 *Journals*, p. 13.
74 Witt, *Brecht as They Knew Him*, p. 41.
75 McTeague, *Playwrights and Acting*, p. 31.
76 *BonT*, p. 144.
77 *Journal*, p. 319.
78 *Journal*, p. 405.
79 *BonT*, p. 45.
80 Brecht, *Poems on the Theatre*, p. 22.
81 Carl Weber, 'Brecht as Director', *Drama Review*, vol. 12, no. 1, Fall 1967, p. 104.

82 *BonT*, pp. 200, 201.
83 *Journals*, p. 411.
84 *Journals*, p. 139.
85 Thomson and Sacks, *Cambridge Companion*, p. 172.
86 *BonT*, p. 283.
87 *BonT*, p. 103.
88 Witt, *Brecht as They Knew Him*, p. 72.
89 Michael Patterson, *The Revolution in German Theatre, 1900–1933*, London: Routledge and Kegan Paul, 1981, p. 167.
90 Witt, *Brecht as They Knew Him*, p. 73.
91 Bertolt Brecht, 'Notes on *The Caucasian Chalk Circle*', *Drama Review*, vol. 12, no.1, Fall 1967, pp. 98–9.
92 *Ibid.*, p. 90.
93 John Willett, *The Theatre of Bertolt Brecht*, London: Methuen, 1959, p. 216.
94 Quoted in Pia Kleber and Colin Visser, *Re-interpreting Brecht: His Influence on Contemporary Drama and Film*, Cambridge: Cambridge University Press, 1990, p. 75.
95 Beumers, *Yuri Lyubimov at the Taganka Theatre*, p. 16.
96 Judith Malina in Bertolt Brecht, *Antigone*, New York: Applause, 1990, p. vii.
97 John Fuegi, *The Life and Lies of Bertolt Brecht*, New York: Grove, 1994.
98 Fredric Jameson, *Brecht and Method*, London: Verso, 1998, p. 177.
99 Sue-Ellen Case, *Contemporary Feminist Theatres*, London: Routledge, 1993, p. 129.
100 Augusto Boal, *Theatre of the Oppressed*, London: Routledge, 1988, p. 141.
101 Thich Nhat Hanh, *Old Path, White Clouds*, London: Rider, 1992, p. 213.

5 Antonin Artaud

1 Brook, *The Empty Space*, p. 54.
2 Stephen Barber, *Antonin Artaud: Blows and Bombs*, London: Faber & Faber, 1993, p. 2.
3 *CW1*, p. 58.
4 *CW1*, pp. 41–2.
5 Naomi Greene, *Antonin Artaud: Poet Without Words*, New York: Simon & Schuster, 1970, p. 11.
6 Ronald Hayman, *Artaud and After*, Oxford: Oxford University Press, 1977, p. 54.
7 *Ibid.*, p. 46.
8 Quoted in Greene, *Antonin Artaud*, p. 30.
9 *CW3*, pp. 20–1.
10 Naomi Greene, 'All the Great Myths are Dark: Artaud and Fascism', in Gene A. Plunka (ed.), *Antonin Artaud and the Modern Theatre*, London and Toronto: Associated University Presses, 1994, pp. 102–16.
11 *CW2*, pp. 24–5.
12 *CW2*, p. 30.
13 All quotations from *CW2*, p. 215.
14 Antonin Artaud, *The Theatre and Its Double*, London: Calder and Boyars, 1970, p. 23.
15 Anaïs Nin, *Diary of Anaïs Nin*, New York: Swallow Press and Harcourt Brace, 1966, p. 192.

16 See Antonin Artaud, Roger Blin *et al.*, 'Antonin Artaud's *Les Cenci*', *Drama Review*, vol. 16, no. 2, June 1972, p. 138.
17 *Ibid,*, p. 110.
18 *Ibid.*, p. 132.
19 Quoted in Hayman, *Artaud and After*, p. 128.
20 Charles Marowitz, *Artaud at Rodez*, London: Marion Boyars, 1977, p. 83.
21 Claude Schumacher and Brian Singleton (eds), *Artaud on Theatre*, London: Methuen, 2001, pp. 232–3.
22 *CW1*, p. 49.
23 Hayman, *Artaud and After*, p. 3; Greene, *Antonin Artaud*, p. 72.
24 Greene, *Antonin Artaud*, p. 72.
25 Schumacher and Singleton, *Artaud on Theatre*, pp. xxi and 71.
26 Greene, *Antonin Artaud*, p. 193.
27 Schumacher and Singleton, *Artaud on Theatre*, p. 193.
28 *CW2*, p. 152.
29 *CW2*, p. 16.
30 *CW2*, p. 26.
31 *CW4*, p. 78.
32 *CW4*, p. 87.
33 *CW4*, p. 94.
34 *CW4*, p. 144.
35 Eric Sellin, *The Dramatic Concepts of Antonin Artaud*, Chicago, Ill.: University of Chicago Press, 1968, p. 129.
36 *CW4*, p. 60.
37 *CW4*, pp. 10, 13.
38 *CW4*, p. 20.
39 *CW4*, p. 17.
40 *CW4*, p. 14.
41 *CW4*, p. 20.
42 *CW2*, p. 17.
43 *CW4*, p. 63.
44 Schumacher and Singleton, *Artaud on Theatre*, p. 83.
45 *CW4*, p. 56.
46 *CW4*, p. 117.
47 Susan Sontag, *Antonin Artaud: Selected Writings*, New York: Farrar, Strauss & Giroux, 1976, p. lvii.
48 Marowitz, *Artaud at Rodez*, p. 80
49 *CW4*, p. 39.
50 Bert O. States, *Great Reckonings in Little Rooms*, Berkeley, Calif.: University of California Press, 1987, p. 109.
51 *CW4*, p. 26.
52 *CW4*, p. 71.
53 *CW4*, pp. 135, 196, 126.
54 *CW4*, p. 47.
55 Schumacher and Singleton, *Artaud on Theatre*, p. 92.
56 *CW3*, p. 217.
57 Richard Southern, *The Seven Ages of Theatre*, London: Faber & Faber, 1962, p. 76.
58 *CW4*, pp. 74, 75.

59 *CW4*, p. 97.
60 *CW3*, p. 215.
61 *CW4*, p. 73.
62 *CW4*, p. 75.
63 Quoted in Sellin, *Dramatic Concepts*, p. 52.
64 Quoted in Hayman, *Artaud and After*, p. 46.
65 Barber, *Antonin Artaud*, p. 28.
66 Artaud *et al.*, 'Antonin Artaud's *Les Cenci*', p. 128.
67 Martin Esslin, *Antonin Artaud, the Man and His Work*, London: John Calder, 1976, p. 9.
68 *CW4*, p. 39.
69 Schumacher and Singleton, *Artaud on Theatre*, p. 78.
70 *CW4*, p. 50.
71 *CW2*, p. 76.
72 *CW2*, p. 76.
73 *CW2*, p. 84.
74 *CW2*, p. 23.
75 Schumacher and Singleton, *Artaud on Theatre*, pp. 78, 166.
76 *CW4*, pp. 109, 210–11.
77 *CW2*, pp. 74–5.
78 *CW4*, p. 30.
79 *CW4*, p. 107.
80 *CW4*, p. 108.
81 *CW2*, p. 38.
82 *CW2*, p. 73.
83 *CW4*, p. 38.
84 *CW1*, p. 62.
85 *CW2*, p. 75.
86 *CW4*, p. 65.
87 Schumacher and Singleton, *Artaud on Theatre*, p. 77.
88 *Ibid.*, pp. 167, 168.
89 Quoted in Albert Bermel, *Artaud's Theatre of Cruelty*, London: Methuen, 2001, p. 73.
90 *CW4*, pp. 38, 43.
91 Schumacher and Singleton, *Artaud on Theatre*, pp. 71–2.
92 Marowitz, *Artaud at Rodez*, p. 76.
93 The text for Act 1 Scene 3 of *The Cenci* is reproduced on the left-hand page with Artaud's blocking and stage directions on the right-hand page, in *The Drama Review*, vol. 16, no. 2, June 1972, pp. 112–25.
94 Charles Marowitz, Tom Milne and Owen Hale (eds), *The Encore Reader*, London: Methuen, 1970, p. 177.
95 Sellin, *Dramatic Concepts*, p. viii.
96 David Williams (ed.), *Peter Brook: A Theatrical Casebook*, London: Methuen, 1988, p. 30.
97 Tom Milne, 'Cruelty, Cruelty', *Encore*, vol. 11, no. 2, March–April 1964, pp. 11–12.
98 Clive Barker, 'Tell Me When It Hurts: The "Theatre of Cruelty" Season, Thirty Years On', *New Theatre Quarterly*, vol. XII, no. 46, May 1996, p. 130.
99 Williams, *Peter Brook*, pp. 356–7.

100 Catherine Itzin, *Stages in the Revolution*, London: Eyre Methuen, 1980, p. 68.
101 Bermel, *Artaud's Theatre of Cruelty*, p. 96.
102 Plunka, *Antonin Artaud*, pp. 252–62.
103 Quoted in Hayman, *Artaud and After*, p. 144.
104 See Jacques Derrida and Paule Thévenin, *The Secret Art of Antonin Artaud*, Cambridge, Mass.: MIT Press, 1998, p. 71.
105 *Ibid*, p. 149.
106 Quoted in Hayman, *Artaud and After*, p. 159.
107 Jacques Derrida, *Writing and Difference*, Chicago, Ill.: University of Chicago Press, 1978, pp. 169–95 and 232–50.
108 CW4, p. 73.

6 Afterwards . . . after words

1 Mikhail Bulgakov, *Black Snow*, London: Flamingo, 1986; Günter Grass, *The Plebeians Rehearse the Uprising*, Harmondsworth: Penguin, 1966; Marowitz, *Artaud at Rodez*; Mark Rozovsky, *Triumphal Square*, unpublished typescript.

Index